Dear Colleague:

Stocks tumble. Subprime exposés grow. The dollar weakens against the Euro and other currencies. When will the gyrations that cause anxiety on Main Street and Wall Street stop?

Possibly never. We live and work in one of the most vital sectors of the economy where investors seek healthy returns and safe investments in a world where "normalcy" is increasingly hard to describe. Policyholders turn to stable companies they trust because they know and expect that honorable companies will stand by the products they sell. Interestingly enough, conservatism has returned as a theme generally desired by insurers as well as the insured. That's what happens when recession talk fills the air.

This second volume of our New York Life Guide to Retirement Income brings together some of the foremost thought leaders who will share with you their wisdom regarding the distribution equation and other key issues. We are especially appreciative to Ted Mathas, President and Chief Executive of New York Life, for continuing to support The Center so that we may provide superb insight to guide agents and advisors.

Please join me in welcoming the new Director of the Center, Kenn Tacchino, JD, LLM. Kenn's superb research and teaching platform in retirement and financial planning brings additional depth to the faculty of The American College. We are delighted to have his energy and insight.

Enjoy this continuing, robust dialogue on retirement and distribution strategies. As the nation's largest accredited non-profit College devoted to your success, we welcome your comments and suggestions throughout the year.

Very truly yours,

Laurence Barton, Ph.D.
President and Chief Executive Officer

New York Life Center's Retirement Income Guide
Second Edition

The American College Press/*Bryn Mawr, Pennsylvania*

The New York Life Center for Retirement Income has been funded by a generous endowment from New York Life Insurance Company. The Center's purpose is to provide fair and balanced educational opportunities to the insurance industry's agents and producers who serve the financial service needs of the senior marketplace.

The opinions presented in this publication are those of the respective authors and do not necessarily represent the opinions or polices of New York Life. New York Life makes no warranties or representations about the accuracy or completeness of the content of this publication or any associated materials appearing on the American College website and assumes no liability for damages resulting from the use of the information contained therein. Nothing in this publication should be construed as sales or promotional material for the products and services sold by New York Life or its affiliates. New York Life is not engaged in rendering legal, accounting, or other professional advice through the use of this book or associated materials. If legal or other expert advice is required, the services of an appropriate professional should be sought.

The purpose of the articles in the Retirement Income Guide is to present retirement income strategies to help financial advisors provide their clients with long-term financial safety and security. The views and opinions expressed in any of the articles do not necessarily reflect the views and opinions of either The American College.

This publication is designed to provide accurate and authoritative information about the subject covered. While every precaution has been taken in the preparation of this material, the authors and The American College® assume no liability for damages resulting from the use of the information contained in this publication. The American College is not engaged in rendering legal, accounting, or other professional advice. If legal or other expert advice is required, the services of an appropriate professional should be sought.

© 2008 The American College Press
270 S. Bryn Mawr Avenue
Bryn Mawr, PA 19010
(888) AMERCOL (263-7265)
www.theamericancollege.edu
All rights reserved

Library of Congress Control Number 2008929423
ISBN 1932819657

Printed in the United States of America

Contents

	Acknowledgments	vii
	Foreword *Kenn B. Tacchino*	ix
	A Gentle Introduction to the Calculus of Sustainable Income: What is Your RisQuotient? *Moshe A. Milevsky*	1.1
	Dynamic Allocation Strategies for Distribution Portfolios: Determining the Optimal Distribution Glide Path *David M. Blanchett*	2.1
	Real Longevity Insurance with a Deductible: Introduction to Advanced-Life Delayed Annuities (ALDA) *Moshe A. Milevsky*	3.1
	Recent Developments in Life Annuity Markets and Products (excerpt) *Mark J. Warshawsky*	4.1
	Planning Required Minimum Distributions for Multiple Beneficiaries *April K. Caudill*	5.1
	Distributions from Stretch IRAs *Kevin J. Sigler*	6.1
	An Examination of Delaying Social Security Retirement Benefits *Clarence C. Rose*	7.1
	When Should Married Men Claim Social Security Benefits? *Steven A. Sass, Wei Sun, and Anthony Webb*	8.1

Factors in Deciding to Relocate After Retirement   **9.1**
John J. McFadden

Age Banding: A Model for Planning Retirement Needs   **10.1**
Somnath Basu

Medicare's Financial Condition: Beyond Actuarial Balance   **11.1**
American Academy of Actuaries

Spending in Retirement: Easing the Reins or Pulling Them In   **12.1**
Richard F. Stolz

Acknowledgments

The American College wishes to acknowledge Kenn B. Tacchino for compiling the material for this book, and retired faculty member John McFadden for his contribution.

The College wishes to thank Larry Barton, president and CEO of The American College, and Walt J. Woerheide, vice president and dean of The American College, for providing continued support and guidance throughout this project.

The College also wishes to thank Virginia Webb, Librarian at The American College, for the comprehensive research she provided, which made it possible to assemble the diverse material in this book.

Special thanks are extended to Todd Denton for editorial coordination, Evelyn Rice for production assistance, Patricia Cheers for assistance in securing reprint permissions, and Patricia Perillo for data processing support. Thanks are also due to Marie Hatkevich and Monica Mockus for their work on the cover design. Thanks are also due to Rebecca Adkins for her help as the New York Life Intern.

Finally, we acknowledge the generosity of New York Life for its commitment to help all agents and advisors have credible, pertinent information in the area of retirement income planning.

Foreword

Welcome to the second volume of the Retirement Income Guide. It is our sincere hope that you find the articles in this publication the type of cutting edge research that can help you provide state-of-the-art service as a planner. The ideas and insights suggested in each article represent some of the newest and most promising strategies in the retirement planning field. They address some of the key questions your clients have about retirement security and financial independence. The following paragraphs provide a thumbnail sketch of concepts contained in the Guide. Let's take a closer look.

Our first two articles focus on evaluating whether a client's savings will be depleted during the retirement liquidation period. "A Gentle Introduction to the Calculus of Sustainable Income: What is Your RisQuotient" has a somewhat scary title if you are math-phobic like me. However, when you get beyond the math there is a straightforward and new approach that can be used to analyze whether a client is able to sustain a chosen withdrawal rate during the retirement liquidation period. In other words, you will be able to analyze the possibility of failure of a client's retirement portfolio based on tables provided. This article deliberately avoids advocating a particular spending rate. Instead, it provides an overview of the analytic relationship of the three key risk variables that determine income sustainability. These are brought together by linking investment characteristics, spending rates, and longevity risk, to provide what is coined the *Retirement RisQuotient*. What's more, the tables indicate how life annuities and embedded put options can increase a portfolio's sustainability by reducing the Retirement RisQuotient.

The second half of our decumulation analysis, "Dynamic Allocation Strategies for Distribution Portfolios: Determining the Optimal Distribution Glide Path," proposes the optimal allocation strategy (referred to as the *distribution glide path*) for a portfolio subject to withdrawals. The paper introduces a risk-adjusted measure called the *success to variability ratio* (once again, not as complicated as it sounds) to incorporate portfolio variability (standard deviation) into the optimal glide path decision process. When considering a variety of distribution periods and real withdrawal rates, as well as the probability of failure and the success of variability ratio, a balanced static allocation, such as 60 percent equity and 40 percent fixed income/cash, is likely one of the most efficient portfolio allocations for retirees.

The next group of articles examines the newest annuity products and concepts. "Real Longevity Insurance With a Deductible: Introduction to Advanced-Life Delayed Annuities (ALDA)" introduces what promises to become a wildly popular retirement product. The ALDA, sometimes called *longevity annuity*, is a variant of a pure deferred annuity contract that is acquired by installments, adjusted for inflation, and pays off toward the end of a client's life. The ALDA concept should go a long way in mitigating the psychological barrier to voluntary lump-sum annuitization.

The second article in our annuity group, "Recent Developments in Life Annuity Markets and Products" lives up to the title's promise. The article looks at some new life annuity products and features such as inflation-indexed annuities, enhanced liquidity (lump-sum payment options), individual defined-benefit pensions, and lifelong distribution products. The article also covers a discussion of the new integrated annuity product with long-term care insurance.

After our annuity discussion is completed, we turn our attention to the required minimum distribution rules. Our first article in this group, "Planning for Required Minimum Distributions for Multiple Beneficiaries" takes an insightful look at the options available in this less-than-perfect tax scenario. Put another way, qualified plans and IRAs are often described as great places to accumulate money but bad places from which to inherit it. They become especially complicated when the deceased has multiple beneficiaries, some of whom are trying to minimize taxable distributions. The article explains a number of strategies for addressing the disadvantageous tax treatment of multiple beneficiaries.

Continuing the trend of a non-spousal beneficiary is our second required minimum distribution article, "Distributions from Stretch IRAs." This article reviews the regulations regarding required minimum distributions (RMD) from traditional IRAs and focuses on the distributions that are made to non-spouse beneficiaries of the IRA after the death of the owner. It appears from the example presented that the beneficiary will substantially increase his total payout by stretching the IRA instead of opting for total payout by the fifth anniversary of the IRA owner's death. Using the assumptions of the analysis provided, if a non-spouse beneficiary desires to maximize his wealth, stretching the IRA is the viable option.

Our next pair of articles focuses on the financial planning implications of delaying receipt of Social Security benefits. Our first article in this group, "An Examination of Delaying Social Security Retirement Benefits" makes the point that clients may be leaving money on the table by taking Social Security at the earliest possible age. Delaying receipt can increase retirement security for the average client. The statistics indicate that many baby boomers will be facing difficult financial times in retirement. The author points out that delaying the start of Social Security retirement benefits beyond age 62 increases the expected economic value for the participant and beneficiaries.

The latter part of this statement (about beneficiaries) is the subject of our second Social Security start-date article, "When Should Married Men Claim Social Security Benefits." Most married men claim Social Security benefits at age 62 or 63. This is well short of the age that maximizes the expected present value of the average household's benefits.

The expected present value for married couples is complicated because of spousal and survivor benefits. Upon a death, survivors (who are not getting their own benefit) are subject to reductions if the benefit was claimed before full retirement age. The spousal benefit recipient is greatest at age 62 from an expected present value analysis. However, the spousal benefit survivor's benefit rises 7 to 8 percent each year the primary Social Security beneficiary postpones claiming Social Security Retirement benefits. In other words, the expected present value of the survivor benefit can be up to 25 percent higher if, for example, the husband waits until full retirement age, rather than starting benefits at age 62.

Our remaining articles do not have companion pieces in this issue of the Guide. "Factors in Deciding to Relocate After Retirement" talks about financial and cost-of-living issues such as the cost of housing and tax implications of moving. In particular, state and local income taxes, sales taxes, and property taxes are examined. Inheritance and estate taxes are another important factor. Finally, job opportunities in retirement and lifestyle issues are considered.

The next topic we examine concerns how much a client needs to accumulate for retirement. "Age Banding: A Model for Planning Retirement Needs" proffers a new approach for determining the amount of savings needed for retirement. Most retirement calculators assume that the client will spend the same inflation-adjusted amount throughout each year of retirement. In this model, the retirement span is parsed into different spending phases to represent different levels of activity during retirement. The end result is a more accurate calculation which is more closely related to dynamic spending patterns.

Our next topic is an overview of Medicare's financial condition. "Medicare's Financial Condition: Beyond Actuarial Balance" paints a bleak picture of the fiscal soundness of this crucial health care system. Financial planners need to understand the long-range financing problems of Medicare because this may become a grave threat to the retirement security of their clients.

Our final topic centers on behavioral finance and provides some practical advice for dealing with clients during retirement. "Spending in Retirement: Easing the Reins or Pulling Them In" talks about both how to confront over-spenders and how to deal with needlessly frugal clients. It seems a fitting way to end our Guide which has focused so much on retirement income.

Kenn Beam Tacchino

New York Life Center's
Retirement Income Guide

A Gentle Introduction To The Calculus Of Sustainable Income: What Is Your Retirement RisQuotient?[*]

by Moshe A. Milevsky, PhD[†]

Abstract: A little over a year ago, on January 1, 2006, the first American baby boomer turned 60. These birthdays are expected to continue at the rate of one per 7–10 seconds over the next 20 years. In anticipation of this demographic wave the financial services industry is bracing for the retirement income revolution, and one of the critical issues is how to build a portfolio that will provide a sustainable income flow over the uncertain length and cost of the human lifecycle. Indeed, a number of recent articles have gained notoriety by advocating spending rates in the 4–6% vicinity as being sustainable for portfolios that contain 70–90% equity exposure.

But prudent risk management involves more than just controlled consumption, and this article deliberately avoids advocating a particular spending rate. Instead it provides an overview of the analytic relationship or calculus among the three key risk variables that determine income sustainability. These are brought together by linking investment characteristics, spending rates, and longevity risk, to provide what is coined the Retirement RisQuotient.[1] And, while statistical formulas will never capture the complex nuances of retirement reality, there are a variety of intuitive insights that can be gleaned from this summary number. Moreover, this calculus illustrates how products with longevity insurance (e.g., life annuities) and downside protection (e.g., embedded put options) can increase the sustainability by reducing the Retirement RisQuotient

The last few years have seen intense research around the topic of retirement income planning. One of the most widely studied issues is how to build a portfolio that will provide a sustainable income flow over the uncertain length and cost of the human lifecycle. Not surprisingly, a number of recent articles have argued that one of the key components to a sustainable retirement is to simply avoid spending too much. A variety of authors have advocated spending rates in the 4–6% vicinity as being sustainable for portfolios that contain 70% to 90% equity exposure. To be clear, a spending rate of x percent is meant to imply withdrawing $x per original $100 nest egg on an annual basis, with each year's spending being adjusted for consumer price inflation.[2]

For example, Bengen; Ho, Milevsky, and Robinson; Cooley, Hubbard, and Walz; Pye; Milevsky; Ameriks, Veres, and Warshawsky; and Guyton have all created financial experiments incorporating historical, simulated, and scrambled returns to quantify the sustainability of various *ad hoc* spending policies and consumption rates

---

[*]Reprinted with permission. Copyright © 2007, Society of Financial Service Professionals. All rights reserved.
[†]Moshe A. Milevsky, PhD, is associate professor of finance at York University in Toronto, Ontario, Canada. He is also the executive director of The IFID Centre, Toronto. He can be reached at milevsky@yorku.ca.

for retired individuals.[3] As a number of financial commentators have emphasized, the problem with such studies is that (1) these simulations are often difficult to replicate by financial practitioners, (2) many conduct only a minimal number of simulations, and (3) most provide little pedagogical intuition on the financial tradeoff between retirement risk and return. More importantly, they focus too much attention on the relationship between spending habits and the composition of the investment portfolio, yet they neglect the many other factors that determine retirement income sustainability. For example, important questions such as: "What are the roles of variable payout (or income) annuities and their guaranteed riders in a sustainable portfolio?" are not addressed in any of these studies.

Therefore, to differentiate this article from the recent simulation-based debate around prudent retirement spending, this article will deliberately avoid advocating a preferred portfolio withdrawal rate. Instead, it provides an overview of the analytical relationship between the key risk variables that determine sustainability. These ingredients are brought together by linking portfolio parameters, spending rates, and longevity risk to an analytic probability of retirement ruin. More specifically, a number of key variables are identified that will determine a retiree's Retirement RisQuotient.

While statistical formulas will never capture the complex nuances of retirement reality, there are a variety of intuitive insights that can be gleaned from this summary Retirement RisQuotient metric. Moreover, this calculus helps illustrate how products with longevity insurance (e.g., life annuities) and downside protection (e.g., the put options embedded within variable annuities) can increase the sustainability of retirement.

The remainder of this article is organized as follows. The basic formula that helps us estimate ruin and sustainability is presented first. Although the underlying mathematics are quite complicated and are described elsewhere, the main formula itself can be implemented using a function that is easily available in Microsoft Excel. Next, a short-cut method for arriving at the Retirement RisQuotient using two summary variables is provided. Some caveats and warnings about the underlying assumptions are discussed, and then illustrations show how this risk measurement system can be extended to include life annuities and various downside protected portfolio strategies, many of which are embedded within variable annuities.

THE MAIN FORMULA: PROBABILITY OF RETIREMENT RUIN

If a retiree is invested in a standard (balanced) portfolio and plans on withdrawing a fixed inflation-adjusted amount every year during retirement, he or she obviously faces the probability that his or her portfolio will be exhausted while still alive. Whether or not these constant static withdrawals are a realistic assumption for the behavior of actual retirees, the underlying paradigm is the foundation of numerous simulation-based studies. Figure 1 provides a graphical illustration. Nevertheless, under basic portfolio-dynamic assumptions, the formula for this *probability of retirement ruin*—the probability that a fixed spending plan will deplete a retirement nest egg prior to the end of the lifecycle—can be expressed in two distinct steps. First, define:

$$\alpha = \frac{2(\mu + 2\lambda)}{\sigma^2 + \lambda} - 1, \beta = \frac{\sigma^2 + \lambda}{2} \qquad \text{(Equation 1)}$$

where μ denotes the retiree's portfolio expected rate of return, σ denotes the volatility or uncertainty surrounding this projected investment return, λ denotes the *mortality rate* of the retiree, and S denotes the inflation-adjusted spending rate as a percentage of the initial portfolio value.

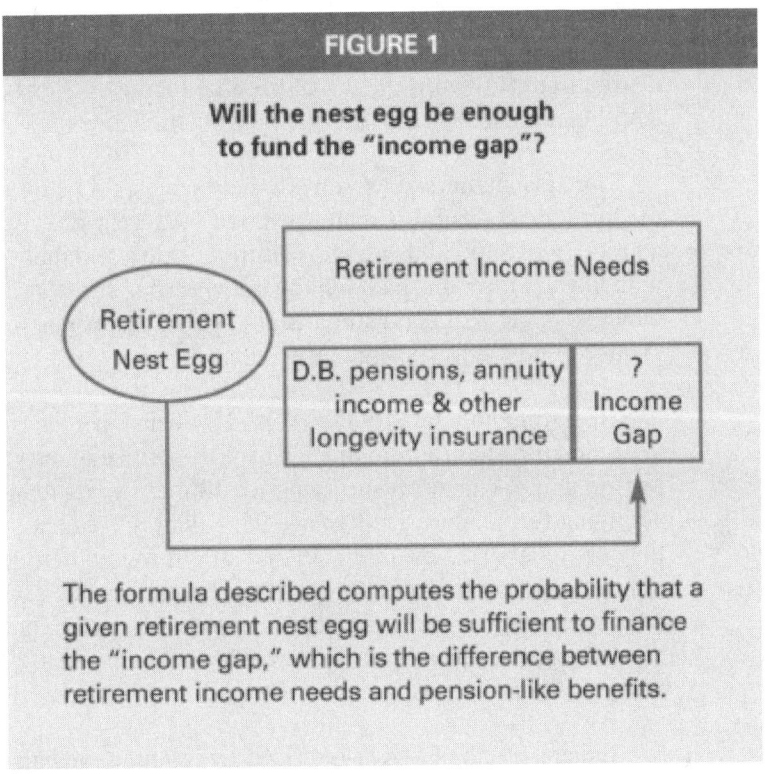

The formula described computes the probability that a given retirement nest egg will be sufficient to finance the "income gap," which is the difference between retirement income needs and pension-like benefits.

The probability of retirement ruin—1 minus the probability of sustainability—can be obtained via the GammaDist formula in Excel:

$$\text{RetirementRuin} = \text{GammaDist}(S/\beta, \alpha, 1, \text{TRUE}) \quad \text{(Equation 2)}$$

where the two intermediary variables (α, β) are defined by equation 1 as explicit functions of the four input variables (μ, σ, λ S), all of which will be explained in greater detail in a moment. Note that the last expression in the formula (TRUE) is meant to indicate to Excel that the user is interested in the cumulative distribution function (CDF) and not the probability mass function (PMF).

First, let's break equation 1 into bite-sized pieces and translate the Greek into English. The formula depends on four input variables (μ, σ, λ, S) that get mapped into the two intermediate variables (α, β), which then get used in the actual formula.

One can think of the underlying problem in the following way. At retirement the individual has a sum of money (nest egg) that must finance a fixed consumption stream over a random investment horizon. This randomness, of course, comes from the uncertainty of the length of one's life. Note that if the entire nest egg itself were invested in a portfolio that earns a fixed inflation-adjusted return forever, and the horizon were deterministic, one could easily calculate the present value of the desired consumption stream and compare with the retirement nest egg (RNE). This is the textbook example of retirement income planning. If the PV < RNE, the income plan is not sustainable. If the PV > RNE, the income plan is sustainable and the retiree will have enough. But—and this is the critical part—when the retirement horizon is random and the future inflation-adjusted returns themselves are random, the PV is random as well. This then leads to a probability that PV < RNE, which is the probability of retirement ruin or 1 minus the probability of sustainability. Indeed, the above-mentioned formula is akin to computing a z-score from a normal distribution, where alpha is related to the "mean" and beta is related to the "variance" of the distribution. However, the PV of lifetime income is most definitely not normally distributed; it is closer to gamma distributed, hence the GammaDist function.

Here is a numerical example to help develop a better understanding of how to use the formula in general. Assume a generic, 65-year-old client who has just retired with a nest egg of $500,000, which is sitting inside a tax-sheltered plan. Any and all withdrawals from this plan will be taxed at the retiree's marginal tax rate, which is why this paper will not distinguish between the various forms of income such as taxable bonds, tax-efficient equity, etc.

According to mortality tables used by pension actuaries, this typically healthy 65-year-old client has (approximately) a 94% chance of surviving for 5 more years to age 70, a 56% chance of surviving for 20 more years to age 85, and a 16% chance of surviving for 30 more years to age 95. Client retirement horizons are random and they obviously face the *longevity risk* of out living their nest eggs if they live longer than anticipated. It is hard to overstate the importance of incorporating longevity risk when preparing a retirement plan. The many research studies (and software algorithms) that focus deterministically on 20, 25, or 30 years of retirement are ignoring the most vexing risk of them all.

Either way, the 65-year-old (healthy) client's median remaining lifespan (MRL)—or median number of years until death—is approximately 23 years, which means that there is 50% chance he or she will live beyond age 88. From a mathematical point of view, if there is a 50% chance of living for 23 more years, an *exponential future lifetime* assumption ($e^{-23\lambda} = 0.5$) leads to a mortality rate of $\lambda = \ln[2]/23 = 0.0301$. The average rate of death is approximately 3% per year. Recall that this number is one of the four input variables in equation 1.

Let's further assume that the same 65-year-old would like to withdraw $40,000 per year, pretax in inflation-adjusted terms, during the course of his or her retirement. This represents $S = 40/500 = 0.08$ or 8% of the initial nest egg and is another one of the four input variables in the retirement ruin formula displayed in equations 1 and 2.

Now, let's emphasize once again up front that it is unrealistic to assume any client will be mechanically adhering to a withdrawal rule of precisely $40,000 per year in inflation-adjusted terms. Every client has the flexibility to modify a plan by spending more or less in any given year. Most likely if the portfolio performs poorly the client will scale back spending and *vice versa* if the portfolio achieves above-average investment performance. However, the point of this exercise is to ascertain whether $40,000 per year withdrawals are sustainable over a random retirement horizon.

In terms of asset allocation, assume the client's investment portfolio is allocated to a mix of balanced mutual funds (or ETFs, SMAs, etc.) and the estimate is that this portfolio will earn $\mu = 0.075$, which is an arithmetic average of 7.5% in any given year, with a standard deviation or volatility of $\sigma = 0.18$, which is 18% per year, both in *inflation-adjusted* terms. These numbers are consistent with the well-known and widely cited numbers by Ibbotson Associates (2004).[4] In some sense, the precise magnitude of these numbers is less important than the general awareness that they can fluctuate and hence are yet another source of retirement risk.

To those who are unfamiliar with investment means and volatilities, what these parameters imply is that in any given year the range of annual investment outcomes is between –10.5% and +25.5% two times out of three, which is one standard deviation away from the mean. For 19 times out of 20 confidence, the range is between –28.5% and +43.5%, which is obviously much wider. Note, also, that all of these numbers are expressed as a continuously compounded rate. Either way, the two numbers 0.075 and 0.18 are the last of the four ingredients needed to use the retirement ruin equation.

The next step is to compute the newly defined *retirement alpha:*

$$\alpha = \frac{2\mu - 4\lambda}{\sigma^2 - \lambda} - 1 = 3.326$$

and the newly defined *beta-adjusted spending* rate:

$$\frac{S}{\beta} = \frac{2S}{\sigma^2 + \lambda} = 2.558$$

as per the instructions in equation 1. Finally, plugging these values into Excel as per equation 2, *GammaDist(2.558,3.326,1,TRUE)* results in the number 39.3%, which is the probability of retirement ruin. Intuitively, a higher retirement alpha will result in a lower risk of retirement ruin, while a higher beta-adjusted spending rate will lead to a higher retirement ruin, or Retirement RisQuotient.[5]

Now, for example, if this retiree was planning on spending only $35,000 per year of retirement (in inflation-adjusted terms), the spending rate would fall to 7% of the initial $500,000 and the beta-adjusted spending rate would be reduced to 2.239 instead of the earlier 2.558 value. It is therefore no surprise that when this value is plugged into the same function *GammaDist(2.239,3.326,1,TRUE)*, the probability of retirement ruin is reduced to 31.3% from 39.3%. A lower beta-adjusted level of spending results in a lower ruin probability. Likewise, if instead of assuming that the portfolio will earn 7.5% in any given year, one is more optimistic and uses $\mu = 0.09$, which is 1.5% per annum above the earlier number, the retirement alpha variable becomes 3.806 instead of the earlier 3.326 value. And, under the earlier $40,000 spending rate and beta-adjusted spending rate of 2.558, we arrive at a retirement ruin probability, using the same formula *GammaDist(2.558,3.806,1,TRUE)* of 29.1% instead of 39.3%. This is an improvement, i.e. a reduction of risk, of close to 10 percentage points. Once again, a higher retirement alpha value will reduce the ruin probability.

Tables 1-4 provide a range of numbers based on equations 1 and 2 assuming differing spending rates, mortality rates, and portfolio characteristics. The four tables correspond with four extremes. Table 1 represents a relatively high spending rate of 8% (i.e. annual $8 withdrawals per $100 nest egg) of a typical retiree with a 23-year median remaining lifespan. Table 2 illustrates the results for the same 8% spending rate, but for a much younger (early) retiree facing a median remaining lifespan of 35 years. Tables 3 and 4 examine the same mortality rates but under a much lower spending rate of 4% of the initial nest egg. All of these rates are adjusted for inflation.

TABLE 1
Random Life and Returns: What Is Your Probability of Retirement Ruin?

(Under various portfolio returns (μ) and volatility (σ) combinations, this table displays the probability of retirement ruin—i.e. the retiree's RisQuotient—under a relatively high spending rate of S = 8% and a median remaining life of 23 years)

Mortality Rate	3.01%	Median Life (years)			23.00
		Retirement Income Spending Rate			8.00%
		The Volatility of Portfolio's Investment Return			
Expected Return	5%	10%	15%	20%	25%
1%	82.8%	84.2%	86.6%	89.7%	93.4%
3%	62.8%	66.5%	71.7%	77.5%	83.6%
5%	40.7%	46.4%	54.1%	62.5%	71.1%
7%	22.6%	28.6%	37.2%	47.1%	57.4%
10%	7.0%	11.0%	18.0%	27.3%	38.0%

TABLE 2
Random Life and Returns: What Is Your Probability of Retirement Ruin?

(Under various portfolio returns (μ) and volatility (σ) combinations, this table displays the probability of retirement ruin—i.e. the retiree's RisQuotient—under a relatively high spending rate of S = 8% and a median remaining life of 35 years. Quite intuitively, the RisQuotient is high.)

Mortality Rate	1.98%	Median Life (years)			35.00
		Retirement Income Spending Rate			8.00%
		The Volatility of Portfolio's Investment Return			
Expected Return	5%	10%	15%	20%	25%
1%	95.7%	95.4%	95.6%	96.7%	98.6%
3%	81.6%	82.8%	85.1%	88.3%	92.0%
5%	57.1%	61.9%	68.1%	74.8%	81.4%
7%	31.5%	39.0%	48.5%	58.4%	67.9%
10%	8.3%	14.1%	23.4%	34.6%	46.4%

TABLE 3
Random Life and Returns: What Is Your Probability of Retirement Ruin?

(Under various portfolio returns (μ) and volatility (σ) combinations, this table displays the probability of retirement ruin—i.e. the retiree's RisQuotient—under a relatively high spending rate of S = 4% and a median remaining life of 35 years. Quite intuitively, the RisQuotient is high.)

Mortality Rate	1.98%	Median Life (years)		35.00
		Retirement Income Spending Rate		4.00%
		The Volatility of Portfolio's Investment Return				
Expected Return	5%	10%	15%	20%	25%
1%	60.0%	67.0%	75.8%	85.2%	94.4%
3%	25.2%	34.8%	47.8%	61.8%	75.7%
5%	7.0%	13.3%	24.4%	38.7%	54.5%
7%	1.4%	3.9%	10.4%	21.3%	35.7%
10%	0.1%	0.4%	2.1%	7.1%	16.3%

TABLE 4
Random Life and Returns: What Is Your Probability of Retirement Ruin?

(Under various portfolio returns (μ) and volatility (σ) combinations, this table displays the probability of retirement ruin—i.e. the retiree's RisQuotient—under a relatively high spending rate of S = 8% and a median remaining life of 23 years. Quite intuitively, the RisQuotients are lower compared to the previous three tables.)

Mortality Rate	3.01%	Median Life (years)	23.00
		Retirement Income Spending Rate	4.00%
		The Volatility of Portfolio's Investment Return				
Expected Return	5%	10%	15%	20%	25%
1%	37.1%	44.8%	55.7%	67.9%	80.3%
3%	15.3%	21.9%	32.4%	45.7%	60.2%
5%	5.0%	8.8%	16.3%	27.5%	41.5%
7%	1.3%	3.0%	7.2%	15.1%	26.5%
10%	0.1%	0.5%	1.7%	5.2%	12.1%

Thus, for example, a portfolio that is expected to earn 5% per annum with a volatility of 10% will result in a 46.4% ruin probability under an 8% spending rate and 23-year median remaining lifespan, but only an 8.8.% probability of ruin under a 4% spending rate. Halving the spending rate reduces the ruin by over 38 percentage points. It is often stated that spending money in retirement is akin to creating your own pseudo "bear market" since each year the withdrawal process reduces portfolio growth by the spending rate S. Notice that, consistent with this heuristic, increasing S from 4 to 8% under a 7% expected investment return and a 20% volatility has the same impact as reducing the expected return from 7 to 3% under an 8% spending rate.

The important take-away is as follows. This paper does not advocate a particular spending/withdrawal rate or equity/bond allocation as being optimal or prudent. In fact, it is doubtful that any spending rate will be adhered to on a constant basis. Rather, the answers to all these important questions are intertwined and depend on the level of risk aversion (or tolerance) of the retiree, compared against the Retirement RisQuotient of the plan.

The point is that spending rates as high as 8–10% can be defended if the forward-looking volatility is low enough and the forward-looking expected return is high enough. One important take-away is that the retirement income debate should be phrased in terms of the anticipated and forward-looking equity risk premium (ERP) as opposed to the historical performance of these asset classes. The formulas in equations 1 and 2 provide this link.

Figure 2 provides a graphical illustration of the retirement ruin probabilities under the same 7.5% expected return and 18% volatility assumption, for a variety of spending rates and at various retirement ages. The differing retirement ages are captured by changing the MRL. At the extreme left of the figure there is a 50% chance of living for five more years and at the extreme right there is a 50% chance of living for 40 more years. Remember that the MRL is used to compute the mortality rate (λ) which is at the heart of equation 1.

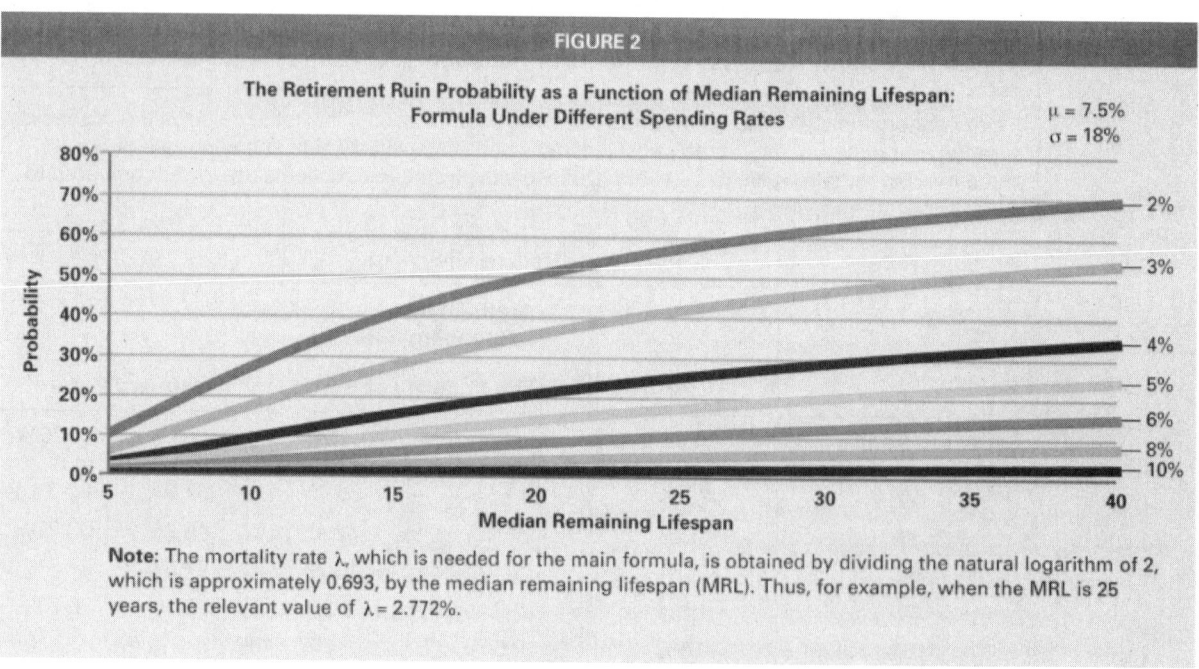

FIGURE 2

The Retirement Ruin Probability as a Function of Median Remaining Lifespan: Formula Under Different Spending Rates

$\mu = 7.5\%$
$\sigma = 18\%$

Note: The mortality rate λ, which is needed for the main formula, is obtained by dividing the natural logarithm of 2, which is approximately 0.693, by the median remaining lifespan (MRL). Thus, for example, when the MRL is 25 years, the relevant value of $\lambda = 2.772\%$.

As one would expect, the greater the spending rate— which ranges from a low of 2% to a high of 10%—the higher the probability of retirement ruin. Likewise, the longer the MRL, the greater is the probability of ruin. Notice that when planning on spending 10% of the initial nest egg each and every year of retirement, the probability of ruin ranges from a low of about 10% to a high of 69% depending on how old one is when one starts retirement spending. In contrast, when planning on spending only 2% of the nest egg during retirement, the ruin probability ranges from a minimal 0.1% to 2.7% depending on age.

Another possible way of interpreting or thinking about the MRL is to treat this number as the 50% mark for a couple's retirement plan. If the couple expects at least one member to be alive for at least 30 years, they should focus on numbers to the right of 30 on the x axis. Those who can tolerate living on the 30% ruin fault line can obviously spend much more than those who prefer a southern climate in the 10% ruin region.

ON THE BACK OF AN ENVELOPE: NO SOFTWARE REQUIRED

It is possible to use and apply the main equations 1 or 2 without having access to Microsoft Excel, or any other statistical software package that does calculus. In fact, using the two key variables of *retirement alpha* (α) and the *beta-adjusted spending rate* (S/β), also called the retirement beta, one can calculate the retirement ruin probability on the back of a (large) envelope. Table 5 provides the main exhibit.

TABLE 5
Back-of-the-Envelope Calculation of Retirement Ruin Risk

Retirement Alpha	Beta-Adjusted Spending Level															
	0.5	0.65	0.8	0.95	1.1	1.25	1.4	1.55	1.7	1.85	2	2.15	2.3	2.45	2.6	2.75	2.9
4.50	0.1[a]	0.2	0.4	0.7	1.2	1.9	2.8	4.0	5.4	7.0	8.9	10.9	13.2	15.7	18.3	21.1	24.0
4.30	0.1	0.2	0.5	1.0	1.6	2.5	3.7	5.1	6.7	8.6	10.8	13.1	15.7	18.4	21.3	24.3	27.4
4.10	0.1	0.4	0.8	1.4	2.23	3.3	4.7	6.4	8.4	10.6	13.0	15.7	18.5	21.5	24.6	27.8	31.1
3.90	0.2	0.5	1.1	1.9	3.0	4.4	6.1	8.1	10.3	12.9	15.6	18.6	21.7	24.9	28.3	31.6	35.0
3.70	0.3	0.8	1.5	2.6	4.0	5.7	7.7	10.1	12.7	15.6	18.6	21.9	25.2	28.7	32.2	35.7	39.2
3.50	0.5	1.2	2.1	3.5	5.2	7.3	9.7	12.4	15.4	18.6	22.0	25.5	29.1	32.8	36.4	40.1	43.7
3.30	0.8	1.7	3.0	4.7	6.8	9.3	12.1	15.3	18.6	22.2	25.8	29.6	33.4	37.2	41.0	44.7	48.3
3.10	1.2	2.4	4.1	6.2	8.8	11.7	15.0	18.5	22.3	26.1	30.1	34.0	38.0	41.9	45.7	49.4	53.0
2.90	1.8	3.4	5.5	8.2	11.3	14.7	18.4	22.3	26.4	30.5	34.7	38.8	42.9	46.8	50.6	54.3	57.8
2.70	2.6	4.7	7.4	10.6	14.3	18.2	22.4	26.7	31.0	35.4	39.7	43.9	48.0	51.9	55.7	59.3	62.6
2.50	3.7	6.5	9.9	13.7	17.9	22.4	26.9	31.5	36.1	40.7	45.1	49.3	53.3	57.2	60.8	64.2	67.4
2.30	5.4	8.9	13.0	17.5	22.2	27.1	32.1	36.9	41.7	46.3	50.7	54.8	58.8	62.5	65.9	69.1	72.0
2.10	7.6	12.0	16.9	22.0	27.3	32.6	37.8	42.8	47.6	52.2	56.5	60.5	64.2	67.7	70.8	73.8	76.4
1.90	10.6	16.0	21.6	27.4	33.1	38.7	44.0	49.1	53.8	58.2	62.3	66.1	69.6	72.7	75.6	78.2	80.6
1.70	14.7	21.0	27.3	33.6	39.6	45.3	50.7	55.6	60.2	64.4	68.2	71.6	74.8	77.6	80.1	82.4	84.4
1.50	19.9	27.1	34.1	40.7	46.8	52.5	57.7	62.4	66.6	70.4	73.9	76.9	79.6	82.1	84.2	86.1	87.8
1.30	26.5	34.4	41.8	48.5	54.4	60.0	64.8	69.1	72.9	76.3	79.2	81.8	84.1	86.2	87.9	89.5	90.8
1.10	34.7	43.1	50.5	56.9	62.6	67.6	71.9	75.6	78.9	81.7	84.2	86.3	88.2	89.8	91.2	92.4	93.4

[a] All numbers are percentages.

The columns of Table 5 represent increasing levels of beta-adjusted spending (retirement beta), while the rows capture decreasing levels of retirement alpha. From any given cell in the table, moving down and/or to the right will increase the probability of retirement ruin. Quite naturally, when spending more or generating a smaller retirement alpha, the probability of ruin and Retirement RisQuotient is higher. Within this table the numbers range from a low of almost zero to a high of

93%. Ideally one wants to position oneself in the upper left-hand corner of this two dimensional risk map.

For example, using the 8% spending rate numbers from the previous section, when the inflation-adjusted portfolio mean return was 7.5%, the return volatility was 18%, and mortality rate was 3.01%, the value of the retirement alpha was 3.326 and the beta-adjusted spending was 2.558. This led to a probability of retirement ruin of 39.3%. Now, if we examine Table 5, the closest value for α is 3.3 and the closest value for S/β is somewhere between 2.45 and 2.6, with equal distance. This leads to a probability of 37–41%, which closely approaches the true 39.3% probability. Likewise, if the spending is reduced from 8% of the initial nest egg to 4% of the nest egg, the retirement alpha value remains unchanged but the beta-adjusted spending rate declines to 1.279 from 2.558. The exact retirement ruin probability is now 9.5% according to equation 1. In Table 5, when the beta-adjusted spending rate falls between 1.25 and 1.4, the ruin probability is between 9.3% and 12.1%.

Those who decide to use such a table instead of the precise formula occasionally might encounter portfolio return variables μ, σ and/or mortality rates λ and/or inflation-adjusted spending rates S that will induce α, S/β values lying beyond the ranges listed in Table 5. In this case, the direction via which one leaves the table should provide a general picture of sustainability. If, for example, the computed retirement alpha value is very low (>1), this is bad news. The ruin probability will be high, and so is a very large (<3) level of your beta-adjusted spending rate. Of course, if one wants a more precise answer compared to what the table's heuristics can provide, then fire up Excel.

In sum, the way to use this table is in two stages. First, estimate the four main variables (μ, σ, λ, S) and convert those into the key variables (α, S/β), based on equation 1. Then, take these two summary numbers to Table 5 and look up the retirement ruin probability based on rows and columns. Obviously, this exercise will not produce the precise number generated by equations 1 and 2 since they are approximating the row and column variable to within two digits, but the results are quite close. In fact, given that this entire exercise hinges on a number of embedded assumptions described in the next section, it is prudent to avoid emphasizing numerical results beyond the first two digits of Table 5.

Using this approach, one can envision a simple questionnaire that clients (users) can complete to measure their Retirement RisQuotient. Soon-to-be retirees would be asked about their gender, age, family history, and health information to arrive at an estimate of their MRL which leads to their implied mortality rate (λ). The same user would then specify an inflation-adjusted retirement income spending rate net of any defined-benefit (DB) pension income, preexisting life annuities, and other longevity-insured income stream, which would lead to an estimate for S. Finally, they would be asked about the specific composition of their investment portfolio that would lead to estimates of μ, σ. All of these together would be fed into a formula or Table 5 that would generate a Retirement RisQuotient. The higher this number the lower the sustainability of the retirement plan.

CAVEATS AND WARNINGS FOR THE QUANTS: KNOW THE LIMITS

For those readers who want to know where this formula comes from, or how accurate it is relative to extensive Monte Carlo simulations, one is encouraged to consult the book by Milevsky (2006)[6] or the paper by Milevsky and Robinson (2005).[7] Both references contain much greater mathematical detail relative to what can be described in a brief article such as this. In a nutshell, however, there are a number of important assumptions upon which equations 1 and 2 are based. It is important to spell them out explicitly.

First, the formula assumes that the underlying investment portfolio value obeys a geometric Brownian motion (GBM). This means that in any given year the one-plus-investment return is not normally distributed and the logarithm of the one-plus-investment return (the continuously compounded return) is normally distributed. And, while this embedded assumption has been used by thousands of practitioners ever since the pioneering days of Markowitz and Merton, it has been questioned by thousands of academics as well. In GBM's defense, it seems the brunt of the criticism has been leveled at the inability of the normal distribution to capture the rare and infrequent tails in market returns over short horizons, as opposed to the (very) long term that would be relevant for the sustainability of retirement portfolios. Thus, the author feels comfortable using the normal distribution within the calculus of retirement income, although it is recommended to use a portfolio volatility estimate (σ) that is slightly higher than historical estimates to take account of the above-mentioned model risk.

Second, the model is predicated on the uncertain length of human life being *exponentially distributed*. This implies that the mortality rate is constant over time and that the probability of living for T more years is precisely where $e^{-\lambda T}$, where λ denotes the instantaneous mortality rate. Indeed, many insurance actuaries will recoil in horror from this assumption knowing that the only organism on earth with an exponential remaining lifespan is a lobster! Human mortality rates increase with age and certainly do not remain constant over time. Yet, interestingly enough, when equations 1 and 2 are calibrated to the actuarially correct median lifespan, the results are remarkably accurate when compared against the true ruin probability under the complete mortality rates.

Third, even under an exponential remaining lifespan and lognormally distributed investment returns, equation 1 is an approximation based on moment matching techniques. In other words, the ruin probability is accurate in the limit and only when $\lambda \to 0$ does the formula converge to the truth. Once again, this approximation has been stress tested quite extensively in a number of other papers (see Milevsky and Robinson for example)[8], and the results indicate errors that are less than 5% in the most extreme cases.

Finally, notwithstanding the above-mentioned caveats, there are a number of important limits to the range of equation 1. For example, the retirement alpha value must be greater than zero, or the underlying integral "blows up" and the formula produces errors. This places restrictions on the *geometric mean*[9] investment return ($\mu - 0.5\sigma^2$) relative to the mortality rate (λ). Specifically, one must obey the relationship $\mu - 0.5\sigma^2 + 1.5\lambda > 0$ in order to satisfy $\alpha > 0$. Thus, when using the formula for any retirement age and any mortality rate, a sufficient condition is that the geometric mean investment return is positive. Notice the critical role of the geometric mean investment return $\mu - 0.5\sigma^2$ relative to the arithmetic mean investment return μ in determining the range of sustainable spending rates. Not only is the difference between the two critical; investment volatility matters.

ENGINEERING SUSTAINABLE INCOME: THE ROLE OF PRODUCT ALLOCATION

In addition to the traditional menu of asset classes such as stocks, bonds, and cash that are available to retirees, there are two important product classes that can further reduce the probability of retirement ruin and increase the sustainability of a retirement plan. The first product class is a life annuity (payout or income annuity) and the second product class consists of exchange-traded put options used to protect the portfolio. And, while many retirees and their advisors might shun exchange-traded options, the closest retail substitute is a variable annuity—manufactured by insurance companies—that contains guaranteed minimum withdrawal benefits (GMWB) and guaranteed minimum income benefits (GMIB). These products effectively create downside protection in the critical early years of retirement, sometimes labeled the retirement risk zone or retirement red zone.

Buying a life annuity that provides lifetime income can greatly improve sustainability. This point was made by Ameriks, Veres and Warshawsky[10] using simulation arguments, or by Chen and Milevsky[11] using utility-based arguments; the same insight can also be extracted from equations 1 and 2 in a number of ways. First, by receiving lifetime income from the insurance company the retiree is exposed to a lower level of longevity risk. This reduces the probability of retirement ruin. More importantly, annuitizing a percentage of one's nest egg generates a mortality subsidy, which increases the portfolio's investment return. This concept has been explained in Milevsky (2005),[12] but can be illustrated using a simple story.

Imagine that a large group of retirees of exactly the same age—and each subject to the same mortality rate (λ)—pool their retirement nest egg into one large portfolio whose value is denoted by the symbol W_t. The members of the pension portfolio invest their collective wealth (W_t) in a mutual fund that is expected to earn μ in any given year. Every day the members of this pension fund, who are still alive, withdraw the exact same $(S/365)W$, stated as a percentage of the original nest egg. However, those who do not survive forfeit their retirement assets to the group. In other words, these funds are not bequeathed to an estate or beneficiary. Now, since this pool of money is being augmented by the assets of the deceased, the money will last longer compared to the situation in which each retiree managed his or her own portfolio independently. In fact, over a short period of time the portfolio will increase by $W(\mu + \lambda)$, which is the sum of the expected investment return and the mortality rate.

Here is another way to justify this issue. So far this entire article has emphasized real (inflation-adjusted) spending. Thus, if one is financing retirement from a basic mutual fund, then conceptually each year the systematic withdrawal plan (SWiP) is adjusted to account for a realized inflation rate. Indeed, one could create the same stable and predictable income stream by purchasing a life annuity from an insurance company and hence completely hedge the longevity risk. However—and this is key—there are very few companies that offer a competitively priced inflation-adjusted life annuity. More importantly, the rate by which one might adjust annual spending would depend on a personal inflation rate, which is unlikely to ever be available from an insurance company.[13] This is why we assume the available annuity is of a variable (tontine) type in which payments fluctuate based on the performance of the stock market, but withdrawals are in constant (personal) inflation-adjusted terms.

From a practical perspective, this implies that we can use the exact same equations 1 and 2 to compute the probability of retirement ruin, except that we substitute the value of $\mu + \lambda$ instead of μ. Clearly this will reduce the risk and increase the sustainability of the portfolio. And, although real-world annuities have additional features that are not quite captured by this framework, the underlying principle is exactly the same.

Table 6 provides some numerical indication of how annuitization will reduce the probability of retirement ruin, i.e. the risk quotient. For example, if a 65-year-old retiree plans on spending 8% (in real terms) and is anticipating a median age at death of 83.9, then the implied mortality rate is $\lambda = \ln[2]/(83.9-65) = 0.03667$. The nonannuitized probability of retirement ruin is 41.15%, under portfolio parameters of 7% expected return and 20% volatility. However, if this person completely annuitizes his or her nest egg, which is obviously the extreme case, the instantaneous expected return will increase from 7% to 10.3667% due to the mortality credits. In other words, since retirees are dying and abandoning their wealth at a rate of 3.667% per year, the portfolio will grow by an extra 3.667% per year. If we then compute the retirement ruin probability using the exact same $\lambda = 0.03667$, $\sigma = 0.20$, $S = 0.08$ variables, but using 10.366% instead of 7% for the input variable μ, one is left with a retirement ruin probability of 20.55%. Hence, life annuities in their most general form will reduce the retirement ruin probability and increase sustainability. And, while we have ignored management and insurance fees, which can easily be incorporated by reducing the magnitude of $\mu + \lambda$, the underlying message remains the same.

TABLE 6
You Retired and Are Planning on Spending 8% of Your initial Nest Egg per Year; Adjusted for Inflation Investment Portfolio is Expected to Earn 7% with a Volatility of 20%

(These assume variable payout annuities with no management or insurance fees.)

Retirement Age	Median Age at Death	Mortality Rate (%)	Ruin Probability with Life Annuities (%)	Ruin Probability without Life Annuities (%)
50	78.1	2.467	34.38	52.80
55	83.0	2.476	34.25	52.71
60	83.4	2.962	27.81	47.63
65	83.9	3.667	20.55	41.15
70	84.6	4.748	13.05	33.02
75	85.7	6.478	6.44	23.61
80	87.4	9.367	2.35	14.22

Note: Using part of your retirement portfolio to purchase variable life (e.g. payout or income) annuities will reduce the retirement ruin or risk quotient. This is achieved by effectively increasing the portfolio's return by the implied longevity yield or the mortality credits contained within the payout annuity.

Just as important as the life annuity product class, downside protection (e.g., portfolio insurance or put options) also reduces the retirement ruin probability. By downside protection I mean having access to derivative products that limit the range of investment outcomes and thus eliminating the "bad tails." These types of guarantees can be purchased in the open market on option exchanges, or the process can be outsourced to intermediaries such as insurance companies that offer withdrawal benefits on variable annuities. All of these GMWBs, GMIBs, and guaranteed minimum accumulation benefits (GMABs) effectively reduce the magnitude of the volatility variable σ, which in turn reduces the retirement ruin probability *assuming the insurance fees charged for this protection are not too high.*

For example, look again at Table 1. In this case a portfolio that is expected to earn 7% with a volatility of 20% will result in a 47.1% ruin probability under an 8% withdrawal rate, for a retiree planning for a median lifespan of 23 years. Note that if the volatility of the portfolio's return can be reduced from 20% to 10%, the probability of retirement ruin will (obviously) be reduced from 47.1% to 28.6%, which is substantial. This reduction in volatility would virtually eliminate the possibility of any large and pleasant (upside) surprises in exchange for avoiding large unpleasant (downside) surprises. And, even if the retiree has to pay an extra (abnormally high) fee of 200 basis points, which reduces the expected return from 7% to 5%, the probability of retirement ruin still declines from 47.1% to 46.4%. In sum, the main formulas 1 and 2 illustrate how two important product classes—life annuities and downside protection—impact the probability of retirement ruin, all in one parsimonious framework.

CONCLUSION: MANAGE YOUR RISK

Simple mathematical formulas in finance can often seduce their users into a false sense of precision regarding the true behavior of the real world. Billions of dollars have been lost by financial scientists who believed markets obeyed formulas. And, while academics might occasionally fall prey to the beauty of formulas, seasoned practitioners know the limits of their relevance. Nevertheless, the author believes this article contains a number of qualitative insights that *do apply* to real people facing retirement.

First and quite obviously, starting retirement early generates a higher Retirement RisQuotient, all else being equal. Likewise, greater retirement spending rates, lower portfolio returns, and higher investment volatility all increase this risk metric. These insights will not come as news to the financial planning profession. However, this framework has also provided a rigorous justification for using life annuities and other riders associated with variable immediate and income annuities in one parsimonious framework, since both these products increase the sustainability of a retirement income portfolio and reduce the Retirement RisQuotient.

The author would like to thank the editor of the Journal and the anonymous referees for providing comments that helped improve an earlier draft. The author would also like to acknowledge Chris Robinson and Tom Salisbury for many helpful discussions and Anna Abaimova for extensive research assistance.

NOTES

1. The Retirement RisQuotient is a trademark of The QWeMA Group and the author.
2. This is very different from the rules and terminology governing required minimum distributions (RMDs) from qualified plans, where a particular spending rate is stated in terms of a percentage of an account value at the beginning or end of a given year.
3. W.P. Bengen, "Determining Withdrawal Rates Using Historical Data," *Journal of Financial Planning* 7 (October 1994):171–181; K. Ho, M. Milevsky, and C. Robinson, "How to Avoid Outliving Your Money," *Canadian Investment Review* 7 (Fall 1994): 35–38; P.L. Cooley, C.M. Hubbard, and D.T. Walz, "Retirement Spending: Choosing a Withdrawal Rate That Is Sustainable," *Journal of the American Association of Individual Investors* 20 (February 1998): 39–47; G. Pye, "Sustainable Investment Withdrawals," *Journal of Portfolio Management* 26 (Summer 2000):13–27; M.A. Milevsky, "Spending Your Retirement in Monte Carlo," *Journal of Retirement Planning* (January/February 2001): 21–29; J. Ameriks, M. Veres, and M. Warshawsky, "Making Retirement Income Last a Lifetime," *Journal of Financial Planning* (December 2001): 60–76; and J.T. Guyton, "Decision Rules and Portfolio Management for Retirees: Is the 'Safe' Initial Withdrawal Rate Too Safe?" *Journal of Financial Planning* (October 2004): 50–60.
4. Ibbotson Associates, *Stocks, Bonds, Bills and Inflation: 2004 Yearbook* (Chicago, IL: Ibbotson Associates).

5. Note that the formula in Excel can also be typed in as GammaDist(S,alpha,beta, TRUE), where instead of the value 1 in the third argument of equation (2) the formula uses beta, but at the same time the spending rate S is not adjusted for beta. The result is the same since mathematically GammaDist (a,b,c,TRUE) is the same as GammaDist (a/c,b,1, TRUE). Other related papers in the literature have used the term beta to describe S/beta.
6. M.A. Milevsky, *The Calculus of Retirement Income: Financial Models for Pensions and Insurance* (Cambridge, U.K.: Cambridge University Press, 2006).
7. M.A. Milevsky and C. Robinson, "A Sustainable Spending Rate without Simulation," *Financial Analysts Journal* 64 (Winter 2005).
8. Ibid.
9. When the investment return is assumed lognormally distributed, the gap between the (larger) arithmetic mean and the (smaller) geometric mean is one-half the volatility squared. Note that all parameters assume continuous compounding.
10. J. Ameriks, M. Veres, and M. Warshawsky, "Making Retirement Income Last a Lifetime," *Journal of Financial Planning* (December 2001): 60–76.
11. P. Chen and M.A. Milevsky, "Merging Asset Allocation and Longevity Insurance: An Optimal Perspective on Payout Annuities," *Journal of Financial Planning* (2003): 64-72.
12. Milevsky, "The Implied Longevity Yield" (2005).
13. For a more detailed discussion of personal inflation rates as they pertain to retirement income, see M.A. Milevsky, "Retirement Income University," *Research Magazine* (May 2007).

Dynamic Allocation Strategies for Distribution Portfolios: Determining the Optimal Distribution Glide Path[*]

by David M. Blanchett, CFP®, CLU, AIFA®, QPA, CFA[†]

Editor's note: We regret that the graphics in this article have not been reproduced in color. This fact should not decrease your understanding of the subject matter.

EXECUTIVE SUMMARY

- The purpose of this paper is to determine the optimal allocation strategy (referred to as the distribution glide path) for a portfolio subject to withdrawals. But unlike most previous research, which uses static allocations, the paper includes a dynamic allocation methodology. It also introduces a methodology to incorporate risk into the decision process.
- Using historical data from four asset categories from 1927 to 2006, 43 different distribution glide paths were considered for 21 different time periods and 51 different real withdrawal rates.
- Despite the expected benefits of more sophisticated dynamic distribution allocation strategies, static equity allocations proved to be remarkably efficient.
- The most optimal glide path from a pure probability-of-success perspective was the 100/0 (100 percent equity and 0 percent fixed income/cash) static allocation portfolio. But due to the underlying variability of a 100/0 portfolio, it is unlikely that this allocation will be appropriate for most retirees.
- The absolute differences in the probability of failure among glide paths for shorter distribution periods and lower real withdrawal rates (less aggressive scenarios) were minor. The absolute differences for longer distribution periods and higher real withdrawal rates (more aggressive scenarios) were considerable.
- The paper introduces a risk-adjusted measure called the Success to Variability ratio in order to incorporate portfolio variability (standard deviation) into the optimal glide path decision process.
- When considering a variety of distribution periods and real withdrawal rates, as well as the probability of failure and the Success to Variability ratio, a balanced static allocation, such as 60 percent equity and 40 percent fixed income/cash, is likely one of the most efficient portfolio allocations for retirees.

Previous research on sustainable real withdrawal rates has focused primarily on appropriate distribution rates given a number of fixed conditions. The purpose of this paper is to provide guidance on sustainable withdrawal rates, as well as to determine the optimal allocation strategy (referred to as the distribution glide path) for a portfolio subject to withdrawals. Unlike previous research, however, this paper also introduces a methodology to incorporate risk (defined as standard deviation) into the

---

[*]Reprinted with permission by the Financial Planning Association, Journal of Financial Planning, December 2007.
[†]David M. Blanchett, CFP® CLU, AIFA®, QPA, CFA, is an institutional consultant at Unified Trust Company in Lexington, Kentucky, where he is responsible for helping 401(k) advisors with fiduciary, compliance, and investment issues relating to Unified Trust's retirement.

optimal portfolio decision process. The most common metric used to gauge the effectiveness of a distribution portfolio is whether it survives the distribution period—its probability of success. While focusing on the probability of success is an approach that certainly has merit, and it is one taken by the author, it ignores the risk of the portfolio necessary to generate the success probability. By combining the underlying risk of the portfolio and its probability of success into one metric (known as the Success to Variability ratio), it becomes possible to compare the overall effectiveness of distribution portfolios by taking both variables into account.

LITERATURE REVIEW

William Bengen is widely regarded as the first person to address the issue of sustainable real withdrawal rates from a financial planning perspective. In his article "Determining Withdrawal Rates Using Historical Data," he found that a "first-year withdrawal rate of 4 percent, followed by inflation-adjusted withdrawals in subsequent years, should be safe. In no past case has it caused a portfolio to be exhausted before 33 years." He goes on to analyze the probability of five different equity portfolios (0 percent, 25 percent, 50 percent, 75 percent, and 100 percent) sustaining various withdrawal rates (1 percent to 8 percent). He concludes that the best starting allocation for retirees is an equity allocation between 50 percent and 75 percent, based on historical returns (Bengen 1994).

The distribution periods of previous research have varied, typically ranging between 20 and 40 years, while the sustainable real withdrawal rate generally has been determined to be in the 4–5 percent range. The highest potential recommended real withdrawal rate the author is aware of, without incorporating any type of decision rules, is the 7 percent real withdrawal rate proposed by Cassaday (2006). But Cassaday's "DIESEL" portfolio is clearly optimized in-sample (that is, during the test distribution period). The future out-of-sample ability for such an allocation, or really any allocation, to provide a 7 percent real withdrawal rate is questionable. Cassaday's findings will be addressed in greater depth later in this paper.

Tezel tested a variety of portfolios over three different periods (10, 20, and 30 years) and found that optimal allocations should include domestic large and small equities, as well as government bonds and Treasury bills. Bengen (1994) and Cassaday have also noted the importance of domestic small equities, while the long-term benefits of small-cap equities (as an asset class) have been well documented by French and Fama (1992, 1993, 1995, and 1996). The importance of international equities for distribution portfolios has differed among studies. Cooley, Hubbard, and Walz (2003) find moderate benefit from including international equities, while Kizer (2005) notes a greater benefit.

In an effort to increase the probability of achieving a particular withdrawal rate, a variety of decision rules and more advanced withdrawal strategies have been introduced by Pye (2000), Bengen (2001), Guyton (2004), Guyton and Klinger (2006), and Robinson (2007). Decision rules are relevant from a common-sense perspective: when faced with the possibility of financial ruin, it is likely a retiree will decrease consumption to ensure continued survival of savings. Yet while it is certainly advantageous to create decision rules, since markets and clients (as well as their advisors) can at times be equally irrational, the ability to consistently follow such decision rules over 30 years or more is questionable. Also, dynamic and sophisticated decision rules are not viable strategies for the generally unsophisticated investing public.

LIFE EXPECTANCY

Before exploring sustainable real withdrawal rates it is important to establish a method to determine the length of the retirement distribution period. Clients not familiar with the nature of life expectancy may question the need to plan for a distribution period of 30 years or more when the current life expectancy for a newborn male is 74.[1] But when life expectancy is viewed correctly, from a probability perspective, it becomes a more dynamic consideration.

Life expectancy is defined as the average number of years of life remaining for a person at a particular age, though many people don't realize that there's a 50 percent chance for the average person to live beyond their average life expectancy. Life expectancies have increased dramatically in developed nations for a variety of reasons, such as improvements in sanitation and nutrition, as well as advances in medical technology.[2] Furthermore, life expectancy is a moving target because it increases as you age. For example, while the life expectancy of a newborn male is 74, the life expectancy for a 74-year-old male is 84—not zero. Consequently, a better way for planners and their clients to determine the length of the distribution period is to determine the acceptable probability of outliving it. Table 1 displays the probability of living to a target age under four different scenarios.

Table 1: Life Expectancy Probabilities for Various Current and Target Ages

Male Life Expectancy: Probability of Living to Target Age

Target Age \ Current Age	50	55	60	65	70	75
60	92%	95%	n/a	n/a	n/a	n/a
65	86%	88%	93%	n/a	n/a	n/a
70	76%	79%	83%	89%	n/a	n/a
75	63%	66%	69%	74%	83%	n/a
80	47%	49%	51%	55%	62%	75%
85	30%	31%	32%	35%	39%	47%
90	13%	14%	14%	16%	18%	21%
95	4%	4%	4%	4%	5%	6%
100	0%	1%	1%	1%	1%	1%

Male and Female (Same Age): Probability of Both Spouses Living to Target Age

Target Age \ Current Age	50	55	60	65	70	75
60	88%	93%	n/a	n/a	n/a	n/a
65	78%	82%	88%	n/a	n/a	n/a
70	64%	68%	73%	83%	n/a	n/a
75	47%	50%	54%	61%	74%	n/a
80	29%	31%	33%	38%	46%	62%
85	13%	14%	15%	17%	21%	28%
90	3%	4%	4%	4%	5%	7%
95	0%	0%	0%	0%	1%	1%
100	0%	0%	0%	0%	0%	0%

Female Life Expectancy: Probability of Living to Target Age

Target Age \ Current Age	50	55	60	65	70	75
60	95%	97%	n/a	n/a	n/a	n/a
65	91%	93%	95%	n/a	n/a	n/a
70	84%	86%	89%	93%	n/a	n/a
75	75%	76%	79%	82%	89%	n/a
80	62%	63%	65%	68%	73%	83%
85	45%	45%	47%	49%	53%	60%
90	25%	26%	26%	28%	30%	33%
95	9%	9%	10%	10%	11%	12%
100	2%	2%	2%	2%	2%	2%

Male and Female (Same Age): Probability of At Least One Spouse Living to Target Age

Target Age \ Current Age	50	55	60	65	70	75
60	100%	100%	n/a	n/a	n/a	n/a
65	99%	99%	100%	n/a	n/a	n/a
70	96%	97%	98%	99%	n/a	n/a
75	91%	92%	93%	95%	98%	n/a
80	80%	81%	83%	86%	90%	96%
85	61%	62%	64%	67%	71%	78%
90	35%	36%	37%	39%	42%	47%
95	12%	13%	13%	14%	15%	17%
100	2%	2%	2%	3%	3%	3%

Source: Social Security Administration Web site: http://www.ssa.gov/OACT/STATS/table4c6.html, note #1.

Once the acceptable probability of living beyond the distribution period has been decided, it is possible to determine the length of the distribution period. For example, if a male age 65 wanted no more than a 5 percent probability of outliving the projected distribution period, the appropriate distribution period would be until age 95. But if the same individual were willing to accept a 20 percent probability of outliving the distribution period, the appropriate distribution would be only to age 89.

The calculation becomes more complex when considering the joint probabilities of a married couple.

For married couples, the probability of either (or both) spouse(s) living beyond the distribution period must be considered. This is a slightly more complex calculation than determining the probability of just one individual living to a certain age. For example, the probability of a male age 60 living to age 95 is only 3.90 percent; however, the probability of at least one spouse of a married couple (both age 60) living to age 95 is 13.18 percent. If this same couple wanted to take only a 5 percent risk that neither spouse would outlive the distribution period, the appropriate distribution period would be until age 98. If only the life expectancy of the wife is considered for a couple both 65 years old (since females have longer life expectancies than males), the projected distribution period would only last until age 84. But there is a 71.38 percent probability that at least one of two spouses will live past the age of 84.

Stout and Mitchell (2006) introduce the concept of life expectancy when determining an appropriate withdrawal rate. The authors found that while a fixed 4.5 percent withdrawal rate has a 7.16 percent probability of ruin before 30 years, it has a 13.44 percent probability of ruin before life expectancy for someone 60 years old. While it is possible to select the length of the distribution period without considering life expectancy (such as 30 years), considering life expectancy allows a financial planning professional to incorporate probability into the distribution period decision.

DISTRIBUTION RATES AND PROBABILITY

The second consideration when determining a sustainable withdrawal rate also relates to probability: determining the acceptable probability of a portfolio failing. Figure 1 includes the maximum withdrawal rates for 11 different equity allocations (decreasing from 100 percent to 0 percent in 10 percent increments) for 20 different distribution periods (ranging from 20 to 40 years in 1-year increments) based on a 5 percent probability of failure. Information on the calculation methodology and the assumptions is discussed at length in the "Analysis" section of this paper.

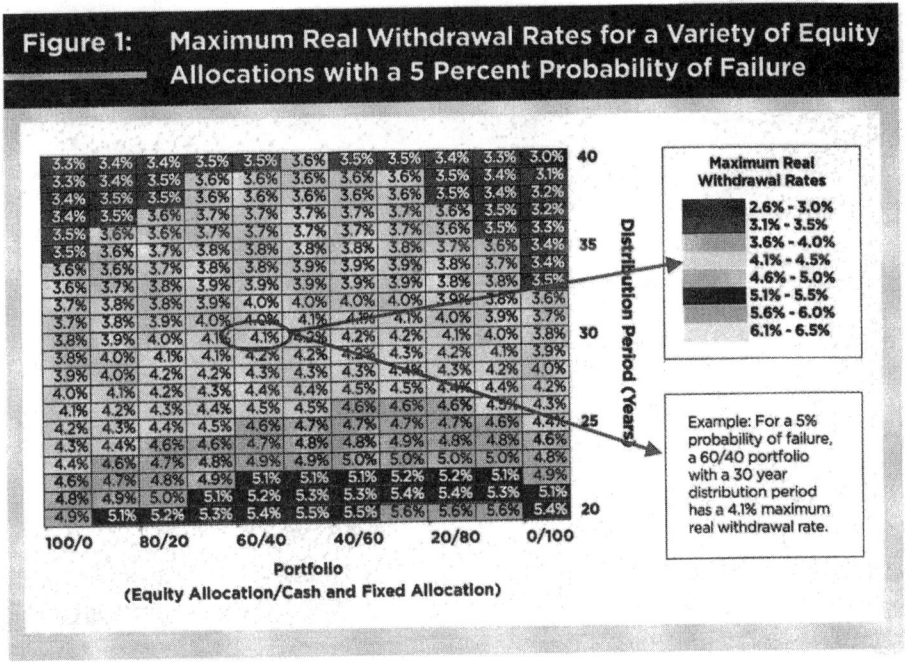

Figure 1: Maximum Real Withdrawal Rates for a Variety of Equity Allocations with a 5 Percent Probability of Failure

As noted earlier, a male age 65 who wants only a 5 percent probability of outliving the distribution period would select a target life expectancy of 95 (or a distribution period of 30 years, assuming the beginning and ending years are not inclusive). Also assume this same male wanted a portfolio of 60 percent stocks and 40 percent bonds. Based on the information in Figure 1, his real maximum withdrawal rate would be 4.1 percent. The withdrawal rate is defined in "real" terms such that the effects of inflation have been removed.

Something interesting to note about Figure 1 is the "humped" nature of the distribution. While one might expect the equity allocations at either extreme (100/0 or 0/100) to have the highest real withdrawal rates, this was not the case (based on a 5 percent probability of failure). In fact, the balanced allocations (such as 50/50 and 40/60) had the highest potential real withdrawal rates for almost every distribution scenario. Therefore, those retirees willing to accept only a 5 percent probability of failure are likely best served with a balanced allocation, regardless of their expected distribution period.

What if, however, a retiree is willing to accept a 20 percent probability of distribution failure? Figure 2 includes the same general information as Figure 1, except the probability of failure has been increased from 5 percent to 20 percent.

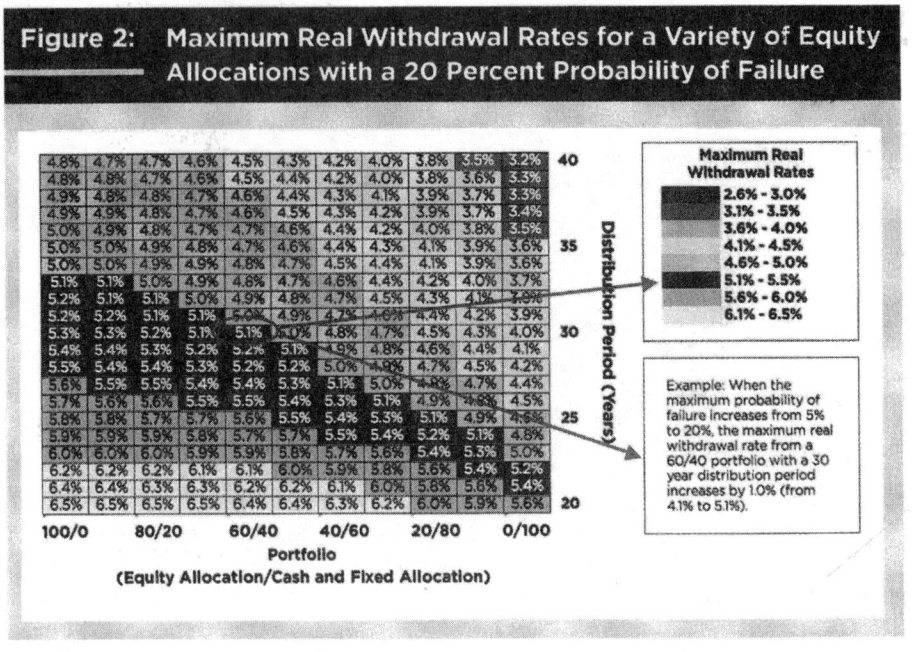

Figure 2: Maximum Real Withdrawal Rates for a Variety of Equity Allocations with a 20 Percent Probability of Failure

Notice that unlike Figure 1, the highest real withdrawal rates based on a 20 percent probability of failure are for those portfolios with higher equity allocations. While the more balanced (such as 50/50) portfolios had the highest real withdrawal rates based on a 5 percent probability of failure, the more aggressive portfolios resulted in higher real withdrawal rates when considering a greater likelihood of failure. The increase in the real withdrawal rates for all scenarios from the 0/100 portfolios to the 100/0 portfolios averaged 1.3 percent. The highest real withdrawal rate (6.5 percent) was for the 100/0 portfolio with a 20-year distribution period, while the lowest real withdrawal rate (3.2 percent) was for the 0/100 portfolio with a 40-year distribution period. The differences in Figures 1 and 2 underscore the importance of determining an acceptable probability of failure for a retiree.

ANALYSIS

The term *glide path* is commonly used to describe the decreasing equity allocation for target-date mutual fund investments. As the target-date investment approaches its retirement date, the overall equity allocation tends to decrease, at an increasing rate (taking the general shape of a concave hyperbola). For this analysis, "glide path" is used to describe the equity allocation throughout the entire distribution period. While past research on sustainable withdrawal rates has tended to focus on more distinct time periods (say 20, 30, or 40 years), this analysis will increase the scope of the distribution period by analyzing distribution periods from 20 to 40 years (in one-year increments) and real withdrawal rates from 3 percent to 8 percent (in .1 percent increments), for a total of 1,071 scenarios.

The rates of return and standard deviations for the asset categories considered for any analysis on sustainable withdrawals will have a dramatic impact on the results. In the attempt to minimize the impact of time-period selection bias, the longest period of returns available to the author was used for the analysis (1927–2006, or 80 years of data). Monthly data from 1927 until 2006 (960 months) was obtained on four asset categories:[3]

1. Cash
2. Intermediate-term bond
3. Domestic large-blend equity
4. International equity

The monthly returns were adjusted into real terms by subtracting the monthly inflation rate, which was defined as the increase in the Consumer Price Index for all Urban Consumers (CPI-U).4 Real returns were considered because people typically seek to maintain a constant level of purchasing power as prices increase with inflation. While there are different types of inflation (such as health care inflation), the CPI-U was used because it is the most common definition of inflation. The average annual geometric inflation rate for the period tested (1927–2006) was 3.51 percent. The annual real returns and annual standard deviations for the four asset categories considered in the analysis are included in Table 2.

Table 2: Annualized Real Returns and Annual Standard Deviations for Selected Asset Categories

	Geometric Real Returns	Arithmetic Real Returns	Standard Deviations
Cash	0.72%	0.81%	4.10%
Intermediate-Term Bond	2.34%	2.52%	6.14%
Domestic Large Blend Equity	7.36%	9.48%	20.99%
International Equity	5.16%	7.25%	21.59%

Data Source: See Endnote 3.

The 9.48 percent average arithmetic real return for large-blend equity over the test period was similar to the 9.17 percent return calculated by Stout and Mitchell (2006) using Ibbotson Associates data over a similar test period (1926–2004). While the historical performance represents the returns an investor could have achieved (before fees) had he or she been able to invest in these asset categories, these were not investable indexes for the entire historical period (for example, it would have been impossible to buy the International Equity proxy).

Some readers may question the exclusion of domestic small-cap equities from consideration in the portfolios despite previous research noting their benefits for distribution portfolios (refer to the "Literature Review" section, earlier in this article). The reason for their exclusion was due to their high return over the test period.

Small-cap equities (defined using the return information available on Kenneth French's Web site) had a 10.46 percent geometric annualized real return (13.89 percent nominal) and a 14.10 percent arithmetic annualized real return over the test period (17.56 percent nominal). Such high returns seem aggressive on a forward-looking basis and would result in an upward bias in the available sustainable withdrawal rate in a portfolio if these returns were not realized in the future.

For the portfolio allocations, the ratio between cash and intermediate-term bond and between domestic large blend equity and international equity was held constant regardless of the overall cash/fixed income and equity allocation. The allocation between cash and intermediate-term bond was split 50 percent each, while the allocation between domestic large-blend equity and international equity was split 66.67 percent and 33.33 percent, respectively. For example, a 60/40 portfolio would have a 20 percent cash allocation, a 20 percent intermediate-term bond allocation, a 40 percent domestic large-blend equity allocation, and a 20 percent international equity allocation.

PORTFOLIO THEORY CONSTANTLY CHANGING

While the test allocation may be viewed as overly simplistic, it is important to note that portfolio theory is constantly changing. Allocations recommended to clients today are considerably different from those recommended 20 years ago and will likely again be different from those implemented 20 years from now. Using overly precise allocations that performed well historically (Cassaday's DIESEL allocation, for example) can lead to overly optimistic withdrawal assumptions. If the original research by Brinson, Hood, and Beebower (1986), and more recently by Tokat, Wicas, and Kinniry (2006), has taught us anything, it is that the overall equity allocation decision should be the primary focus during the portfolio construction process, not the more precise allocations to different asset categories.

The actual returns used for testing purposes were created through a process known as bootstrapping. Bootstrapping is a type of simulation analysis where the in-sample test period returns are randomly recombined to create sample annual returns. For the analysis, the 960 monthly returns were randomly recombined to create hypothetical real annual rates of return for the analysis. For example, the monthly real returns for each of the four categories for the same month (for example, June 1961) would be recombined with monthly real returns from 11 other months (for example, March 1930, January 1995, May 1979, and so on) to create each hypothetical annual real return.

A benefit of using the actual historical monthly returns (through bootstrapping) is that no assumption needed to be made regarding the distribution of returns (such as lognormal or leptokurtic). A potential problem with bootstrapping, however, is that it assumes that the cross correlations among asset categories are maintained for each recombined bootstrapped sub-period. But since the recombination period was small (monthly) and the recombination sample was large (960 months spanning 80 years), this was not considered to be a significant issue.

The annual distribution was assumed to have been taken from the portfolio once a year, at the beginning of each year. Each test scenario (for example, 60/40 Constant portfolio, 30-year distribution period, and 4 percent real withdrawal rate) was subjected to a 10,000-run Monte Carlo simulation. Note that the Monte Carlo simulator (that is, bootstrap simulator) used for the analysis was built in Microsoft Excel since the author was not aware of any existing programs that could incorporate dynamic asset allocation changes (on an annual basis) during the distribution period. Also, it was important that the test used geometric returns instead of arithmetic returns, since arithmetic returns with higher standard deviations are biased downward on a geometric-return basis.

A portfolio was considered successful if it did not run out of money during the distribution period. The amount of the ending balance was not considered. The portfolios were assumed to be held in tax-deferred accounts and any tax implications of the withdrawals were ignored. Based on the bootstrapping methodology, it is implicitly assumed that the portfolios were rebalanced back to their target allocations monthly. Any potential costs associated with the rebalancing were ignored. Tax considerations were also ignored for the analysis.

TEST DISTRIBUTION GLIDE PATHS

Five primary types of distribution glide path strategies were tested. Table 3 includes each of the 43 glide paths tested.

Table 3: Beginning Allocations (Equity/Fixed) and Names of the 43 Different Distribution Glide Paths Tested

Constant	Linear	Stair	Convex	Concave
0/100 Constant	30/70 Linear	30/70 Stair	30/70 Convex	30/70 Concave
10/90 Constant	40/60 Linear	40/60 Stair	40/60 Convex	40/60 Concave
20/80 Constant	50/50 Linear	50/50 Stair	50/50 Convex	50/50 Concave
30/70 Constant	60/40 Linear	60/40 Stair	60/40 Convex	60/40 Concave
40/60 Constant	70/30 Linear	70/30 Stair	70/30 Convex	70/30 Concave
50/50 Constant	80/20 Linear	80/20 Stair	80/20 Convex	80/20 Concave
60/40 Constant	90/10 Linear	90/10 Stair	90/10 Convex	90/10 Concave
70/30 Constant	100/0 Linear	100/0 Stair	100/0 Convex	100/0 Concave
80/20 Constant				
90/10 Constant				
100/0 Constant				

1. Constant: static allocation for the entire period.
2. Linear: the equity allocation decreases by 1 percent a year throughout the distribution period.
3. Stair: the equity allocation decreases by 10 percent each 10 years throughout the distribution period.
4. Concave: the equity allocation decreases at an increasing rate and resembles a concave hyperbola throughout the distribution period.[5]
5. Convex: the equity allocation decreases at a decreasing rate and resembles a convex hyperbola throughout the distribution period.[6]

Any type of equity reduction for the distribution glide paths was assumed to begin during the second distribution year. For example, a 70/30 Linear strategy would have a 70 percent allocation during the first year, a 69 percent allocation in the second year, a 68 percent allocation in the third year, and so on. Figure 3 includes a chart that contains the equity allocations for each of the 43 different distribution glide paths considered for the analysis over the entire 40-year distribution period.

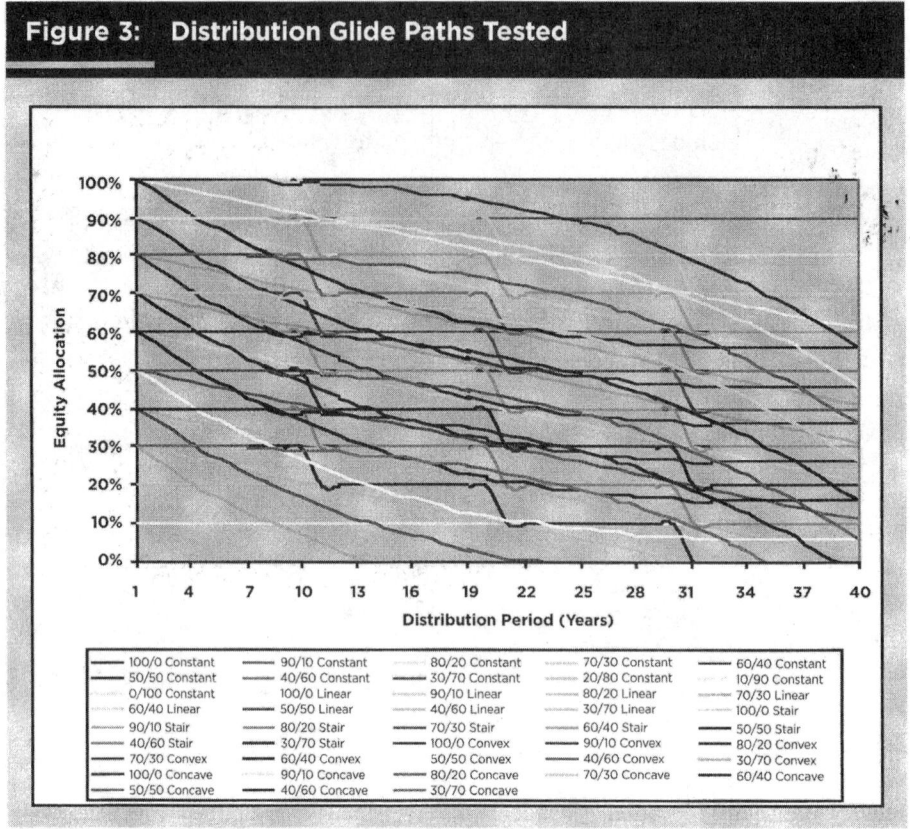

Figure 3: Distribution Glide Paths Tested

The distribution glide paths tested represent a number of potential equity reduction strategies. To give the reader a scope of the analysis conducted for this paper, each of the 43 different test glide paths was tested for distribution periods between 20 and 40 years (in one-year increments, inclusive) for withdrawal rates between 3 percent and 8 percent (in .1 percent increments, inclusive) at 10,000 runs per scenario. This means that each glide path had a total of over 10 million different test runs, and the overall analysis conducted over 450 million different test runs.

DISTRIBUTION GLIDE PATHS: GENERAL RESULTS

Table 4 contains the results for 9 of the 1,071 scenarios tested. While the paper will later address a more thorough analysis covering each of the tested scenarios, Table 4 provides the reader with a general insight into the overall efficiency of the 43 different distribution glide paths for a select few scenarios. The best distribution glide path for each scenario is highlighted in green, while the worst glide path for each scenario is highlighted in blue. Note, if multiple glide paths had the same probability of failure and were either the best or worst for the scenario (for example, a 4 percent real withdrawal rate and a 20-year distribution period), they would both be highlighted.

A variety of general conclusions can be reached from Table 4.

Table 4: Probabilities of Failure for a Variety of Scenarios for Each of the 43 Distribution Glide Paths

	Scenario								
Distribution Rate	4.00%	4.00%	4.00%	5.00%	5.00%	5.00%	6.00%	6.00%	6.00%
Distrib. Period (Years)	20	30	40	20	30	40	20	30	40
Glide Path	Probability of Failure								
0/100 Constant	0.00%	14.81%	98.25%	0.08%	99.67%	100.00%	63.99%	100.00%	100.00%
10/90 Constant	0.00%	3.01%	65.53%	0.07%	84.03%	99.94%	26.35%	99.99%	100.00%
20/80 Constant	0.00%	2.10%	32.77%	0.10%	52.53%	93.44%	16.76%	96.60%	99.93%
30/70 Constant	0.00%	2.06%	18.07%	0.51%	32.55%	70.74%	12.51%	81.27%	96.41%
40/60 Constant	0.00%	2.66%	13.73%	1.02%	24.44%	53.35%	11.79%	65.16%	86.42%
50/50 Constant	0.09%	3.29%	10.97%	1.75%	19.28%	37.96%	11.16%	49.84%	70.06%
60/40 Constant	0.17%	3.58%	10.13%	2.23%	17.52%	32.61%	11.38%	42.49%	60.35%
70/30 Constant	0.33%	4.21%	9.77%	3.16%	16.34%	27.10%	11.97%	36.16%	50.14%
80/20 Constant	0.77%	4.64%	9.42%	3.80%	15.66%	25.06%	12.20%	33.10%	44.21%
90/10 Constant	1.00%	5.39%	9.83%	4.52%	15.48%	23.30%	12.62%	30.58%	40.58%
100/0 Constant	1.56%	6.10%	10.11%	5.14%	15.58%	22.26%	13.32%	28.80%	37.55%
30/70 Linear	0.00%	3.64%	38.57%	0.50%	49.28%	92.76%	16.16%	93.75%	99.69%
40/60 Linear	0.00%	3.31%	23.10%	0.77%	33.93%	72.58%	13.84%	77.20%	95.75%
50/50 Linear	0.01%	3.59%	16.16%	1.50%	25.31%	53.98%	12.45%	61.54%	84.58%
60/40 Linear	0.13%	4.26%	13.62%	2.41%	21.29%	41.65%	12.72%	50.02%	70.94%
70/30 Linear	0.45%	4.56%	11.85%	3.04%	18.39%	34.00%	12.39%	41.92%	60.03%
80/20 Linear	0.52%	4.86%	10.61%	3.73%	17.04%	28.81%	12.42%	36.29%	51.05%
90/10 Linear	0.92%	6.71%	13.78%	4.31%	17.77%	28.22%	12.94%	34.05%	45.04%
100/0 Linear	1.36%	5.81%	10.84%	4.99%	15.98%	24.09%	13.42%	30.43%	40.74%
30/70 Stair	0.00%	3.07%	29.14%	0.41%	40.83%	85.09%	14.00%	87.91%	98.99%
40/60 Stair	0.00%	3.09%	18.78%	0.92%	28.54%	64.24%	12.21%	70.71%	92.45%
50/50 Stair	0.06%	3.55%	14.16%	1.63%	22.06%	47.13%	12.00%	55.03%	78.16%
60/40 Stair	0.11%	3.82%	12.02%	2.06%	18.90%	37.52%	11.61%	46.10%	65.86%
70/30 Stair	0.36%	4.51%	11.29%	3.10%	17.68%	31.30%	12.62%	38.75%	54.69%
80/20 Stair	0.67%	4.97%	10.34%	3.68%	16.19%	27.37%	12.36%	34.58%	47.73%
90/10 Stair	1.16%	5.90%	10.82%	4.75%	16.04%	25.19%	13.23%	32.34%	43.64%
100/0 Stair	1.51%	6.04%	10.45%	5.16%	15.94%	23.23%	13.31%	29.69%	39.12%
30/70 Convex	0.00%	6.86%	67.72%	0.27%	74.96%	99.44%	25.13%	99.33%	100.00%
40/60 Convex	0.00%	5.50%	45.66%	0.87%	53.30%	92.78%	18.18%	92.56%	99.55%
50/50 Convex	0.01%	4.73%	28.93%	1.19%	36.46%	74.87%	15.39%	77.10%	95.50%
60/40 Convex	0.04%	4.71%	19.40%	2.08%	27.23%	57.15%	13.86%	62.40%	85.48%
70/30 Convex	0.13%	4.87%	15.38%	2.93%	22.55%	43.35%	14.04%	49.96%	72.12%
80/20 Convex	0.33%	4.99%	12.57%	3.53%	19.32%	35.29%	12.64%	42.11%	60.59%
90/10 Convex	0.71%	5.50%	11.96%	4.03%	17.52%	29.62%	13.12%	36.84%	52.04%
100/0 Convex	1.05%	5.99%	11.43%	4.92%	17.15%	26.77%	13.56%	33.48%	46.07%
30/70 Concave	0.00%	2.45%	24.14%	0.47%	36.22%	78.64%	13.46%	84.05%	97.93%
40/60 Concave	0.01%	2.99%	16.69%	0.95%	26.23%	59.31%	12.21%	67.73%	89.26%
50/50 Concave	0.08%	3.25%	12.39%	1.63%	19.68%	42.50%	11.14%	51.09%	73.69%
60/40 Concave	0.04%	4.71%	19.40%	2.08%	27.23%	57.15%	13.86%	62.40%	85.48%
70/30 Concave	0.36%	4.54%	10.55%	3.12%	16.54%	29.19%	11.75%	37.25%	52.02%
80/20 Concave	0.58%	4.82%	10.20%	3.74%	15.93%	26.19%	12.60%	33.93%	46.50%
90/10 Concave	1.03%	5.55%	10.30%	4.50%	15.56%	24.13%	12.70%	30.64%	41.22%
100/0 Concave	1.55%	6.15%	10.37%	5.13%	15.70%	22.69%	13.35%	29.13%	38.23%
Minimum	0.00%	2.06%	9.42%	0.07%	15.48%	22.26%	11.14%	28.80%	37.55%
Maximum	1.56%	14.81%	98.25%	5.16%	99.67%	100.00%	63.99%	100.00%	100.00%
Range	1.56%	12.75%	88.83%	5.09%	84.19%	77.74%	52.85%	71.20%	62.45%

Best glide path for scenario   Worst glide path for scenario

A variety of general conclusions can be reached from Table 4.

The best distribution glide path now might be the worst distribution glide path later. The distribution period and the real withdrawal rate can be extremely important when determining the optimal glide path. For example, the 0/100 Constant portfolio was one of the best glide paths for the 4 percent real withdrawal rate and 20-year distribution period but was the worst glide path for the 4 percent real withdrawal rate and the 40-year distribution period. Therefore, studies based on different distribution periods (say 20 years versus 40 years) are likely to have varying conclusions if multiple periods are not considered.

Die soon enough and the allocation doesn't matter. The absolute differences in the probability of failure for lower real withdrawal rates and for shorter distribution periods (less aggressive scenarios) was minor compared with the differences in the probability of failure for higher real withdrawal rates and longer distribution periods (more aggressive scenarios). For example, the range of failure probabilities for the 20-year distribution period with a 4 percent real withdrawal rate was only 1.56 percent (between .00 percent and 1.56 percent), while the range of failure probabilities for the 40-year distribution period with a 6 percent real withdrawal rate was 62.45 percent (between 37.55 percent and 100 percent). This represents an extreme difference in probability of success and underscores the importance of using higher equity allocations, at least initially, during the distribution period.

Static allocations did very well. The Constant (static) distribution glide paths were remarkably efficient despite their simplicity. While one would think that a more dynamic asset allocation strategy (such as the Concave distribution glide path) might result in a lower probability of failure (higher probability of success), the Constant portfolios had the lowest probabilities of failure for all but one of the above test scenarios (apart from the 20-year, 4 percent scenario, which had multiple "best" distribution glide paths).

While the probabilities of failure tended to be slightly lower than previous research on an absolute basis, the overall results of the analysis were similar. For example:

1. Stout and Mitchell (2006) found that a 65/35 Constant allocation, assuming a 4.5 percent real withdrawal rate and a 30-year distribution period, has a 13.44 percent probability of failure over 30 years. This author found a 65/35 Constant allocation (not included above) has a 10.04 percent probability of failure (an absolute difference of 3.40 percent).
2. Ameriks and Warshawsky (2001) found that a 60/40 Constant allocation, assuming a 4.5 percent real withdrawal rate and a 30-year distribution period, has a 12.60 percent probability of failure in 30 years. Based on the same criteria, this author determined the probability to be 8.72 percent, for an absolute difference of 3.88 percent.
3. Bengen (2001) found that a 63/37 Constant allocation, assuming a 5 percent real withdrawal rate and a 30-year distribution period, has a 19 percent probability of failure in 30 years. This author found a 60/40 Constant allocation has a 17.52 percent probability of failure (an absolute difference of 1.48 percent).

The greatest disparity among the results of this analysis and previous published research was by Cassaday. He contends that his DIESEL portfolio is able to sustain a 7 percent withdrawal rate over a 33.5-year distribution period with a 9.1 percent probability of failure. The most similar distribution glide path tested for this analysis, the 80/20 Constant, had a 57.92 percent probability of failure over a 34-year distribution period. This represents a probability of failure that was *six times greater* than the probability of failure determined by Cassaday.

Two key problems with Cassaday's research were the inflation assumption and the clearly in-sample optimized portfolio. First, Cassaday assumed a 3 percent inflation rate for the test period (January 1, 1972, through July 31, 2005), despite the fact that the actual geometric annualized inflation rate during the test period (as measured by the increase in the CPI-U) was 4.75 percent. Second, while Cassaday's DIESEL allocation clearly performed well historically (that is, in-sample), the out-of-sample (future) benefits of such are still unknown. Determining the best historical allocations is easy—predicting which allocations will do best in the future is an entirely different matter.

BEST DISTRIBUTION GLIDE PATHS

For the general results, the 100/0 Constant was the distribution glide path that had the lowest probability of failure for the nine scenarios considered in the "General Results." This relationship was consistent when all 1,071 scenarios were considered. Figure 4 shows the best distribution glide path for each distribution period and withdrawal rate tested. The color for each scenario (or cell) represents the respective optimal glide path for that scenario. For example, the color pink, which represents the 30/70 Constant distribution glide path, covers the 4.0 percent real withdrawal rate for the 30-year distribution period. This means the 30/70 Constant distribution glide path was the glide path with the lowest probability of failure (or highest probability of success) among the 43 glide paths tested for that scenario.

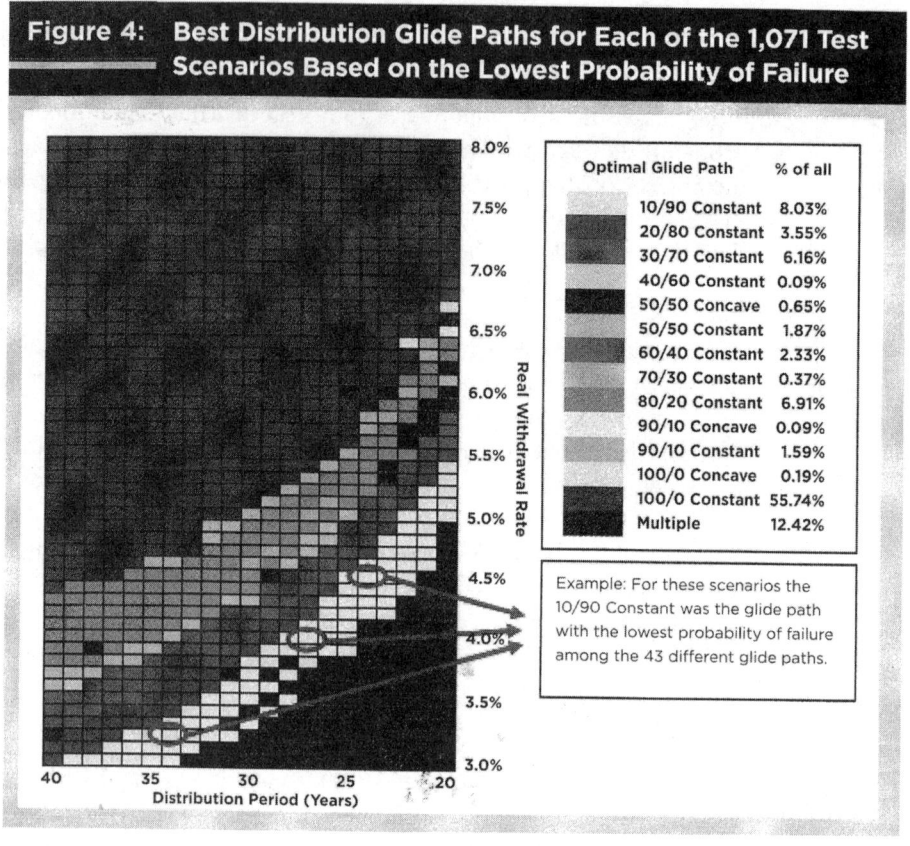

Figure 4: Best Distribution Glide Paths for Each of the 1,071 Test Scenarios Based on the Lowest Probability of Failure

Of the 43 different distribution glide paths considered, only 14 were distinctly better than the other glide paths for any given scenario. If multiple glide paths had the same (lowest) probability of failure for a given scenario, the term "Multiple" is used since no one methodology was optimal. The Multiple category was prevalent primarily for only the least aggressive scenarios (that is, the ones with the lowest withdrawal rates and the shortest distribution periods).

While 100/0 Constant was the most common optimal distribution glide path, the 0/100 Constant distribution glide path was not uniquely the best for any of the 43 distribution glide paths. The lack of congruence among the portfolios for the different test scenarios was also somewhat alarming. For example, there is a "jump" for scenarios where the 30/70 Constant portfolio is the optimal distribution glide path to where the 80/20 Constant is the optimal glide path if the real withdrawal rate is increased by a mere .2 percent or the distribution period is increased by two years. The long-term differences in both return and risk for a 30/70 and an 80/20 portfolio are considerable. This suggests that a more balanced allocation, with a slightly higher equity allocation, such as a 60/40 Constant distribution glide path, would likely be a more practical allocation for retirees compared with either extreme.

BEST DISTRIBUTION GLIDE PATHS EXCLUDING CONSTANT PORTFOLIOS

Because an equity reduction strategy is a likely methodology for a number of retirees who will want to reduce their equity exposure (risk, in other words) throughout retirement, a second analysis was conducted to determine the optimal distribution glide path where the Constant glide paths were removed. Figure 5 contains the results of this analysis.

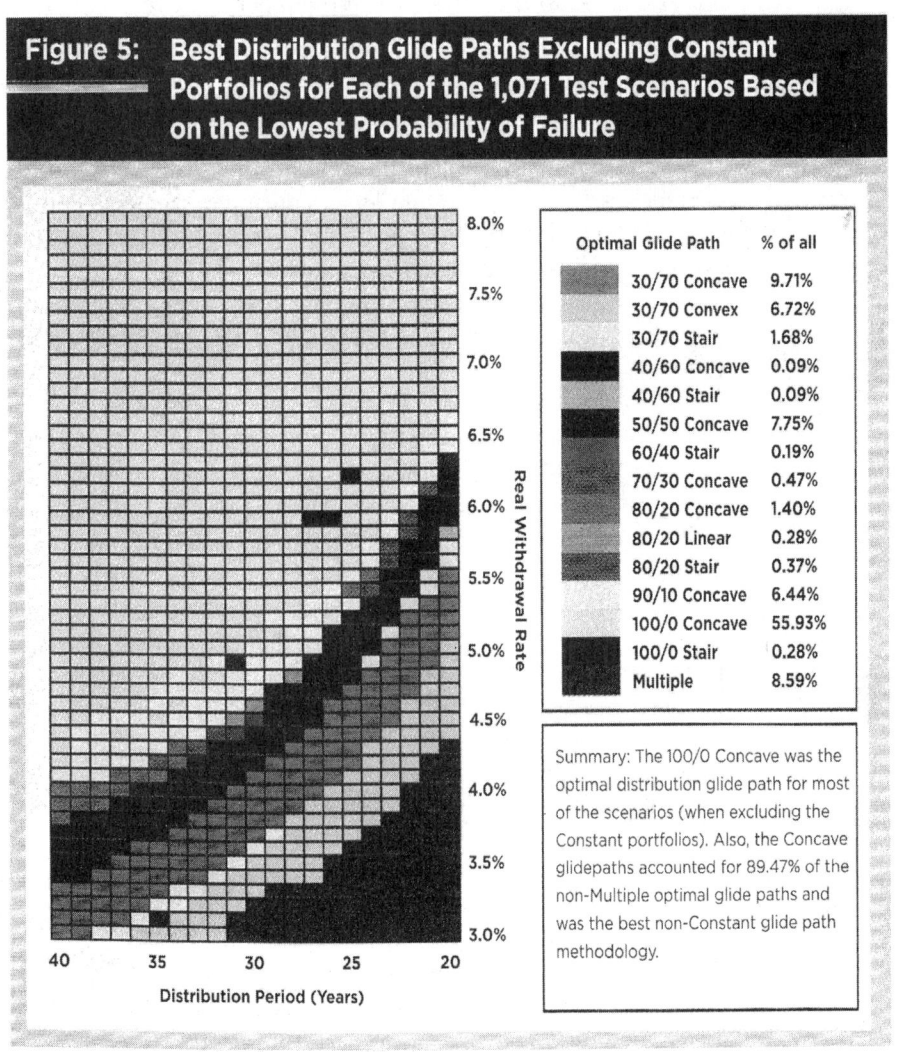

Figure 5: Best Distribution Glide Paths Excluding Constant Portfolios for Each of the 1,071 Test Scenarios Based on the Lowest Probability of Failure

Optimal Glide Path	% of all
30/70 Concave	9.71%
30/70 Convex	6.72%
30/70 Stair	1.68%
40/60 Concave	0.09%
40/60 Stair	0.09%
50/50 Concave	7.75%
60/40 Stair	0.19%
70/30 Concave	0.47%
80/20 Concave	1.40%
80/20 Linear	0.28%
80/20 Stair	0.37%
90/10 Concave	6.44%
100/0 Concave	55.93%
100/0 Stair	0.28%
Multiple	8.59%

Summary: The 100/0 Concave was the optimal distribution glide path for most of the scenarios (when excluding the Constant portfolios). Also, the Concave glidepaths accounted for 89.47% of the non-Multiple optimal glide paths and was the best non-Constant glide path methodology.

When the Constant portfolios are removed, the 100/0 Concave portfolio proved to be the most optimal distribution glide path and the Concave methodology was clearly the best distribution strategy. The 100/0 Concave glide path was the best glide path for 55.93 percent of all scenarios, while the Concave methodology accounted for 89.47 percent of scenarios that were not considered Multiple. The Concave methodology has an equity reduction methodology that is highest at the beginning and then starts to decrease at a faster and faster rate throughout the distribution period. The shape of the Concave glide path is very similar to the shape of the glide path for most target-date mutual funds.

INTRODUCING THE SUCCESS TO VARIABILITY RATIO[7]

From a probability-of-failure perspective, the Constant portfolios proved to be far from inefficient. If one were to select a portfolio based entirely on the probability of success, the 100/0 Constant distribution glide path (the most aggressive glide path tested) would likely be considered the most optimal. This is because although the 100/0 Constant glide path tended to have the lowest probability of success for shorter distribution periods and lower real withdrawal rates, the absolute differences were small for those scenarios, and it proved to be a much more advantageous strategy (on an absolute basis) for longer distribution periods and higher real withdrawal rates.

But selecting an optimal distribution glide path based entirely on the probability of success ignores the underlying risk associated with the portfolio. The 100/0 Constant distribution glide path has nearly seven times the variability (or risk) of the 0/100 Constant glide path (17.08 percent versus 2.20 percent). While retirees are concerned with having enough money during retirement (that is, a high probability of success), they are also concerned with the variability of their portfolios. High portfolio variability can lead to sleepless nights for clients, which can then result in poor investment decisions (exiting the market after a large loss). Therefore, the underlying variability of a portfolio should be considered when selecting the optimal portfolio for a retiree.

To incorporate variability into the optimal distribution glide path decision, a risk-adjusted method for determining the optimal Constant distribution glide path is introduced. This method, called the Success to Variability ratio, uses standard deviation as the definition of risk because standard deviation is the most common definition of risk among investment professionals.[8] Although financial markets exhibit non-normal characteristics, such as kurtosis and skewness, standard deviation is nevertheless a useful tool to describe the distribution of returns for investments financial markets (DiBartolomeo 1993).

Based on logic similar to that of the Sharpe ratio,[9] the numerator is adjusted (using the probability of success instead of the excess return) to create a success-to-variability ratio:

$$\text{Success to Variability Ratio} = \frac{\text{Probability of Success}}{\text{Standard Deviation of the Portfolio}}$$

The Success to Variability ratio allows the user to assign a risk-adjusted score to a distribution portfolio, which considers both the probability of success and the underlying risk of the portfolio. The higher the Success to Variability ratio score, the more optimal the portfolio. As an example, the 100/0 Constant distribution glide path was very efficient on a probability-of-success basis. But when variability is included in the optimal decision process, it becomes much less optimal. Figure 6 includes the optimal Constant distribution glide paths based on the highest Success to Variability ratio for each of the 1,071 scenarios tested. Table 5 compares the overall distribution of the portfolios. Note, Figure 4 provides a good reference for Figure 6 if the reader is interested in comparing the Success to Variability ratio results to the pure probability of success results.

When the Success to Variability ratio is used to define the optimal distribution glide path, the less aggressive portfolios become much more efficient. The 0/100 Constant glide path had the highest Success to Variability ratio for most of the 1,071 scenarios (267 or 24.93 percent). In contrast, the 0/100 Constant glide path was never defined as the uniquely optimal portfolio based entirely on the probability of success. The 100/0 Constant distribution glide path, which had the highest probability of success for 56.02 percent of the scenarios, was only optimal on a Success to Variability ratio basis for 7.38 percent of the scenarios.

Table 5: Comparison Between the Probability of Success and the Success to Variability Ratio for the Optimal Portfolio Decision

Glide Path	Portfolio Standard Deviation	Pure Probability of Success		Success to Variability Ratio	
		#	%	#	%
0/100 Constant	2.20%	0	0.00%	267	24.93%
10/90 Constant	2.76%	86	8.03%	117	10.92%
20/80 Constant	3.96%	38	3.55%	69	6.44%
30/70 Constant	5.49%	66	6.16%	81	7.56%
40/60 Constant	6.93%	1	0.09%	48	4.48%
50/50 Constant	8.56%	28	2.61%	127	11.86%
60/40 Constant	10.04%	27	2.52%	59	5.51%
70/30 Constant	11.92%	4	0.37%	98	9.15%
80/20 Constant	13.72%	74	6.91%	65	6.07%
90/10 Constant	15.31%	18	1.68%	61	5.70%
100/0 Constant	17.08%	600	56.02%	79	7.38%
Multiple	n/a	129	12.04%	0	0.00%
Total		1,071	100.00%	1,071	100.00%

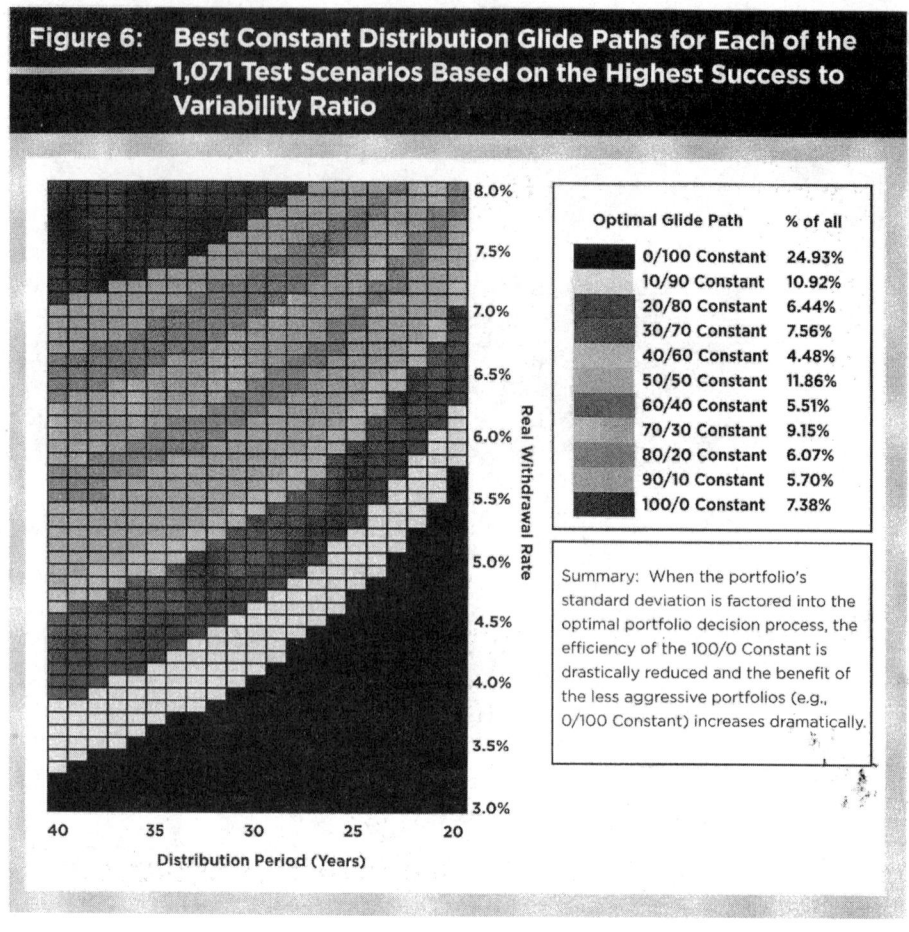

Figure 6: Best Constant Distribution Glide Paths for Each of the 1,071 Test Scenarios Based on the Highest Success to Variability Ratio

Optimal Glide Path	% of all
0/100 Constant	24.93%
10/90 Constant	10.92%
20/80 Constant	6.44%
30/70 Constant	7.56%
40/60 Constant	4.48%
50/50 Constant	11.86%
60/40 Constant	5.51%
70/30 Constant	9.15%
80/20 Constant	6.07%
90/10 Constant	5.70%
100/0 Constant	7.38%

Summary: When the portfolio's standard deviation is factored into the optimal portfolio decision process, the efficiency of the 100/0 Constant is drastically reduced and the benefit of the less aggressive portfolios (e.g., 0/100 Constant) increases dramatically.

The difference between the optimal portfolio definitions for the two methods emphasizes the importance noted earlier of taking a balanced approach to selecting the equity allocation for a client. While the 100/0 Constant distribution portfolio was the portfolio with the highest overall probability of success and the 0/100 Constant distribution portfolio was the portfolio with the highest overall Success to Variability Ratio, neither extreme is likely the best for most clients. Instead, a more balanced approach to investing, such as a 60/40 portfolio, is likely a good starting place for most retirees since it has a good balance of success and risk.

LIMITATIONS WITH THE SUCCESS TO VARIABILITY RATIO

While the Success to Variability ratio provides the user with a methodology to introduce risk in the optimal distribution portfolio process, it has three limitations:

1. It would be difficult to use the Success to Variability ratio for a distribution glide path with a non-constant equity allocation. This is because unlike the Constant, or static glide paths, non-constant glide paths (such as Concave) would have non-constant standard deviations throughout the distribution period.

2. While standard deviation is the most common definition of risk for investment purposes, investors do not fear making too much money (upside deviation), which is why other definitions of risk (such as downside risk) may prove to be more useful.

3. The difference between a probability of failure of 5 percent and 10 percent, or the difference between a standard deviation between 6 percent and 9 percent, is not constant across investors. Incorporating more advanced risk-matching strategies (such as Lower Partial Moments) may prove useful in solving this problem.

Despite its limitations, the Success to Variability ratio is a useful tool in determining the optimal distribution portfolio.

While future research is likely necessary to further refine the concept, the concept of considering both the probability of success and the underlying risk of a portfolio is an important one.

OUR CLIENTS AND OUR PROFESSION

A key assumption of the analysis was that the distribution glide paths tested were followed for the entire retirement period. Given the demographics of our profession and the often irrational nature of clients, this may be a questionable assumption. Currently, the average approximate age of a CFP practitioner is 49 and only 25 percent of CFP certificants are under the age of 40.[10] If we assume a distribution period of 20-plus years, it is likely that only a handful of financial planning professionals who determine the initial withdrawal strategy will likely be around to determine the strategy's success.

Furthermore, the analysis assumed that a client actually sees the distribution glide path strategy through to completion. Adverse market conditions can lead to irrational investing, such as buying high and selling low, which is common among individual investors (one only needs to refer to one of the many DALBAR studies). Such behavior can have a dramatic negative impact on the success of any given distribution strategy. This suggests that equity allocations should not be overly aggressive and that the underlying variability of the portfolio should be considered when determining the optimal distribution portfolio for a client.

FEES AND EXPENSES

Investment fees and expenses such as advisory fees and fund expenses must be taken into consideration when projecting a real withdrawal rate because, like the retiree's distribution income, such fees represent fixed outflows that must be deducted from a portfolio regardless of market conditions. Although this is a topic that was covered at length by Pye (2001), it is important to understand the impact that fees and expenses can have on retirement income when determining an appropriate withdrawal rate for a retiree.

For example, if a retiree needs a 4 percent real withdrawal rate for 30 years, the probability of failure for a 60/40 static portfolio is only 3.58 percent. But if we assume a 1 percent advisory fee and an average expense ratio of .5 percent (for an aggregate cost of 1.5 percent), the real withdrawal rate necessary to meet the client's 4 percent distribution goal would need to be increased by 1.5 percent to 5.5 percent (ignoring any additional tax considerations).[11] The probability of failure for a 5.5 percent real withdrawal rate and a 30-year distribution period (with a 60/40 portfolio) is 28.99 percent, which is more than eight times the probability failure for the 4 percent withdrawal rate. If the client's initial distribution goal was 5 percent, there is a 17.52 percent probability of failure; however, a real withdrawal rate of 6.5 percent (again assuming an increase of 1.5 percent for fees and expenses) has a probability of failure of 56.32 percent. In summary, fees and expenses are very important and must be considered during the sustainable real withdrawal rate for a client portfolio.

CONCLUSION

Despite their simplicity, Constant (static allocation) distribution glide paths proved to be remarkably efficient distribution strategies, followed by the Concave distribution glide path strategy. But in order to determine the true optimal distribution glide path, a variety of factors must be considered. If the distribution period and real withdrawal rate are both known, it is possible to determine the optimal distribution glide path based entirely on probability of failure. However, focusing entirely on the probability of failure ignores the potential variability of the portfolio allocation, which is likely an important consideration for most retirees.

While the unique facts and circumstances associated with each client should dictate the appropriate distribution portfolio, it is likely that an overly aggressive portfolio (say 100/0) will prove to be too risky for most clients, while an overly conservative portfolio with a higher Success to Variability ratio (say 0/100) will not provide an adequate probability of success when addressing the likelihood of longer distribution periods. Therefore, based on the research conducted for this paper, as well as other qualitative and practical considerations, the optimal allocation for most retirees is likely a balanced portfolio, such as a 60 percent equity and 40 percent fixed income/cash allocation.

ENDNOTES

1. Social Security Administration Web site: http://www.ssa.gov/OACT/STATS/table4c6.html.
2. Life Expectancy by Age, 1850–2004, Web site: http://www.infoplease.com/ipa/A0005140.html.
3. Data definitions:
   Intermediate-term bond. Defined as the return on the Moody's Seasoned AAA Corporate Bond Yield, assuming a ten-year duration. Data obtained from the St. Louis Federal Reserve: http://research.stlouisfed.org/fred2/.
   Cash. Defined as the yield on the 3-Month Treasury bill. Secondary Market Rate, data obtained from Tradetools.com (1927–1933) and the St. Louis Federal Reserve (1934–2006): http://research.stlouisfed.org/fred2/.
   Domestic large-blend equity. Defined as the return on the "Big Neutral" portfolio based on the 2 x 3 portfolio return information publicly available on Kenneth French's Web site: http://mba.tuck.dartmouth.edu/pages/faculty/ken.french/data_library.html.
   International equities. Defined as the return on the Global Financial Data World ex-USA Return Index, data obtained from Global Financial Data.
   Since pure historical data is used for this analysis, as is common among distribution research, the author would caution the reader that if future returns are lower than historical returns, the actual result of a distribution portfolio may be materially different from what this research suggests.
4. Data obtained from the Bureau of Labor Statistics: http://data.bls.gov/PDQ/servlet/SurveyOutputServlet.
5. The equity reduction for the concave allocations was determined using the following formula: ((Previous Year's Equity Allocation) – ((Distribution Year)^2)*.00002)). All allocations were rounded to the nearest whole percentage.
6. The convex allocation formula was determined using the mirror image of the concave hyperbola.

7. Credit for this portion must be given to Dr. Gregory W. Kasten, who after working with the author on the paper, recognized the importance of combining both the probability of success (or failure) and the underlying variability of the portfolio and suggested such a metric.
8. Familiarity was one of the original reasons (along with cost and convenience) that Markowitz (1959) selected variance (or standard deviation) as the definition of risk (as opposed to semi-standard deviation, which also referred to as downside risk). Familiarity and convenience are two of the primary reasons for its continued popularity, despite its noted shortcomings. See, for example, Nawrocki (1999), Sortino and Satchell (2001), and Swisher and Kasten (2005).
9. For readers not familiar with the Sharpe ratio, it is a reward-to-variability (or risk) calculation that is a common method for comparing portfolios and investments on a risk-adjusted basis. The calculation is the excess return (return minus the risk-free rate) divided by the standard deviation.
10. Based on the demographic information obtained from the CFP Board Web site (updated as of January 31, 2007): http://www.cfp.net/media/profile.asp.
11. Assuming that the investment fees increase the necessary real withdrawal rate as opposed to decreasing the real returns of the portfolio.

REFERENCES

Ameriks, John, Robert Veres, and Mark J. Warshawsky. 2001. "Making Retirement Income Last a Lifetime." *Journal of Financial Planning* 14, 12 (December): 60–76.

Bengen, William P. 1994. "Determining Withdrawal Rates Using Historical Data." *Journal of Financial Planning* 7, 1 (January): 14–24.

Bengen, William P. 1996. "Asset Allocation for a Lifetime." *Journal of Financial Planning* 9, 4 (August): 58–67.

Bengen, William P. 1997. "Conserving Client Portfolios During Retirement, Part III." *Journal of Financial Planning* 10, 6 (December): 84–97.

Bengen, William P. 2001. "Conserving Client Portfolios During Retirement, Part IV." *Journal of Financial Planning* 14, 5 (May): 110–118.

Brinson, Gary P., L. Randolph Hood, and Gilbert L. Beebower. 1986. "Determinants of Portfolio Performance." *Financial Analysts Journal* 42, 4 (July/August): 39–44.

Cassaday, Stephan Q. 2006. "DIESEL: A System for Generating Cash Flow During Retirement." *Journal of Financial Planning* 19, 9 (September): 60–65.

Cooley, Phillip L., Carl M. Hubbard, and Daniel T. Walz. 1998. "Retirement Savings: Choosing a Withdrawal Rate That Is Sustainable." *Journal of the American Association of Individual Investors* 20 (February): 16–21.

Cooley, Phillip L., Carl M. Hubbard, and Daniel T. Walz. 2003. "Does International Diversification Increase the Sustainable Withdrawal Rates from Retirement Portfolios?" *Journal of Financial Planning* 16, 1 (January): 74–80.

DiBartolomeo, Dan. 1993. "Portfolio Optimization: The Robust Solution." White Paper. www.northinfo.com/documents/45.pdf.

Fama, Eugene F. and Kenneth R. French. 1992. "The Cross-Section of Expected Stock Returns." *Journal of Finance* 47, 2 (June): 427–465.

Fama, Eugene F., and Kenneth R. French. 1993. "Common Risk Factors in the Returns on Stocks and Bonds." *Journal of Financial Economics* 33, 1 (February): 3–56.

Fama, Eugene F., and Kenneth R. French. 1995. "Size and Book-to-Market Factors In Earnings and Returns." *Journal of Finance* 50, 1 (March): 131–155.

Fama, Eugene F., and Kenneth R. French. 1996. "Multifactor Explanations of Asset Pricing Anomalies." *Journal of Finance* 51, 1 (March): 55–84.

Guyton, Jonathan T. 2004. "Decision Rules and Portfolio Management for Retirees: Is the 'Safe' Initial Withdrawal Rate Too Safe?" *Journal of Financial Planning* 17, 10 (October): 54–61.

Guyton, Jonathan T. and William J. Klinger. 2006. "Decision Rules and Maximum Initial Withdrawal Rates." *Journal of Financial Planning* 19, 3 (March): 49–57.

Kizer, Jared. 2005. "Drawing Down and Looking Abroad: International Diversification and Sustainable Withdrawal Rates." *Journal of Indexes* (May/June): http://www.indexuniverse.com/JOI/index.php?id=535.

Markowitz, H. M. 1959. *Portfolio Selection: Efficient Diversification*

Real Longevity Insurance with a Deductible: Introduction to Advanced-Life Delayed Annuities (ALDA*)

Moshe A. Milevsky[†]

This paper explores the financial properties of a concept product called an advanced-life delayed annuity (ALDA). The ALDA is a variant of a pure deferred annuity contract that is acquired by installments, adjusted for consumer price inflation, and pays off toward the end of the human life cycle. The ALDA concept is aimed at the growing population of North Americans without access to a traditional defined benefit (DB) pension plan and the implicit longevity insurance that a DB plan contains. I show that under quite reasonable pricing assumptions, a consumer can invest or allocate $1 per month, while saving for retirement, and receive between $20 and $40 per month in benefits, assuming the deductible in this insurance policy is set high enough. The ALDA concept might go a long way in mitigating the psychological barrier to voluntary lump-sum annuitization.

1. INTRODUCTION

There appears to be universal agreement among financial economists and pension actuaries about the substantial social welfare benefits from payout (or immediate) annuity contracts. But the public and media have yet to embrace this risk-management instrument as being equally important as a well-diversified retirement portfolio of stocks and bonds. Part of the low acceptance and take-up rates for annuitization can be attributed to the fact that a strong consensus has yet to emerge regarding the optimal age at which to annuitize as well as the optimal design of the ideal payout annuity. Indeed, the global trend away from defined benefit (DB) and toward defined contribution (DC) pension plans, in conjunction with exceptionally low levels of voluntary annuitization, cry out for a new way—or revisiting old ways—of thinking about the provision of lifetime retirement income.

This paper promotes, advocates, and explores the financial risk-and-return properties of a *concept product* called an advanced-life delayed annuity (ALDA), which is a variant of a *pure* deferred annuity contract that is paid by installments, linked to consumer price inflation, while locking in longevity insurance. Reduced to its essence, the ALDA would be acquired at a young age—and small premiums would be paid over a long period of time—but the ALDA would begin paying an inflation-adjusted life-contingent income only at the advanced age of 80, 85, or even 90. The product would contain zero cash value and no survival or estate benefits and could not be commuted for cash at any age. Of course, these stringent (no forfeiture benefits) design requirements might be impossible to attain, given the

---

*Copyright © 2008 by the Society of Actuaries, Schaumburg, Illinois. Reprinted with permission.
[†]Moshe A. Milevsky, PhD, is an Associate Professor of Finance at the Schulich School of Business at York University and the Executive Director of the Individual Finance and Insurance Decisions (IFID) Centre in Toronto, Canada, 4700 Keele St., Toronto, Ontario, Canada, M3J1P3, milevsky@yorku.ca.

current regulatory environment. But, in theory, these features, combined with standard actuarial, interest, and (possibly) lapsation discounting, would reduce the ongoing premium for this insurance to mere cents on the dollar. The ALDA and its derivatives would be a close relative to a DB pension and are intended for those who don't have one, possibly even as an option within a DC (or 401k)–style pension.

From a slightly different perspective, this type of product is akin to buying auto, home, or health insurance with a large deductible, which is also the optimal strategy—and common practice— when dealing with catastrophic risk. By analogy, the ALDA's longevity insurance would kick in only once the longevity risk became substantial and financially unsupportable. Indeed, the raison d'être of life-contingent annuities is the acquisition of mortality credits, which at advanced ages are substantial and unavailable from any competing asset class. During the early years of retirement—when most pension decisions are made— the magnitude of these credits is quite small once survivor benefits, insurance fees, and antiselection (i.e., annuitant versus population) costs are included. In contrast, the ALDA would entitle the holder to insurance against the risk of outliving assets, but only when the assets actually run the risk of being depleted, which is later in life.

As King Solomon said, "there is nothing new under the sun," and the intellectual origins of this particular idea can be traced to a 25-year-old article in the *Journal of Risk and Insurance* by Stephenson (1978). It has doubtlessly been toyed with, contemplated, and possibly even designed by many pension actuaries ever since. Currently, though, these products are unavailable on a stand-alone basis, although a number of companies in the United States—such as MetLife and GenWorth—have recently started offering variants of ALDA. Stephenson criticized existing annuity products in the marketplace and argued in favor of adopting designs that contain high ratios of "protection to investment." He developed a concept called the *index of protection* and demonstrated that properly designed deferred annuities could provide greater inflation-protected value to consumers. This paper continues that line of thought by arguing that the fairly low actuarial premium for providing longevity insurance, together with well-known facts about individual behavior, make a compelling case for offering—and perhaps even imposing the purchase of—ALDAs in DC pension plans, as a substitute for a DB pension.

From a microeconomic (consumer welfare) framework, the ALDA would transform the portfolio choice and asset-allocation problem from a stochastic date of death to a deterministic one in which the terminal horizon becomes the annuity's payment commencement date. From a practical point of view, retirees no longer would have to worry about the "risk" of outliving their assets. They should be secure in the knowledge that if and when they reach an extreme (to be defined) age, their longevity insurance would begin. In fact, this might create interesting incentive effects in their own right.

I believe that the ALDA is preferable to a pure endowment policy that would (mature and) pay a lump sum at age 80, 85, or 90 since it would continue to provide periodic lifetime income regardless of how long the annuitant lived beyond the endowed age. This continual flow of income would serve as a better hedge for the household's liabilities and would reduce the (psychological, behavioral) risk of misspending the lump sum once it became available. Indeed, a pure endowment's embedded longevity insurance is terminated as soon as the policy matures. And it is highly unlikely the policyholder would (again) annuitize the lump sum at age 80, 85, or 90 for the same behavioral reasons individuals are reluctant to annuitize at retirement. The main thesis underpinning this paper is that engaging in irreversible financial transactions—that is, annuitization—involving large sums of money will *never* be appealing to individuals regardless of (whether they grasp) the importance of longevity insurance.

The remainder of the paper is organized as follows. Section 2 provides a brief review of the academic literature on the gains from annuitization and discusses some of the empirical evidence regarding the aversion to voluntary annuitization. Section 3 is the theoretical core of the paper; it describes the financial, economic, and actuarial properties as well as the different design possibilities for the ALDA contract. Section 4 discusses some related annuity products that recently have been made available to the public and describes an attempt by the author to get the ALDA introduced by a large insurance company in Canada. Section 5 discusses some of the issues surrounding longevity risk management, and Section 6 concludes the paper with some general comments.

2. Gains from Annuitization

The industry as well as scholars in the field are aware of—and continue to puzzle over—the extremely low levels of voluntary annuitization exhibited among new and elderly retirees. From a theoretical perspective, this aversion to annuitization is inconsistent with a standard Modigliani life-cycle model of savings and consumption as described by Yaari (1965). In a life-cycle model with no bequest motives, Yaari demonstrated that all consumers hold actuarial notes (a.k.a. life contingent annuities) as opposed to liquid and marketable assets. This implies that when given the chance, retirees should convert their liquid assets into lifetime payout annuities that provide longevity insurance and protection against outliving one's money. The rationale behind Yaari's results is that returns from actuarial notes (life annuities) dominate all other assets, since the *living* inherit the assets of the *deceased*. Moreover, having access to life annuities enables the rational consumer to better smooth his or her planned consumption over the life cycle and hence gain greater lifetime utility of wealth. And, although some might react to the failure of this utility-based argument to sway retirees, by dismissing the economic theory itself, there are a number of more intuitive ways to explain the benefits of annuitization.

A simple example can help convert the problem into the language of investments. Suppose, according to population mortality tables, that there is a 20% chance that a 95-year-old female will die during the next year and before she reaches her 96th birthday. If 1,000 such females enter into a one-year term-life annuity (a.k.a. tontine) agreement by investing $100 each in a pool yielding 5%, the funds will grow to $105,000 by the end of the year. Of the initial 1,000 females, 800 are expected to survive, with a rather small variance around the expected value, leaving an average of $105,000/800 = $131.25 per survivor. This is a total return of 31.25%. This quite obviously far exceeds the interest rate (or investment return) of 5% used to ''store'' the funds, because the annuitants have seceded control of assets in the event of death.

The powerful algebra of longevity credits can be stated symbolically as follows: If r denotes the effective interest rate per year and if p is the probability of survival per year, then the return for the survivors from the one-year annuity is expected to be $(1 + r)/p - 1 > r$. The expectation will become reality as long as the group of annuitants participating in this risk-mitigating scheme is large enough. The gap between the one-year returns to the survivors and the interest rate is the so-called mortality credits. Table 1 illustrates some numerical values for these credits at different ages, using a unisex annuitant mortality table.

To put these numbers in perspective, a (unisex) 85-year old who decides *not* to annuitize and instead *take his or her chances* investing in traditional (nonmortality contingent) asset classes and finance consumption from discretionary wealth would have to earn 725 basis points (which is 7.25%) above the risk-free rate of 6% during the next year, in order to be as well-off as someone who decided to annuitize at age 85. Think of this (6% + 7.25% =) 13.25% number as a hurdle rate that must be earned by the self-annuitizer to keep up with the "annuitizer." At age 90 this hurdle rate increases to 18.56%, which becomes virtually unachievable using any conventional investment products. Of course, different interest rates and mortality tables will lead to different numerical results, but the order of magnitude is always the same. *At advanced ages nothing beats the implied yield from a payout annuity.*

As many actuaries understand and appreciate, the risk-sharing principle of a tontine is in fact the concept underlying all immediate annuities, and all pension plans for that matter. In practice, the risk-sharing agreement is made over a series of years, as opposed to just one. Think of it as term longevity insurance versus *whole-life* longevity insurance. The mechanics remain the same, and the survivors derive a higher return—which is then amortized over one's life—compared to placing the funds in a conventional (nonmortality-contingent) asset. See the paper by Milevsky (2005) for an in-depth discussion of how to calculate the implied longevity yield—akin to the above mortality credits—from a multiple-period payout annuity versus a one-period tontine.

TABLE 1
Investment Benefits from Annuitization Assuming 40/60 Male/Female Split for Annuity 2000 Table under 6% Interest

Age	Mortality Credits (b.p.)
55	35
60	52
65	83
70	138
75	237
80	414
85	725
90	1,256

Also, while the example assumes that r is fixed, in theory, the exact same principle applies with a variable investment return. In fact, the ex post returns might be even higher. For example, the 1,000 females, who are 95 years old, can invest their $100 in a stock mutual fund that earns the random return R. They do not know in advance what the fund/pool will earn. At the end of the year the annuitants will learn (or realize) their investment returns, and then split the gains among the surviving pool. Moreover, in the event the investment earns a negative return—and loses money—the participants will share in the losses as well, but the effect will be mitigated by the mortality credits. Algebraically, the expected return will be the same $(1 + R)/p - 1 > R$. In fact, this concept is the foundation of a *variable* immediate annuity. See Milevsky (2006) for more detailed information about the mechanics of variable immediate annuities, which are also referred to as variable payout or index-linked annuities.

In practice, most insurance companies go one step further than the above (participating annuity) example and actually *guarantee* that the annuitant will receive the mortality credit enhancements even if the mortality experience of the participants is better than expected. In other words, in the above-mentioned example for fixed annuities, with an expected 20% mortality rate, the insurance company would guarantee that all survivors receive 31.25% on their money, regardless of whether or not 20% of the group died during the year. See Poterba (1997) for a history of the development of the variable annuity in the United States.

Nevertheless, despite the highly appealing arguments in favor of annuitization there is little evidence that retirees are voluntarily embracing this arrangement. Modigliani (1986), Friedman and Warshawsky (1990), and Brown (2001), among others, have carefully documented that very few people consciously choose to annuitize their marketable wealth. In the comprehensive Health and Retirement Survey (HRS) conducted in the United States, only 1.57% of the HRS respondents reported annuity income. Likewise, only 8.0% of respondents with a DC pension plan selected an annuity payout. The Society of Actuaries and LIMRA, as reported in Sondergeld (1997), conducted a study showing that only 0.3% of variable annuity contracts were annuitized during the 1992–94 period. According to the National Association of Variable Annuities, of the $909 billion invested in variable annuities during 2003, only 2% were annuitized. It remains to be seen whether the high take-up rates the industry has experienced lately for guaranteed minimum income benefits (GMIBs)—which are additional riders available on variable annuities— will translate into increased annuitization activity in the future.

Indeed, the frustratingly low appreciation of the welfare benefits of annuitization has led some researchers to advocate mandatory annuitization for a fraction of discretionary pension savings that benefit from income-tax sheltered growth. See, for example, Bateman, Kingston, and Piggott (2001).

In the face of poor empirical evidence, various theories have been proposed to salvage this aspect of the life-cycle hypothesis and to justify the low demand for longevity insurance. For example, in one of the earlier papers on this "puzzle," Kotlikoff and Spivak (1981) argued that family-risk pooling may be preferred to public annuity markets, especially given the presence of adverse selection and transaction costs. Indeed, a married couple functions as a mini-annuity market, as elaborated by Brown and Poterba (2000). Friedman and Warshawsky (1990) showed that average yields on individual life annuities during the late 1970s and early 1980s were lower than plausible alternative investments. The reduced yield was largely attributed to actuarial loads and profits, which have declined over time, according to work by Mitchell et al. (1999).

Bernheim (1991) argues that large preexisting annuities in the form of Social Security and government pensions might serve as an additional deterrent to voluntary annuitization. In a distinct line of reasoning, Yagi and Nishigaki (1993) argue that the actual design of annuities impedes full annuitization. One cannot obtain a life annuity that provides arbitrary payments contingent on survival, which is dictated by Yaari's (1965) model. They must be either fixed (in nominal or real terms) or variable (linked to an index). This constraint forces consumers to hold both marketable wealth and annuities.

In summary, many explanations exist for why people do *not* annuitize further wealth. Although these justifications have explanatory power, they fail to provide financial advice on optimal product design as well as normative strategies for the elderly. Furthermore, they cannot account for the casual observation that most people shun life annuities simply because they want to maintain control of their assets.

This paper takes the approach that consumers will remain reluctant to annuitize a large lump sum at retirement—regardless of *if and when* academics manage to solve the so-called annuity puzzle. What is needed is to accept that a sudden irreversible transaction will never be popular, especially when the underlying funds were under complete discretionary control of the annuitant up to the point of retirement. The alternative is perhaps slow annuitization over a very long period of time[1] or the gradual purchase of longevity insurance that start providing income only at any advanced age. The ALDA could be offered as an additional rider on existing saving and insurance products or could be sold as a stand-alone product. The critical factor would be to take the edge off a daunting and irreversible annuitization decision.

3. Pricing the ALDA

Although the pricing and valuation of life annuities are the bread and butter of the pension actuary, this section will briefly review the mathematics, if only to increase the accessibility and reach of this article. With some slight abuse of actuarial notation—and my apology to the profession—I start by letting $\bar{a}_{x:u}$ denote the continuous time *annuity factor at age x*. In my simple model it represents the price, value, and cost of acquiring a financial contract that pays an inflation-adjusted life contingent $1 per annum from time zero (i.e., age x) to time u (i.e., age $x + u$). Implicit in the expression is a real interest rate (or curve) denoted by r. The retirement or pension income flow is adjusted for realized inflation each and every year. Thus, in nominal terms, the life annuity initially pays $1 per annum and then increases by the realized rate of the consumer price index. When the pricing or valuation rate r is constant (i.e., no term structure effects) the expression for the annuity factor reduces to the familiar

$$\bar{a}_{x:u} := \int_0^u e^{-rs} \left(_s p_x\right) ds, \qquad (3.1)$$

where $(_s p_x)$ denotes the conditional survival probability, also in continuous time. Without any loss of generality, I will suppress the symbol $u = \infty$ and use $\tilde{a}x$ when I am dealing with a complete life annuity that pays until death. In this paper and the subsequent numerical examples, the ALDA purchase age will range from $x = 35$ to 45, while the ALDA commencement age will range from age $x + u = 70$ to 90.

By construction the net single premium (NSP) at age $x < (x + u)$ for a $1 per annum ALDA benefit is the annuity factor in equation (3.1) discounted for the probability of survival and the time value of money. Mathematically,

$$\text{NSP} = e^{-r(u)} \bar{a}_{x+u}(_u p_x), \qquad (3.2)$$

where the first term captures the u years of interest, the second term represents the annuity factor that commences at age $x+u$, and the third term is the conditional probability that someone currently aged x will survive for u more years. Note that equation (3.2) is consistent with the idea that there are no benefits provided to beneficiaries in the event the primary annuitant dies between the initial acquisition age x and the benefit commencement age $x + u$. Adding a survivorship benefit would increase the NSP and reduce the appeal of the product from a risk management perspective. This idea was also stressed by Stephenson (1978). Note that some of the ALDA-like products that have recently been created by insurance companies for the 401k (DC pension) market contain survivorship benefits and cashable options—for example, the ability to sell the units at some commuted value—that completely eliminate the mortality credits during the accumulation phase.

TABLE 2
Theoretical Net Single Premium for Advanced Life Delayed Annuity

Purchase Age (x)	Annuity Commencement Age			
	$x + u = 70$	$x + u = 75$	$x + u = 80$	$x + u = 85$
r = 3.25% (Real) Pricing Rate				
35	$3.642	$2.376	$1.412	$0.731
40	4.294	2.802	1.665	0.861
45	5.070	3.308	1.965	1.017
r = 2% (Real) Pricing Rate				
35	6.346	4.325	2.687	1.456
40	7.029	4.790	2.976	1.612
45	7.796	5.313	3.301	1.788
r = 1% (Real) Pricing Rate				
35	9.951	7.013	4.509	2.532
40	10.484	7.388	4.750	2.667
45	11.061	7.795	5.012	2.814

Note the focus on real (after inflation) versus nominal returns in the pricing and valuation of the annuity factor. The interest rate r is used in two places in equation (3.2). The first is to discount a single cash flow prior to the annuity commencement date—which covers the next u years—and the second is to price the annuity and discount the repeated cash flows that occur after age $x + u$. Thus, in practice one could envision using slightly different interest rates during the deferral period versus the payout period. Indeed, as I alluded to earlier, one could go a step further and use a real yield curve r_t—implied perhaps from REAL TIPS—as opposed to a single interest rate, which would conform to capital market pricing techniques.

To provide some numerical intuition for the NSP of the ALDA, I offer the following example under a continuous Gompertz approximation to discrete mortality. This law of mortality has been used extensively in the pricing of "academic" life annuities—see, for example, Frees, Carrière, and Valdez (1996)—and is a reasonable approximation for the purposes of the exposition in this paper.

Recall that under a Gompertz law of mortality, the (natural logarithm) of the conditional survival probability is defined equal to

$$\ln(_sp_x) = e\left(\frac{x-m}{b}\right)\left(1 - \frac{s}{b}\right), \tag{3.3}$$

where m and b are the "modal" and "scale" parameters of the remaining lifetime distribution. Thus, for example, if we start (i.e., purchase the ALDA in one lump sum) at age $x = 35$, with benefits commencing at age $x + u = 85$ under Gompertz parameters of $m = 90$ and $b = 9.5$, and a real interest rate of $r = 3.25\%$, the NSP from equation (3.2) is $0.731 in current dollars. This *pure* deferred lifetime annuity will pay $1 in inflation-adjusted terms each year, commencing at age 85, in exchange for a premium payment of less than $1 today. The $0.731 came about from multiplying the age 85 annuity factor of $\bar{a}_{85} = 6.679$ by the 0.556 probability of survival to age 85 and then by the 0.1969 time-value-of-money factor.

Using the formula, Table 2 displays the NSP of a *unisex* annuity purchase age (x) and a variety of annuity commencement ages ($x + u$) under the same Gompertz approximation to mortality and a variety of different real interest rate assumptions r.

For reference purposes, the assumed life expectancy was 84.7, 84.8, and 84.9 at ages 35, 40, and 45, respectively. Likewise, the implied life expectancy at the annuity commencement age was 87.6, 88.9, 90.7, and 92.9 at ages 70, 75, 80, and 85, respectively. No improvement factors or any other dynamic projection methodologies were used to generate these (illustrative) numbers. The above calculation is trivial from an actuarial point of view since this type of ALDA, that is, one that is paid by a lump sum up front, is a well-known deferred annuity. I now proceed to computing the periodic premium for the ALDA, which eventually involves some subtle assumptions about lapsation behavior.

Payment for the ALDA will not be made in one lump sum; rather, the annuitant makes a series of real (after inflation) nonrefundable and noncashable payments between the ages of x and $x + u$, which would then entitle him or her to a real $1 per annum for life, commencing at age $x + u$. In practice, this would be implemented by linking both the periodic premiums and the benefits to the same consumer price index so that all cash flows could be discounted using the same unit of account. I emphasize that the pure actuarial pricing of this product would *not* require any assumptions about future inflation or nominal rates. The *premiums* would be variable in nominal terms, but fixed in real terms. Likewise, the *benefits* would be variable in nominal terms, but fixed in real terms. From a purely financial economic perspective, the lack of any asset-liability mismatch between the units of account should not require any additional reserves or capital requirements. Of course, the current regulatory environment might impede this theoretical invariance and further increase the cost of the product. A full discussion of these important yet complex issues would take us well beyond the scope of this brief article.

In either event, the NSP must be actuarially amortized over the next u years, contingent on survival. Using our previous notation and assuming no lapsation, the net periodic premium (NPP) for the ALDA is

$$\text{NPP} = \frac{e^{-r(u)}\bar{a}_{x+u}\left({}_{u}p_{x}\right)}{\bar{a}_{x:u}}, \qquad (3.4)$$

where the numerator is the NSP and the denominator effectively spreads these payments over the u years between the initial purchase age and the ALDA commencement period. Equation (3.4) is the standard method of converting single premiums into periodic life-contingent premiums. Note that the annuity factor in the denominator is subscripted by the purchase age x, while the factor in the numerator is subscripted by the commencement age $x + u$. Intuitively, for any given purchase age x, the longer the deferral period u, the greater the annuity factor $\bar{a}_{x:u}$, and the lower the ongoing periodic premium. Similarly, as emphasized in the earlier discussion, it is quite conceivable that the pricing interest rate r in the denominator's factor will differ from (be greater than) the pricing rate in the numerator's factor. This is because a non-flat-yield curve in practice will result in different (constant) interest rate approximations, depending on the period that is being discounted. Regardless, they are both real (after inflation) rates.

Here are some examples under the same pricing conditions that I considered in the NSP case. When the initial purchase age is $x = 35$ and the annuity commencement age is $x + u = 85$, then under an $r = 3.25\%$ real interest rate, the NPP needed to create a $1 per annum real lifetime annuity is precisely $0.0312 per annum. In other words, a mere three cents on the dollar per annum—paid over a period of 50 years—will generate an income flow of $1 per year for life. This is a factor of 32 times the ongoing premium. I can scale this quantity up (or down) and declare that, for each $100 of inflation-adjusted premium per week, month, or year, the ALDA will pay an inflation-adjusted pension of $3,200 per week, month, or year. If instead of using ages 35 and 85, I use ages 40 and 80, while retaining the same interest rate of $r = 3.25\%$, the NPP becomes $0.0779, which is a factor of 12.8 times the ongoing premium. Finally, if I increase the interest rate to 4%, the NPP becomes $0.061, which is a factor of 16.2. Table 3 converts the NSP numbers in Table 2 into payout factors that are the reciprocal of the NPP.

Table 3 also includes the extreme case in which the commencement age is 90. In this case, a 35-year-old, for example, would receive $77.7 real dollars starting at age 90 for each real dollar paid from age 35 under an $r = 3.5\%$ pricing rate. The number would drop by more than half to $32.5 real dollars per year for life under a lower $r = 1\%$ pricing rate. Thus, with yields on inflation-protected zero-coupon bonds (a.k.a. TIPS) in the 2–2.5% vicinity at the time of writing, one would be expected to see ''real'' prices for ALDA in the marketplace somewhere between the lower and upper bounds of 3.5% and 1% provided in the table. Of course, whether or not a 35-year-old would actually persevere and pay premiums for 55 years is debatable, which leads us to the topic of lapsation, which I will return to later.

TABLE 3
Theoretical ALDA Income Payout Factors Lifetime Retirement Income per Premium Dollar

Purchase Age (x)	Annuity Commencement Age				
	$x + u = 70$	$x + u = 75$	$x + u = 80$	$x + u = 85$	$x + u = 90$
r = 3.25% Pricing Rate					
35	5.6	9.2	16.1	32.0	77.7
40	4.4	7.2	12.8	25.7	62.6
45	3.3	5.6	10.1	20.4	49.9
r = 2% Pricing Rate					
35	3.9	6.2	10.5	20.2	47.3
40	3.1	5.1	8.7	17.0	39.9
45	2.4	4.1	7.1	14.0	33.2
r = 1% Pricing Rate					
35	2.9	4.5	7.6	14.3	32.5
40	2.4	3.8	6.5	12.4	28.3
45	1.9	3.2	5.5	10.5	24.3

3.1 WHO TAKES THE MORTALITY AND INTEREST RATE RISK?

The above description and pricing mechanics are predicated on the ability of the insurance company to guarantee the pricing rate and the mortality table. In practice, if the insurance company offering the ALDA were to earn less than the pricing rate, and/or experience mortality that was worse than assumed, the company would obviously face the potential of severe losses. This raises the question of whether the ALDA should have a participating structure in which a minimal income payout factor would be guaranteed, and then depending on investment performance and mortality experience, the income would be increased. Indeed, this kind of arrangement—which involves an additional level of risk sharing—is at the heart of some products that have recently been introduced in the North American marketplace. Thus, for example, a commercially viable version of the ALDA would guarantee an implicit real rate of *at least* 2% applied to the Annuity 2000 mortality table, and then, depending on future financial and economic conditions, the benefits could be ratcheted up (increased) on a periodic basis. The extent to which this minimum guarantee is calibrated would depend on a number of factors including the ability of the insurance company to hedge part of its mortality risk (i.e., the risk of underestimating longevity) using life and health insurance products in their portfolio with the opposite exposure. I will return to this issue in Section 5.

3.2 LAPSATION CONSIDERATIONS

Although everyone who purchases (or starts) an ALDA likely has the full intention of holding the product to maturity, it is unreasonable to assume that 100% of all survivors will continue to pay premiums until the commencement date. In fact, if the product is structured with absolutely no cash value and/or no ability to scale down the income benefit by reducing premiums, there is a high probability that people will lapse the product prior to the benefit commencement age.

Therefore, the lapsation phenomena might be taken into account in the original design. From a pricing perspective, one can assume the existence of an instantaneous lapse-rate curve, which is akin to a force of mortality, which determines the probability that the contract will be lapsed as a function of the number of years since initiation. This curve will most likely start at a level close to zero and then increase as time goes on, but will start to decline again as the ALDA nears the commencement date. The psychological justification would be that on an aggregate level as individuals "see" the payoff horizon approaching, they are likely to reduce the rate at which they become disillusioned with the product.

Lapse-adjusted pricing would impact the NPP of the ALDA in two partially offsetting ways. First, it would reduce the numerator in equation (3.4) by virtue of the smaller number of people who will utilize the product, but it would also reduce the denominator of equation (3.4) by virtue of the reduced size of the group who will actually cover the actuarial present value of the ALDA benefit. It is relatively easy to prove—and is a textbook case in multiple decrement theory—that the net effect will be a total reduction in the relevant NPP in equation (3.4), regardless of the precise shape of the lapsation curve. Indeed, for most reasonable specifications, the premiums will decline quite substantially.

One could envision a wide number of specifications, each leading to their own premiums. For illustrative purposes, Table 4 takes a simple approach and displays the relevant income payout factors assuming a constant 2% lapse rate each year. In other words, the difference between Tables 4 and 3 includes the assumption that each year 2% (in continuous time) of the ALDA population ceases to make payments, but for nonmortality-driven reasons. I emphasize again that this is a very crude approximation, and that actual lapsation behavior and intensity in such a product would depend on the number of years remaining until the product commencement date as well as number of health-related factors. Despite the simplicity, a number of interesting facts emerge from Table 4. Income multiples increase by a factor of two to three, but this impact is even further pronounced as the commencement date becomes later.

TABLE 4
Lapse-Adjusted ALDA Income Payout Factor Lifetime Retirement Income per Premium Dollar

Purchase Age (x)	Annuity Commencement Age				
	$x + u = 70$	$x + u = 75$	$x + u = 80$	$x + u = 85$	$x + u = 90$
r = 3.25% Pricing Rate; 2% Lapse Rate					
35	8.7	15.3	29.2	63.4	168.4
40	6.3	11.2	21.6	47.0	125.3
45	4.4	8.1	15.7	34.5	92.3
r = 2% Pricing Rate; 2% Lapse Rate					
35	5.9	10.0	18.4	38.5	98.0
40	4.4	7.7	14.3	30.1	76.8
45	3.3	5.8	10.9	23.2	59.5
r = 1% Pricing Rate; 2% Lapse Rate					
35	4.3	7.2	12.9	26.2	64.8
40	3.4	5.7	10.4	21.3	52.7
45	2.6	4.4	8.2	17.0	42.4

3.3 SCALING DOWN BENEFITS

If the insurance company is unwilling to price the product using a lapse curve (assumption), one could envision an ALDA design in which the premiums could be voluntarily stopped at some age z prior to age $x + u$. The benefit would then be reduced accordingly, perhaps with the same benefit commencement date, to avoid antiselection problems. The benefit would be scaled down by computing the *ex post* actuarial present value of the premiums at the lapse age z and then scaled into the original NSP to arrive at a fractional scaled-down percentage of the originally guaranteed payout factor from Table 2. There are a number of compelling reasons why this particular incarnation of the ALDA would be the most popular from a consumer standpoint, and I envision variants of this design as having the best chance of survival in the marketplace.

In sum, I have described and motivated the basic *actuarial chassis* of the ALDA product, which, despite its actuarial simplicity, contains a number of important economic benefits. The main features can be summarized as follows: (a) real inflation-adjusted benefits, (b) an annuity commencement date that is irreversible and well into the retirement years akin to a deductible on an insurance policy, together with (c) slow and prolonged premium payments that counteract the ingrained reluctance of consumers to annuitize in one lump sum.

4. DOES THIS PRODUCT EXIST ALREADY?

The answer to this question is *yes, but* . . . Indeed, as mentioned earlier, a number of North American insurance companies have recently launched variants of ALDA under numerous guises and incarnations. In fact, some of the older long-term-care (LTC) insurance policies also had an element of the ALDA as part of their benefit structure. I refer the reader to a recent article in *Best's Review* (February 2004, pp. 70–74) for a review of the industry in the payout annuity market. For example, Prudential Financial and Genworth as well as MetLife and Principal Financial are just some of the named companies that are in the process of developing, or already offer, a financial vehicle that allows one to acquire lifetime income using a dollar-cost averaging strategy. And, although it is beyond the mandate of this paper to critique the merits and pitfalls of each, it seems the emphasis on real (after-inflation) income has been neglected by most of the current manufacturers. Furthermore, as I mentioned above, some of the inherent flexibility and choice embedded in these products may "kill" the mortality credits and detract from the ultimate objective, which is to *encourage annuitization at the lowest possible cost*.

On a more pessimistic note, it seems that industry innovation around retirement income (payout) products has been taking place for decades, but with very few noticeable successes. In the late 1980s, the IDS Life Insurance company in Minneapolis (an American Express company) offered a variant of the ALDA called IDS retirement assurance. Under this product, the annuity premiums were paid in one lump sum upon initiation, the deferral or delay period lasted for 30 or 40 years, and the benefit commenced at age 80. This product paid out in nominal terms, included a survivor and/or surrender benefit of premiums paid (without interest), and included a participating structure linked to mortality credits. The policy statement contained a fairly complicated schedule of mortality credits that would be added to the account on attaining certain ages. And, despite the differences with the ALDA product described above, this product did in fact come close to achieving the objectives of longevity insurance with a deductible. The sales literature created by IDS stated that "this product is designed for your later retirement years, and does this at a cost that is far lower than conventional annuities." Unfortunately, despite the sound theoretical foundations, this product was a commercial failure, and the company withdrew sales soon after.

In the same spirit, in the lead-up to the writing of this paper, the author approached one of the largest insurance companies in Canada with a proposal to develop an ALDA product. The author also volunteered to be the first to purchase the product (at age 35) and assist in the public marketing and promotion campaign once the product was launched. Initially, there was much excitement about the concept, and the insurance company's actuaries produced the pricing schedule displayed in Table 5, the number of which are well within the range of the numbers presented in Table 3. In general, the payout multiples were lower than the numbers obtained using our theoretical model, although at higher ages the numbers do seem excessively lower than what theory would dictate. For example, an ALDA purchased at age x = 35, whose benefit would commence at age $x + u = 85$ would entitle a male to 25.9 times multiple and a female to a 20.5 multiple. Note that these are not model values but actual prices at which the insurance company was (initially) willing to sell the ALDA to the public. Unfortunately, as the ALDA proposal made its way up the chain of command it encountered a number of institutional and regulatory obstacles, and finally the initiative was abandoned in early 2004. The general concerns offered by the company can be broadly categorized as follows:

Monthly or weekly premiums: When long-dated annuities are sold, these types of annuities are based on the payment of one single lump-sum premium. In the ALDA case, the (small) premiums would be paid monthly or weekly until the annuity commencement date. This is an administration limitation since most insurance company software systems are not currently set up to handle such a long period of premium collection, or determine the new premium each year based on the current inflation rates.

Delayed period: The delayed period is the period between the payment of premiums and the commencement of annuity payments. In this case the annuity payments commence at age 70 to 90, which results in a deferred period of up to 55 years. Currently, the maximum deferred period of any annuity product offered by insurance companies in North America is 30 years. Most ALDAs are over this limit, and thus very long horizons result in both pricing and administrative issues since the company must track the annuity for quite a long period, and finding matching long-term investment is unlikely.

Inflation indexing: The fact that the annuity in question is an inflation-indexed annuity causes additional complications. For these annuities, the usual deferred (or delay) period accepted is even shorter—10 years. Again, this is due to the availability of matching investments (vis-à-vis reserving requirements), which would be limited to real bonds or taking on the risk component of inflation predictions.

No death benefit: Although this is possible, it means that the annuitant can be paying premiums for up to age x minus one day, pass away, and receive nothing. After 40, 45, or 50 years of premium payments, the product provides no death benefit. Most insurance companies do not feel comfortable from a public relations (a.k.a. legal or possibly fiduciary) perspective offering such a product and go so far as to argue that it would have limited popularity in the general marketplace.

In sum, there seem to be a number of institutional and regulatory impediments to offering such long-dated inflation-adjusted products. Furthermore, even if these obstacles can be overcome in an economically viable manner, it remains to be seen whether there is a market for the ALDA. Quite likely, a costly and prolonged marketing effort—undertaken by the industry as a whole as opposed to a particular company—will be required to make this concept a commercial success. Corporate patience and long managerial horizons will be necessary, but not sufficient, for success in this market.

TABLE 5
Actual Payout Factors: Male/Female Income per Premium Dollar Quoted by Large Insurance Company in Canada (October 2003) Assuming 3.225% Real (after Inflation) Pricing Interest Rate

Purchase Age	Annuity Commencement Age			
	70	75	80	85
35	5.13/4.47	8.16/6.91	13.82/11.31	25.90/20.53
40	4.08/3.54	6.65/5.60	11.51/9.36	22.08/17.35
45	3.15/2.73	5.30/4.44	9.42/7.61	18.54/14.45

5. MORTALITY RISK CONSIDERATIONS

As mentioned earlier, the insurance company selling an ALDA would be taking a *long* position in mortality rates by fixing the life-contingent payments for up to half a century in advance. Indeed, if experienced mortality (hazard) rates were to decline to a level that is lower than what was priced in advance—that is, if people live longer than expected—the insurance company could be facing the potential for substantial losses. Thus, even if the pricing assumed a very conservative (real) interest rate, and even if the reinvestment risk were mitigated by hedging in the capital markets, it would be difficult if not impossible to do so with uncertain mortality rates.

In fact, this is not just a concern for ALDAs. Insurance companies and reinsurers alike are concerned about guaranteeing mortality on the sale of immediate (let alone delayed) annuities. This is due to the perceived risk that unknown (and nonquantifiable) medical discoveries might increase human lifespans beyond currently projected mortality tables, perhaps even leaving the insurance company paying annuities to infinitely lived Methuselahs. It is common to see insurance companies imposing an explicit mortality risk charge, on a perpetual asset basis, to cover this contingency when selling variable payout annuities.

And, although some actuaries and financial economists argue that in-force life insurance might serve as a hedge against this (diversifiable) risk, others are quick to dismiss the so-called basis risk implicit in this strategy since the target group for both class of policies is distinct. Immediate annuities are sold to the old, while life insurance is purchased by the young (for the most part). Thus, it is plausible that an increase in population longevity will adversely impact the liabilities of the annuity book of business, but marginally impact the profitability of the insurance book. Furthermore, another concern is that the duration and especially the lapsation behavior of the opposing liabilities are mismatched and hence cannot properly hedge each other. Thus, it is unclear to what extent one side of the business could offset the other, and I therefore leave this particular issue for further research.

Yet, oddly enough—and this is the point of the current section—ALDAs might not be terribly sensitive to changes (or misestimates) in mortality assumptions and hence might not pose as much longevity risk to the insurance company as one would expect a priori. Most actuaries will be familiar with the counterintuitive argument that a book of payout annuities sold to a 35-year-old is less exposed to mortality risk compared to selling payout annuities to a 75-year-old. The former's price or value is similar to that of a fixed-income perpetuity—where the annuity factor is: $\bar{a}_x \approx 1/r$—whereas the latter is closer to a medium-term bond. At early issue ages and for long deferral periods, the dominant concern is reinvestment and interest rate risk. The same is true for ALDAs, and I offer the following numerical example to illustrate this concept.

Assume that an insurance company has just sold an ALDA to a (unisex) 45-year-old, whose benefit pays an inflation-adjusted $10,000 per year starting at age 90. Long-term interest rates in the market are 3% (real), and the insurance company prices the ALDA by subtracting off a spread or profit margin of 1 percentage point from the 3% to arrive at annual premium of $301.47 per year for the next 45 years: that is, using equation (3.2), under the same Gompertz (without lapsation) parameters displayed in Tables 2 and 3, but under an adjusted $r = 2\%$ pricing rate.

Now, let us further assume that the insurance company misestimated mortality and, in fact, hazard rates decline by 20% more than anticipated. Or, stated differently, mortality improves by 20% more than what was projected at the time of sale. The 20% can be modeled as a shock to the instantaneous force of mortality (IFM) curve, one that immediately shifts the IFM from μ_x to a modified 0.8 x at all ages. This might appear simplistic, but it has the desired effect. To put this in perspective, the shifting of the hazard rate curve translates the conditional probability of survival to age 90, from the assumed ($_{45}p_{45} = 37.11\%$) to a realized ($_{45}p_{45} = 45.25\%$), for an individual who is currently 45 years old. These numbers are obtained under the usual methods, by integrating only 80% of the IFM curve in equation (3.3), and then evaluating the integral between zero and the survival time and then raising to the exponent.

If we translate this into prices—under the same $r = 2\%$, which is 3% minus the 100 basis point spread—the insurance company *should have* charged a $412.15 premium for the ALDA as opposed to the $301.47 per year it is committed to. Stated differently, if we solve for the implied interest rate that equates the $301.47 premium to the model price under the modified mortality curve 0.8 x, the insurance company's 100 basis point profit spread is reduced to a mere 4.2 basis points. This should not come as a surprise since a 20% improvement in experienced mortality— a.k.a. reduction in hazard rates—will obviously reduce profits. Our model simply quantifies this intuition by converting the 20% number into basis points.

However, the interesting fact is what happens when I do the exact same exercise—pricing the ALDA under one mortality assumption and then immediately shocking the IFM curve to lower level—at younger issue ages. One would think that the longer the deferral period, the greater the so-called risk to the insurance company in misestimating the true curve. It turns out that all else being equal, the situation is reversed, which is my main point. An ALDA that commences paying $10,000 at age 90, but assuming a purchase age of 35 (instead of 45), leads to an annual premium of $211.50 (instead of $301.47) under the full x curve used earlier. If the company misestimates mortality by the same 20% factor, with hindsight the ALDA premiums should have been $291.13 at age 35. In other words, under the true (new) mortality curve, the insurance company undercharged the 35-year-old by the difference between $291.13 and $211.50 per year. The company is "losing" $79.63 per year, relative to what they should have charged. Finally, if we invert and solve for the implied interest rate under the shifted IFM curve, the equivalent profit spread drops from 100 to 19 basis points. Obviously, the product is less profitable ex post, but the interesting and relevant fact is that the spread has dropped to by *less* than when the ALDA was sold to the 45-year-old. Recall that for the 45-year-old the same "mistake" led to a 4 basis points profit spread. And, although there are many ways to quantify the profitability—or lack thereof—of an ALDA, I interpret this evidence to imply that a longer deferral period per se does not necessarily lead to greater longevity risk for the insurance company.

Table 6 provides a summary of this analysis by comparing the revised profit spread under a variety of ALDA purchase and commencement ages. Thus, although misestimating mortality obviously can be very costly—and should be a concern in the pricing of any life contingent instrument—my main argument is as follows. All else being equal, an earlier ALDA purchase age reduces the sensitivity to misestimating experienced mortality. Longer deferral periods do not necessarily translate into greater mortality risk for the insurance company. I refer the interested reader to the report by Fliegelman, Robinson, and Milevsky (2002) for a broader analysis of this important topic.

TABLE 6
You Sold an ALDA under a 100 Basis Point Spread: What Is the Actual Spread if You Misestimate Mortality by 20%?

Purchase Age	Starting Age 85	Starting Age 90
35	38.4 b.p.	19.0 b.p.
40	32.9	12.2
45	26.6	4.1

Note: Assumptions: Gompertz mortality with $m = 90$ and $b = 9.5$, with 0.8 μ_x curve.

6. CONCLUSION

Despite valiant efforts by finance and insurance professionals to educate the public about the benefits of annuitization, the industry must recognize that few people will consciously choose to hand over a lump sum in exchange for lifetime income when given the choice. Numerous experiments involving "live" money have consistently documented consumers' hyperbolic levels of implied time preference when discounting future needs and cash flows during retirement. This is not to say that all consumers *take the money and run* when offered the choice to leave a DB pension plan. Rather, when the default status quo option is to continue maintaining full control of the funds—as in most DC plans—it is extremely hard to give up such control.

Therefore, in the face of a continuing erosion of traditional DB pension plans with their implicit life annuities, the industry must do more to create, promote, and explain viable alternatives. This paper provides another step in that direction by describing the actuarial mechanics of a product called ALDA. In its simple form, the ALDA would allow individuals to voluntarily acquire a lifetime payout annuity in small increments over long periods of preretirement saving. The ALDA could be offered as an additional rider on existing saving and insurance products or together with a phased withdrawal program, or it could be sold as a stand-alone product. The critical factor would be to take the edge off a daunting and irreversible annuitization decision. Likewise, this article emphasized the importance of framing the discussion in real (after inflation) terms, even though the extent to which the current CPI-U captures the basket of goods demanded by retirees is debatable.

While an introductory (motivational) article such as this leaves many details to complete, it is hoped that the ensuing dialogue will move the industry away from yet another generation of complex secondary guarantees such as GLBs on variable annuities—or finite maturity withdrawal benefits that masquerade as longevity insurance—toward a strategy that recognizes the consumer's ingrained reluctance to annuitize.

ACKNOWLEDGMENTS

The author would like to thank Steve Cooper-stein, Martine Duclos, Jeremy Gold, Jerry Golden, Josephine Gurreri, Steven Siegel, Kathleen Vandenberg, and two anonymous referees as well as the Associate Editor at the *NAAJ* for helpful comments and suggestions. An earlier version of this paper was presented at (and published as part of) the Managing Retirement Income symposium organized by the Society of Actuaries in March 2004.

NOTES

1. This idea—which is a form of dollar cost averaging into annuities—has also been adopted by Principal Financial Group in their recently launched income IRA program, in which tax sheltered funds are transferred over a 10–15 year period from equity-based investments to fixed payout annuities.

REFERENCES

BATEMAN, HAZEL, GEOFFREY H. KINGSTON, AND JOHN PIGGOT. 2001. *Forced Saving: Mandating Private Retirement Incomes.*
Cambridge: Cambridge University Press. BERNHEIM, B. DOUGLAS. 1991. How Strong Are Bequest Motives? Evidence Based on Estimates of the Demand for Life Insurance and Annuities. *Journal of Political Economy* 99(5): 899–927.
BLAKE, DAVID, ANDREW J. CAIRNS, AND KEVIN DOWD. 2000. PensionMetrics: Stochastic Pension Plan Design during the Distribution Phase. Pensions Institute Working Paper.
BOWERS, NEWTON L., HANS U. GERBER, JAMES C. HICKMAN, DONALD A. JONES, AND CECIL J. NESBITT. 1997. *Actuarial Mathematics.* 2nd ed. Schaumburg, Ill.: Society of Actuaries.
BROWN, JEFFREY R. 2001. Private Pensions, Mortality Risk, and the Decision to Annuitize. *Journal of Public Economics* 82(1): 29–62.
BROWN, JEFFREY R., OLIVIA S. MITCHELL, JAMES M. POTERBA, AND MARK J. WARSHAWSKY. 2001. *The Role of Annuity Markets in Financing Retirement.* Cambridge, Mass.: MIT Press.
BROWN, JEFFREY R., AND JAMES POTERBA. 2000. Joint Life Annuities and Annuity Demand by Married Couples. *Journal of Risk and Insurance* 67(4): 527–54.

BROWN, JEFFREY R., AND MARK J. WARSHAWSKY. 2001. Longevity-Insured Retirement Distributions from Pension Plans: Market and Regulatory Issues. NBER Working Paper 8064.

BRUGIAVINI, AGAR. 1993. Uncertainty Resolution and the Timing of Annuity Purchases. *Journal of Public Economics* 50: 31–62.

FINKELSTEIN, AMY, AND JAMES POTERBA. 1999. Selection Effects in the Market for Individual Annuities: New Evidence from the United Kingdom. NBER Working Paper 7168.

FLIEGELMAN, ARTHUR, SCOTT ROBINSON, AND MOSHE A. MILEVSKY. 2002. The U.S. Payout Annuity Market: For Life Insurers the Risks Are Real, but Manageable. *Moody's Investors Service Special Comment*, August. Reprinted in *The Pension Challenge: Risk Transfers and Retirement Income Security*, edited by Olivia S. Mitchell and Kent Smetters. Oxford: Oxford University Press, 2003.

FREES, EDWARD W., JACQUES CARRIE` RE, AND EMILIANO VALDEZ. 1996. Annuity Valuation with Dependent Mortality. *Journal of Risk and Insurance* 63(2): 229–61.

FRIEDMAN, BENJAMIN M., AND MARK WARSHAWSKY. 1990. The Cost of Annuities: Implications for Saving Behavior and Bequests. *Quarterly Journal of Economics* 105(1): 135–54.

KOTLIKOFF, LAURENCE J., AND AVIA SPIVAK. 1981. The Family as an Incomplete Annuities Market. *Journal of Political Economy* 89(2): 373–91.

MILEVSKY, MOSHE A. 1998. Optimal Asset Allocation towards the End of the Life Cycle: To Annuitize or Not to Annuitize? *Journal of Risk and Insurance* 65(3): 401–26.

———. 2001. Optimal Annuitization Policies: Analysis of the Options. *North American Actuarial Journal* 5(1): 57–69.

———. 2005. The Implied Longevity Yield: A Note on Developing an Index for Payout Annuities. *Journal of Risk and Insurance* 75(2): 300–325.

———. 2006. *The Calculus of Retirement Income: Financial Models for Pension Annuities and Life Insurance.* Cambridge: Cambridge University Press.

MILEVSKY, MOSHE A., AND VIRGINIA R. YOUNG. 2003. Annuitization and Asset Allocation. Working Paper. Online at www. ifid.ca.

MITCHELL, OLIVIA S., JAMES M. POTERBA, MARK J. WARSHAWSKY, AND JEFFREY R. BROWN. 1999. New Evidence on the Money's Worth of Individual Annuities. *American Economic Review* 89(5): 1299–1318.

MODIGLIANI, FRANCO. 1986. Life Cycle, Individual Thrift, and the Wealth of Nations. *American Economic Review* 76(3): 297–313.

POTERBA, JAMES M. 1997. The History of Annuities in the United States. NBER Working Paper 6004.

SONDERGELD, ERIC. 1997. *Annuity Persistency Study.* Schaumburg, Ill.: LIMRA International and the Society of Actuaries.

STEPHENSON, J. B. 1978. The High-Protection Annuity. *Journal of Risk and Insurance* 45(4): 593–610. YAARI, MENAHEM E. 1965. Uncertain Lifetime, Life Insurance and the Theory of the Consumer. *Review of Economic Studies* 32: 137–50.

YAGI, T., AND Y. NISHIGAKI. 1993. The Inefficiency of Private Constant Annuities. *Journal of Risk and Insurance* 60(3): 385–412.

Discussions on this paper can be submitted until April 1, 2006. The author reserves the right to reply to any discussion. Please see the Submission Guidelines for Authors on the inside back cover for instructions on the submission of discussions.

Recent Developments in Life Annuity Markets and Products (excerpt)[*]

by Mark J. Warshawsky[†]

Recently, there have been a number of innovations in annuity products. Some of these innovations are incremental changes in product design, while others represent complex financial engineering arrangements.

Inflation-Indexed Annuities.

A straightforward product development that had to await the issuance in the late 1990s and early 2000s of Treasury inflation-protected securities (TIPS) in the United States, is the inflation-indexed life annuity. This annuity is essentially a SPIA with the same features and options as a fixed life annuity, but whose income payments track the consumer price index (CPI). There are apparently several companies now issuing inflation-indexed annuities in the U.S. market. In the United Kingdom, these products have been issued for more than two decades by a few companies, consistent with the greater length of time that the U.K. government issued "gilt linkers."

Specifically, for one insurance company in the United States, payments are adjusted each year on January 1 for changes in the nonseasonally adjusted cost-of-living index (CPI-U). The increase in payments, however, is limited annually to 10% and any decrease will never reduce the payment below the initial benefit amount. Any negative changes in the CPI not applied to the payment will be used to offset CPI increases.

For example, on July 13, 2006 the insurance company quoted an initial monthly payment of $501.72 on the Internet for an inflation-indexed annuity, purchased with $100,000 in a single premium by a man aged 65. This may be compared to $685.47 for a fixed SPIA, issued by the same company on that date.

Figures 5–8 for the inflation-indexed annuity correspond to Figures 1–4 [not included in this excerpt] for the nominal SPIA. Clearly, a shorter time period is covered, as the TIPS market did not exist until the late 1990s. Figures 5 and 6 show that simulated volatility in initial inflation-indexed monthly payments picked up, and the general level of payments declined as the TIPS market itself developed and rates declined, particularly following the announcement of the permanence of TIPS issuance by the U.S. Treasury in 2002.

---

[*]Copyright © 2007, International Society of Certified Benefits Specialists. Reprinted with permission.
[†]The author, Mark J. Warshawsky, Ph.D., is director of retirement research at Watson Wyatt Worldwide in Arlington, Virginia. He was assistant secretary for economic policy at the Treasury Department, director of research at TIAA-CREF and senior economist at the Internal Revenue Service and Federal Reserve Board. Warshawsky is the author of many published articles, books, conference volumes and papers covering several areas of economic research including retirement plans, insurance products and life annuities.

► **FIGURE 5**

MONTHLY INFLATION-INDEXED PAYMENT PER $100,000 SINGLE PREMIUM, INFLATION-INDEXED IMMEDIATE LIFE ANNUITY, DAILY SIMULATIONS, 4/15/99 TO 12/11/06

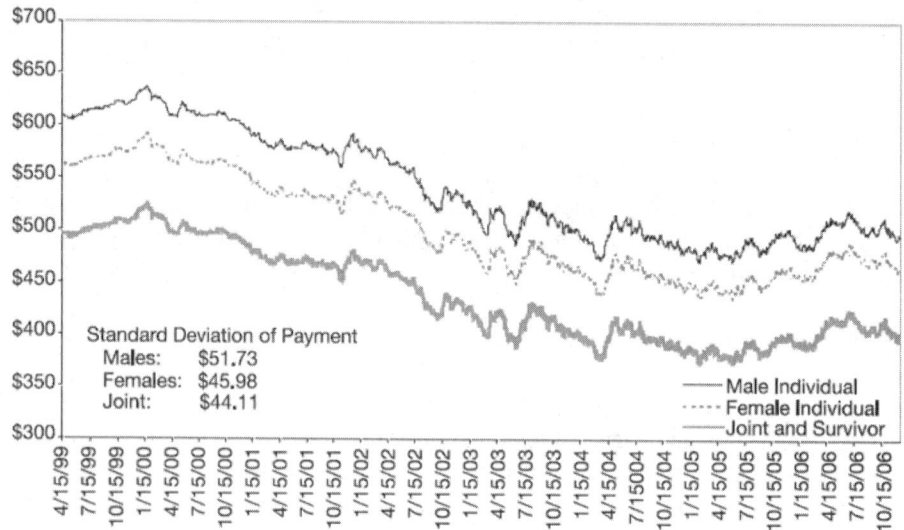

Source: Watson Wyatt Worldwide.

► **FIGURE 6**

ONE-YEAR DIFFERENCES IN INITIAL MONTHLY PAYMENTS FOR JOINT AND SURVIVOR INFLATION-INDEXED LIFE ANNUITIES, DAILY SIMULATIONS 4/19/00 TO 12/11/06

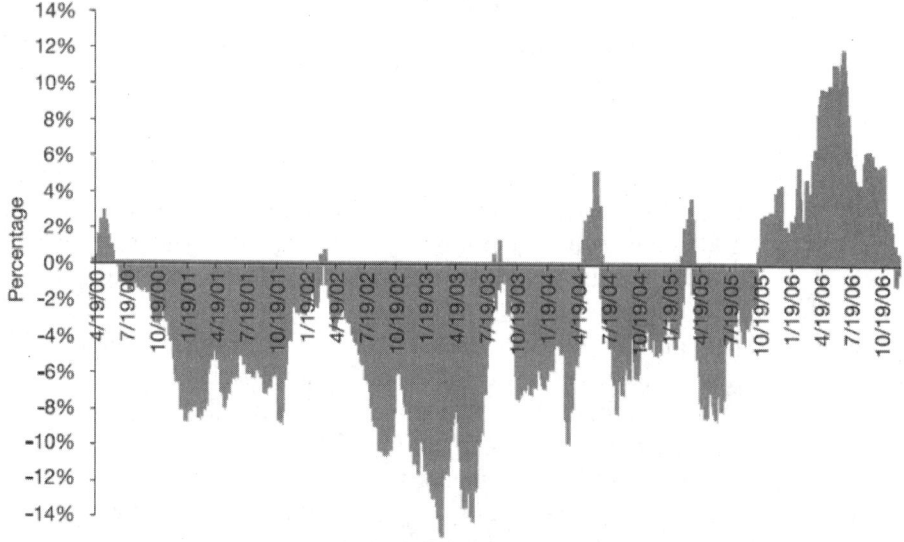

Source: Watson Wyatt Worldwide.

Figure 7 shows Internet quotes for inflation-indexed life annuities issued by one highly rated insurance company over the period since its issuance began, in February 2005; Figure 8 gives the corresponding money's worth ratios. In general, the money's worth ratio has hovered around 0.95, although there is some volatility around that, perhaps owing to changes in pricing policy for a new product or perhaps owing to some incompleteness in the model. This ratio is consistent with what has been found in the U.K. market; the ratio is lower than in the nominal market, which may be explained by a lack of inflation-indexed corporate bonds to afford more competitive annuity rate quotes.

▶ **FIGURE 7**

INITIAL MONTHLY PAYMENTS PER $100,000 PREMIUM, INFLATION-ADJUSTED LIFE ANNUITY DAILY INTERNET QUOTES, HIGHLY RATED LIFE INSURANCE COMPANY, 2/2/05 TO 12/11/06

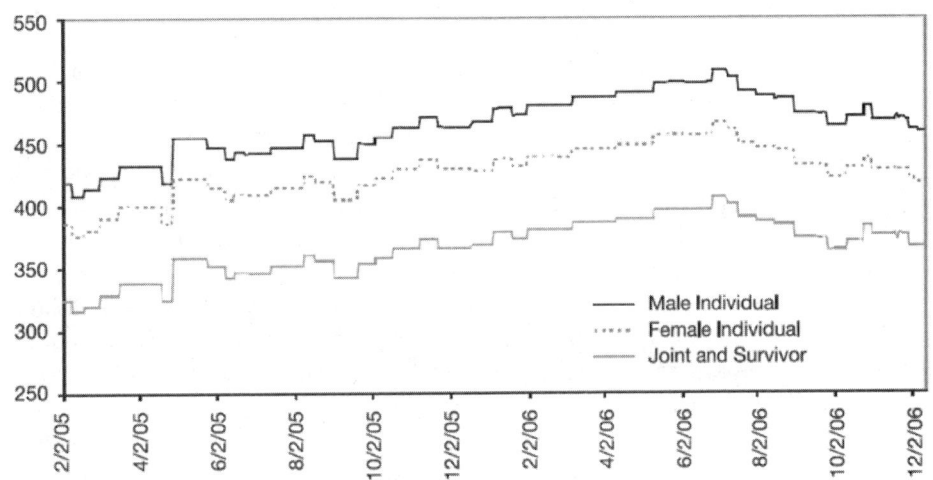

Source: Watson Wyatt Worldwide.

▶ **FIGURE 8**

MONEY'S WORTH FOR INFLATION-INDEXED LIFE ANNUITY (RATE OF QUOTED PAYMENT TO SIMULATED PAYMENT) 2/2/05 TO 12/11/06

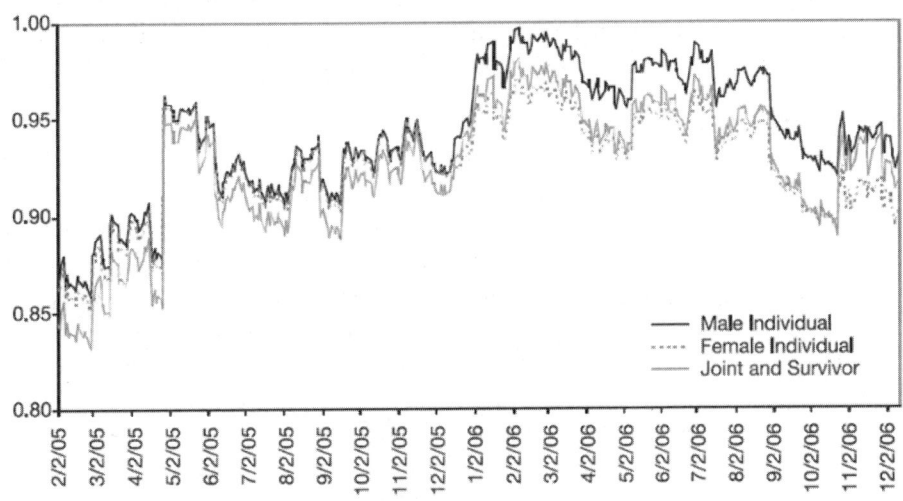

Source: Watson Wyatt Worldwide.

Enhanced Liquidity.

Another recent innovation in individual immediate life annuity products is the offering of enhanced liquidity, the ability to convert some of the value of the stream-of-income payments into a lump-sum payment after the start of payment flows. There is a risk to the issuing company of some additional, dynamic adverse selection from such provisions that presumably are reflected in product pricing (and hence it is unclear how much better in terms of income these products are than partial annuitization), but liquidity is indeed a strong desire among plan participants.

For example, for a fixed life annuity, one insurance company offers a product with the following features. It allows for the withdrawal on a one-time-only basis, of 30% of the expected present value of the remaining payments, based on life expectancy factors set at the time when the annuity was purchased. The option can only be exercised on the fifth, tenth or 15th anniversaries of the first payment from the life annuity, or upon a significant, nonmedical financial loss. Once the option is exercised, future income payments are reduced by 30%. The insurance company calculates the present value for the withdrawal amount by adjusting the interest rate extant at time of purchase, so as to pass through to the annuitant on an approximate basis any capital gains or losses experienced by bonds held in the general investment account.

Another company gives enhanced liquidity for its variable immediate life annuity only in a qualified plan or individual retirement account (IRA). It allows withdrawals of present value through a period set for life expectancy at the time of purchase. The original single premium is divided into two parts representing the present value of annuity payments before and after the year of life expectancy, respectively. The first part is essentially a benefit for a guaranteed period of the length of life expectancy where an acceleration of payments occurs. The second part, which is available only for the first five years of the contract, is a withdrawal of present value of annuity payments after life expectancy, but on a declining scale over the five years. Because no proof of health status or explicit individual liquidity draw needs to be demonstrated, the company is clearly exposed to some additional adverse selection.

Individual DB Pensions.

These products are actually deferred annuities, but unlike most individual deferred annuities currently marketed, individual DB pensions are expected to be distributed as life annuities and not as lump sums. These products have cash values (the market values in the policy can be distributed or transferred to another asset product) unlike pure form deferred life annuities, which have no cash value and can only be distributed as a life annuity upon a set date, age or retirement.

One company offers a fixed-income product purchased with a single premium, or through regularly scheduled premium payments lasting up to 30 years. Income payments will begin on a predetermined fixed date as soon as ten years from the date the annuity was issued, beginning as early as age 55. The level of future income payments is determined based on the age of the annuitant and prevailing interest rates at the time premium payments are made; the interest crediting rate is guaranteed to be at least 3%.

For example, the interest rate credited on April 4, 2006 was 4%. The cash value of the life annuity prior to the start date for income payments is 87.5% of premium payments accumulated at 3% interest.

Another insurance company offers an annuity product that, in explicit intent, is designed to replicate many of the features of a traditional DB pension plan but is offered as an investment option for a 401(k) plan as a group variable annuity. Each contribution to the product purchases a specific amount of guaranteed retirement income. The income is not received, however, unless the policy holder annuitizes on or after the 401(k) plan's stated retirement age. Transfers and withdrawals are allowed, according to general 401(k) and specific plan rules, but any withdrawals from the annuity reduce guaranteed retirement income in proportion to the account value removed. The guarantee is preserved if there is a rollover to an individual variable annuity offered by the insurance company.

Contributions to this product are invested in a fund that mimics a large corporate pension trust. There is an annual investment charge as well as annual guarantee charges. Prior to retirement, the account value reflects the investment performance of the funds, less the charges just mentioned. After retirement, the guaranteed income payments are made (there is no cash value then) based on the age of the annuitant and the account balance. The income payments can increase if investment performance exceeds the benchmarks, as in an immediate variable life annuity.

Lifelong Distribution.

Lifelong distribution is an increasingly common option offered on individual deferred variable annuities. It is not a life annuity distribution; there is still cash value even in the distribution phase. Nevertheless, there is an aspect of life contingencies for the issuing company that is covered by a separate charge.

As a prototypical example, one company guarantees a 5% annual stream of withdrawals for life, or 7% for at least 14.2 years based on an account value, which is the greater of (1) the initial balance compounded at 5% for ten years from the initial election of the option or until the first withdrawal if sooner, (2) the highest anniversary value for the first ten years or until the first withdrawal if sooner, or (3) the account value at first withdrawal. Only certain asset investment fund combinations are allowed when the option is selected.

As early as three years after income withdrawals begin and for every three years thereafter if investment performance causes an increase in the account value, the protected account value and the withdrawal stream will increase. The protected account value is reduced by the amounts withdrawn until it reaches zero. If the amounts withdrawn are cumulatively equal to the 5% stream of withdrawals, then the insured must choose whether to receive 5% income payments for life or at the 7% level for the remainder of the 14.2 years. This insurance company currently charges annually for this distribution option, 60 basis points for an individual and 75 basis points for a couple, in addition to the regular insurance and investment charges that a policy holder will have to pay for a variable annuity bought from this insurance company.

AN IDEA TO INTEGRATE THE LIFE ANNUITY WITH LONG-TERM CARE INSURANCE

The author has put forward a product innovation idea to reduce the adverse selection extant in immediate life annuities, while simultaneously improving a market failure of sorts in the market for long-term care insurance (LTCI).[10] This product, called a *life care annuity*, would integrate a SPIA with a significant pop-up benefit (ideally a cash and not an indemnity approach) when the annuitant becomes disabled with the common triggers found in LTCI policies (unable to perform two of the six activities of daily living or cognitively impaired).

This integration would substantially reduce the need for, and the cost of, LTCI underwriting, allowing those retirees currently shut out from LTCI—as many as a third of the population—to get coverage. And it is precisely the attraction to the integrated product of those adversely affected by underwriting, which enables a reduction in adverse selection for the life annuity segment, thereby increasing the income stream payable by about 5%. Empirical research has established these findings. Indeed, this "pooling equilibrium" should be self-sustaining. Moreover, some flexibility in product design is appropriate to reflect geographic differences in the cost of care, to add desirable inflation-indexing features, and so on.

The Pension Protection Act of 2006 (PPA) gave this type of combination product a tax advantage (beginning in 2010) as an after-tax annuity because, essentially, the implied premium for the LTCI segment will become deductible from taxable income. This tax advantage is not yet available in a qualified retirement plan; there may be other regulatory and legal hurdles for the life care annuity in a qualified plan or an IRA, such as minimum distribution requirements.

It is thought that giving less restrictive standards will engender more competition in the market for life annuities for plan sponsors, thereby encouraging the use of life annuities in DC plans

POSSIBLE IMPLICATIONS OF EMPIRICAL RESULTS

It is still the case that activity in the immediate annuity market is quite modest. Yet, the interest of public policy makers in this area is growing, as evidenced by legislative proposals to incent the choice of a life annuity and by discussions among policy experts to require the offering of life annuity distributions in DC plans.[11] In addition, there has been some activity among a few large DC plan sponsors in offering participants annuity-buying services. Media attention to this area has increased as, reportedly, has the interest of the large financial services companies. But the case for the individual life annuity would be even more compelling if its deficiencies were also addressed.

There are methods for dealing with the risks arising from the volatility of traditional fixed (or inflation-indexed) life annuity payouts. These methods have their drawbacks as well. For example, one could reduce the timing risk by phasing withdrawals from the DC plan and purchases of life annuities over a few years. But this approach requires discipline, liquidity, knowledge and, most significantly, the ability to finance consumption in retirement from other sources in the phase-out period. Another way to manage timing risk would be to defer annuitization until interest rates peaked. This approach perhaps requires even more discipline, liquidity, holdout ability and, especially, more knowledge than the first one.

Alternatively, the plan participant could reallocate assets as retirement draws near, shifting more assets to long-duration bonds whose prices move inversely to interest rates. This is the defining feature of life-cycle mutual funds, which are indeed becoming more popular investments for participants in DC plans. Of course, at least in expectation, this method sacrifices return for the lowered risk, as compared to the steadier asset allocations held by DB plans. Moreover, many life cycle funds also move a substantial share of assets into money market funds as retirement approaches; this feature reduces the natural hedging benefits of the product for the purchase of a life annuity. Variable immediate annuities with monthly payouts that vary with returns on a participant-chosen underlying asset portfolio avoid the point-in-time risk of purchasing fixed annuities. The downside, however, is pushing income volatility risk toward the end of the lifecycle, where it may be particularly hard to bear. A few plan sponsors allow participants to transfer their 401(k) account balances to the DB plan, sometimes on favorable terms, thus securing a life annuity with a fixed payment level. This approach helps avoid marketing costs, but still generally leaves interest rate risk to the plan participant.

As previously mentioned, policy makers are examining the need to encourage the use of life annuities by participants in DC plans. A small step in that direction was taken in the recently enacted PPA, whereby an old DOL regulation requiring plan sponsors to use the safest available annuity was vacated. It is thought that giving less restrictive standards will engender more competition in the market for life annuities for plan sponsors, thereby encouraging the use of life annuities in DC plans. It is unclear whether this legal change will effect much change in the behavior of plan sponsors or participants, and hence more policy analysis using some of the methodologies and information contained in this article will likely be needed.

With the passage of time and rising demand by baby boomers, other enhanced formal lifelong distribution programs and products are being created, and will be created, as shown in this article. These products must be evaluated as to the value of the enhancements and extra features, especially whether these new products are desirable to and understandable by plan participants, compared to their costs and other alternatives. It is possible that the prospect of financial risks and regrets at retirement will foster a greater appreciation among workers and retirees for the risk-reduction properties of traditional DB plans. In a DB plan, the asset return and interest rate risk is held by the plan sponsor, which by virtue of its longer investing horizon, economies of scale and ability to design retirement plan features, is generally better able to manage the investment risks than individuals.

Ben Weitzer and Susie Farris assisted ably in the annuity model simulations and quote collections, respectively, updating work done with Chris Soares and Chris Devlin in model simulation and quote collections, respectively, while the author was assistant secretary for economic policy at the US. Treasury Department. Jeff Brown, Alex Dike and Tomeka Hill provided helpful comments on the article. Any opinions expressed are those of the author alone and not of Watson Wyatt Worldwide.

NOTES

1. Even in traditional DB plans, however, there has been a trend away from life annuity payments and toward lump-sum distributions. In part, because the law prior to the passage of PPA in 2006 encouraged them by requiring the use of abnormally low interest rates for purposes of calculated legal-minimum lump-sum distributions, if allowed by the plan. Under the recently passed PPA, sponsors of DB plans will calculate lump-sum distributions using a corporate bond spot curve rather than long-

term Treasury rates. Because corporate bond rates are almost always higher than long-term Treasury rates, lump sums are likely to go lower. When these issues emerge into public awareness, as they surely will, the great value and benefit found in the life annuity distribution from traditional DB plans will be demonstrated anew.

2. See Mark Warshawsky, "The Market for Individual Life Annuities and the Reform of Social Security: An Update and Further Analysis," Benefits Quarterly, Fourth Quarter 2001, pp. 24-43.
3. This tendency increases the cost of annuities by about ten percentage points compared to a life annuity provided to the entire distribution of mortality expectations (general population), according to several research studies, including Olivia Mitchell, James Poterba, Mark Warshawsky and Jeffrey R. Brown, "New Evidence on the Money's Worth of Individual Annuities," American Economic Review, December 1999, pp. 1299-1318. This is aside from the usual marketing and sales costs and margins for profits and reserves, and the need to search for the best value. Deferred annuities also have extra insurance charges. The reliability of the promise by the issuing insurance company to pay future income benefits may be judged by the rated claims-paying ability of the company, as well as the insurance limits of the various state guarantee funds where the annuity product is backed explicitly by the general account of the insurance company.
4. A good recent demonstration and explanation of the risk-reduction properties for retirement distributions of the fixed life annuity may be found at www.fidelityresearchinstitute.com (Insight Reports: Beyond Conventional Wisdom).
5. The obverse of this trend; the market value of accrued benefits in traditional DB plans has increased in the last few years as interest rates have declined. Described in "DB Plans Become Significantly More Valuable," Watson Wyatt Insider, September 2005.
6. See Chris Soares and Mark Warshawsky, "Annuity Risk: Volatility and Inflation Exposure in Payments From Immediate Life Annuities," in Developing an Annuity Market in Europe, Edward Elgar, London, 2004. Elsa Fornero and Elisa Luciano, editors.
7. That being said, there is still some variance in prices across insurer issuers at any given time.
8. The couples have joint annuities with full benefits payable to the survivor.
9. Some companies use the terminology of assumed investment return (AIR).
10. See Christopher Murtaugh, Brenda Spillman and Mark Warshawsky, "In Sickness and In Health: An Annuity Approach to Financing Long-Term Care and Retirement Income," Journal of Risk and Insurance, 68(2), June 2001, pp. 225-254.
11. See Jeffrey Brown and Mark Warshawsky, "Longevity-Insured Retirement Distributions From Pension Plans: Market and Regulatory Issues," in Private Pensions and Public Policies, Washington, D.C. Brookings Institution Press, 2004, pp. 332-369. William Gale, John Shoven and Mark Warshawsky, editors.

Planning Required Minimum Distributions for Multiple Beneficiaries[*]

April K. Caudill, JD, CLU, ChFC[†]

Many professionals describe qualified plans, IRAs, and other sources of "qualified" retirement funds[1] as great places to accumulate money but bad to inherit. This is because of the devastating combined effect of an estate tax of up to 45% and federal income tax at top marginal rates of 35% on retirement funds.[2] The situation is dramatically worsened by the 50% penalty[3] for failing to satisfy the minimum distribution requirements.[4]

When an IRA owner or plan participant has multiple beneficiaries, particularly if they receive their shares through a trust, the result can be a sharp reduction of income tax deferral for the younger beneficiaries. Fortunately, there are several strategies that can help achieve the lowest possible required minimum distributions (RMDs) for all beneficiaries.

MULTIPLE BENEFICIARIES RULE

If the IRA owner or plan participant names multiple beneficiaries (or a trust with multiple beneficiaries, as explained below), the shortest life expectancy must be used to measure the payout period.[5] This can be highly disadvantageous to the other beneficiaries.

Example: Alexander died in 2007 with an IRA valued at $3 million. He was widowed and had named three beneficiaries of his account to receive equal shares: his sister Alice, age 59, and his two daughters, Robin and Debbie, ages 23 and 12. Under the regulations, since payouts must be made using the shortest life expectancy, which is Alice's, each beneficiary would be required to take a distribution of $38,314 per year ($1 million ÷ 26.1). Assuming that the family does not need the funds and that their objective is to defer income taxation of the account proceeds for as long as possible, this creates an unsatisfactory result. If each of the beneficiaries could elect to use her own life expectancy as the payout period, Robin's payout could drop to $16,639 per year ($1 million ÷ 60.1 years) and Debbie's payout could drop to $14,124 per year ($1 million ÷ 70.8 years).[6] Meanwhile, the underlying account could continue to compound on a tax-deferred basis.

---

[*]Reprinted with permission. Copyright © 2008, Society of Financial Service Professionals. All rights reserved.
[†]April K. Caudill, JD, CLU, ChFC, is an Advanced Marketing Director at The Prudential Insurance Company of America, Newark, NJ, a Prudential Financial company. She is also an associate editor of this Journal. Ms. Caudill's areas of expertise include qualified plans, ERISA, and distribution planning. She may be reached at april.caudill@prudential.com

Since one of the beneficiaries is a minor, the application of these rules also must be considered in the context of naming a trust as beneficiary.

TRUSTS AS BENEFICIARIES

While it may seem at times that the planning world revolves wholly around taxes, the reality is that there are many nontax reasons for naming a trust as beneficiary of an IRA or plan account. Probably the most common is where parents of minor children include a trust clause in their wills (i.e., a testamentary trust) to handle custodianship of funds left to their children. The trust receives taxable RMDs each year and contains provisions governing the administration of those funds for the trust beneficiaries. Trust ownership may be necessary for other reasons, such as avoidance of probate, special needs planning, asset protection, for spendthrift beneficiaries, or to accomplish various tax or estate planning strategies.

If income tax deferral is an objective of the client, one of the critical planning steps in the drafting of a trust to be named as beneficiary of retirement assets is to satisfy the "see-through trust" requirements.7 It is important to note that these requirements include an October 31 deadline (i.e., October 31 of the year after the year death occurs) for providing trust documentation to the plan administrator or IRA custodian. If the see-through requirements are met, the individual beneficiaries can be treated as "designated beneficiaries" under the RMD regulations. If the requirements are not met, the account owner or participant is treated as having no beneficiary, and the payout period will likely be much shorter, thus accelerating income tax.

There are several strategies for avoiding the accelerated payout associated with multiple beneficiaries: (1) separate accounts, within certain limits, (2) a qualified disclaimer, (3) payout of the older beneficiary before the beneficiary determination date, (4) a master trust strategy, and (5) separate IRAs.

SEPARATE ACCOUNTS

Under limited circumstances, separate accounts may be created post-death, which allow each beneficiary to use his or her own life expectancy to calculate distributions. However, this technique generally does not allow trust beneficiaries to use their own life expectancies (to the extent of their trust share).8 For trust beneficiaries, one of the other techniques will be necessary.

For outright beneficiaries of the retirement account to use their own individual life expectancies, the separate accounts must be created by December 31 of the year after the year of death.9 This is also the deadline for a nonspouse beneficiary to receive his or her first distribution if electing a single life expectancy payout.10 If the distribution is not received by this point, the beneficiary's tax deferral opportunities become much more limited.

It is important to note that there are some key nontax reasons to create separate accounts, even if multiple beneficiaries are not permitted to use their own life expectancies (either because they are taking their shares through a trust or because they missed the December 31 deadline).

For example, separate accounts allow beneficiaries to invest in different assets and avoid responsibility for one another's minimum distributions.11 Even if the beneficiaries simply have different investment horizons or cannot get along, the accounts may be separated and retitled in the names of the separate beneficiaries at any time.12

The separation must be "vertical"; in other words, all investment gains, losses, contributions, and forfeitures occurring postdeath must be allocated pro rata between the accounts in a reasonable and consistent matter, and any after-death distributions to one of the beneficiaries must be allocated to his or her account.13 For obvious reasons, this could become more challenging as the amount of time that has elapsed since death increases. It should be noted that a pecuniary bequest (i.e., a specified dollar amount to one beneficiary) might not qualify for separate account treatment, since it may require segregation of a specified amount without allocating the foregoing items pro rata. For planning purposes, a percentage gift is much more likely than a pecuniary gift to qualify for separate account treatment.14

QUALIFIED DISCLAIMER OR PAYOUT

A qualified disclaimer is a second option for dealing with the varying life expectancies in the example above. If the account owner's sister (or another older beneficiary) does not need or want the account benefit, she can be removed as a beneficiary by executing a qualified disclaimer15 of her interest in the account. The RMD regulations state that if disclaimer meets the requirements of IRC Section 2518 and is made by September 3016 of the year after the year of death, the person executing the disclaimer will not be taken into account as a designated beneficiary. However, it should be noted that IRC Section 2518 requires a qualified disclaimer to be executed by nine months after the date of death. The IRS has held that the fact that the disclaiming beneficiary has received a payment of his or her own postdeath RMD from the account in the year after death will not result in being treated as a beneficiary in subsequent years.17

Similar to a qualified disclaimer, a payout of the "undesirable" beneficiary's interest (the "entire benefit to which the person is entitled") prior to the September 30 deadline will remove him or her as a beneficiary.18 This strategy is also available in the event a charity or estate19 was designated to receive a portion of the account. The advantage of both a qualified disclaimer and a payout is that they are employed after death, when it is too late for some of the other techniques.

MASTER TRUST

In a 2005 private letter ruling, the IRS approved one "master trust" arrangement in which multiple trust beneficiaries received shares in an IRA through a trust, yet were permitted to use their own life expectancies.20 The trust contained a number of individual subtrusts, governed by one master trust. While many IRS letter rulings have struck down the availability of separate account treatment for various trust clauses subdividing IRA proceeds after the death of the owner, what set Letter Ruling 200537044 apart was the use of the individual subtrusts as the actual named beneficiaries of the decedent's IRA. This unique design allowed each beneficiary to have his or her own trust, while a master trust provided terms applying to all. Each beneficiary could then use his or her own life expectancy as the payout period.

While private letter rulings are not binding and may not be cited as precedent, there appears to be no reason multiple trusts (one benefiting each beneficiary) could not be used to accomplish the same purpose. However, in many cases, the preparation of multiple trust documents might not be cost effective.

SEPARATE IRAS

Splitting an IRA owner's account into separate IRAs prior to death and naming one individual beneficiary for each account may create the same effect that separate accounts would offer. In the event one of the beneficiaries is a minor child, a trust for only that child could be named as beneficiary, allowing that child to use his or her own life expectancy as the measuring payout period.

The disadvantages of this strategy are primary logistical: paperwork and account fees are multiplied, and the accounts may grow at different rates. If the account values are not rebalanced regularly, the IRA owner's intentions of leaving equal or specified shares to multiple beneficiaries could be thwarted. Furthermore, some custodians do not permit multiple IRAs of the same type to be maintained with different beneficiaries. One provider reportedly has taken the step of actually changing the beneficiaries on IRA owners' accounts of the same type to the name of the last (the most recently named) beneficiary. This would seem to be a recipe for planning disasters and litigation.[21]

CONCLUSIONS

There are a number of strategies for addressing the disadvantageous treatment of multiple beneficiaries. While some of these techniques may be relevant primarily for wealthier individuals, some are cost effective and manageable for accounts of any size where the account beneficiaries want to enjoy income tax-deferred compounding for as long as possible.

Ms. Caudill is not engaged in the practice of law for Prudential. Prudential Financial and its representatives cannot provide tax or legal advice. Such advice should come from an individual's personal tax and legal advisors. Prudential Financial is not affiliated with this journal.

NOTES

1. In addition to qualified plans (including 401(k) plans) and contributory IRAs, the minimum distribution requirements apply to simplified employee pensions (SEPs), SIMPLE IRAs, 403(b) tax-sheltered annuities, and eligible Section 457 governmental plans. Treas. Reg. §1.401(a)(9)-1, A-1.
2. Distributions from a qualified plan, IRA, or tax-sheltered annuity are "income in respect of a decedent" (IRD). An income tax deduction is generally allowed for estate and generation-skipping taxes paid on IRD. See IRC §691(c).
3. The penalty is 50% of the amount that should have been taken but was not taken.
4. The minimum distribution requirements are explained in *Tax Facts on Life Insurance and Employee Benefits* (2008), Q 233 to 237 (IRAs), Q 339 to Q 348 (qualified plans), and Q 493 to Q 496 (tax-sheltered annuities), The National Underwriter Company. For a comprehensive analysis, see Natalie Choate, *Life and Death Planning for Retirement Benefits* 6th Ed. (Ataxplan Publications, 2007).
5. See Treas. Reg. §1.401(a)(9)-5, A-7(a)(1).
6. Life expectancies are taken from the single life table set forth at Treas. Reg. §1.401(a)(9)-9, A-1.
7. There are four requirements that must be satisfied for the beneficiaries of a trust to be treated as "designated beneficiaries." See Treas. Reg. §1.401(a)(9)-4, A-1, A-5(b). A trust that satisfies these requirements is sometimes referred to as a "see-through trust":

a. The trust must be valid under state law, or would be except for the fact that there is no corpus.
   b. The trust must be irrevocable or, by its terms, become irrevocable upon the death of the employee.
   c. The beneficiaries of the trust with respect to the trust's interest in the account benefit must be identifiable from the trust instrument. (They do not have to be specified by name, so long as the individual who is to be the beneficiary is identifiable under the plan as of the date the beneficiary is determined). The members of a class of beneficiaries that could expand or contract (for example "my grandchildren") will be treated as identifiable so long as it is possible, as of the date the beneficiary is determined, to identify the class member with the shortest life expectancy.
   d. Documentation of the trust (e.g., copy of the trust or a list of the beneficiaries and the conditions of their entitlement) must be provided to the plan administrator or IRA custodian by October 31 of the year after death.
8. See Treas. Reg. §1.401(a)(9)-4, A-5(c).
9. Treas. Reg. §1.401(a)(9)-8, A-2(a)(2).
10. Treas. Reg. §1.401(a)(9)-3, A-3.
11. Treas. Reg. §1.401(a)(9)-8, A-2(a)(2).
12. See T.D. 8987, 67 Fed. Reg. 18988, 18992 (April 17, 2002).
13. Treas. Reg. §1.401(a)(9)-8, A-3.
14. For a thorough discussion of this issue, see Natalie Choate, *Life and Death Planning for Retirement Benefits*.
15. See IRC Sec. 2518(b).
16. As of September 30 of the year after the year of death, the identity of the designated beneficiaries is final. Treas. Reg. §1.401(a)(9)-4, A-4(a).
17. See Rev. Rul. 2005-36, 2005-26 IRB 1368.
18. Treas. Reg. §1.401(a)(9)-4, A-4(a).
19. See e.g., Let. Rul. 200432027.
20. See Let. Rul. 200537044.
21. See Ashlea Ebeling, "Disinherited by Vanguard," *Forbes* (September 3, 2007).

Distributions from Stretch IRAs[*]

Kevin J. Sigler, Ph.D.[†]

When the owner of the tax deferred IRA account dies, the beneficiary of the account is liable for the tax on the deceased's traditional IRA. If the beneficiary is the spouse of the owner, she has a variety of ways to receive funds from the IRA. A very popular option is placing the funds in the spouse's own IRA and beginning fresh which means not having to take distributions from IRA until age 70.5 years. If the owner dies, a non-spouse beneficiary, on the other hand, has two ways of receiving the money from the owner's IRA: 1) the beneficiary may take the money by December 31 of the year of the five year anniversary of the death of the owner; or 2) the non-spouse beneficiary may also take payments over his life expectancy starting no later than December 31 of the year following the owner's death. The second option of distribution is referred to as stretching the IRA. The funds are subject to federal and state income tax when distributed with either method. This article reviews the regulations regarding required minimum distributions (RMD) from traditional IRAs and focuses on the distributions that are made to non-spouse beneficiaries of the IRA after the death of the owner. The two distribution options available to the non-spouse beneficiary are analyzed.

RMDs

According to the United States Internal Revenue Service, withdrawals from tax deferred IRAs, 403-B and qualified retirement plans must begin the year an individual reached age 70.5. The first Required Minimum Distribution (RMD) may be delayed three months to April 1 of the next year. The second RMD and all of the rest must be taken by December 3J for the year in which they are calculated. The 2002 regulations require the calculation of the Required Minimum Distribution using one of three tables: Single Life Expectancy, Joint Life Expectancy or the Uniform Life Expectancy. Unless the owner of the IRA has a spouse more than 10 years younger than he, the Uniform Life Expectancy Table is normally used for the owner's RMD each year.[1]

The regulations allow the retirement plan owner to recalculate the RMD each year. For example, a 70-year-old would find his factor on the Uniform Life Expectancy Table (Table 1) to divide into his tax deferred balance. In this case the factor is 27.4 (if he had tuned 70.5 years that year). Assuming a prior year-end balance of $700,000 on his tax deferred retirement accounts, the retirement fund owner would have a RMD of $38,168 ($700,000/27.4 = $25,548). With the recalculation method he would again go to the table the next year at age 71 and find a factor of 26.5 and divide it into the balance of all tax deferred accounts as of the prior

---

[*]Copyright © 2007. Reprinted with permission from Thomson-West Publishing. Reproduction prohibited without publisher's written permission.

[†]Kevin Sigler is a professor of finance at the University of North Carolina Wilmington in the Department of Economics and Finance in the Cameron School of Business. He received a Ph.D. in finance from the University of Nebraska.

December 31. If we assume a prior year-end balance of $720,000, his RMD in year two is $27,170 ($720,000/26.5 = $27,170).

REQUIRED DISTRIBUTIONS FOR THE BENEFICIARY

A non-spouse beneficiary of the account is responsible for the tax due on the deceased's traditional IRA once the owner has died. A non-spouse beneficiary has two ways of receiving the money from the owner's IRA: 1) the beneficiary may take the money by December 31 of the year of the fifth anniversary of the death of the owner; or 2) the non-spouse beneficiary may also take payments over his life expectancy starting no later than December 31 of the year following the owner's death. The second option of distribution is referred to as stretching the IRA. The funds are subject to federal and state income tax when distributed with either method.

For example, if the non-spouse beneficiary is 57 years old the year following the owner's death and wanted to stretch the IRA, he could take a payment using the balance from the end of the prior year and dividing it by the Single Life Expectancy factor of 27.9. It the owner dies at age 80 and has a balance in the retirement account of $200,000 at the end of that year, the beneficially can take a required beneficiary distribution, RED, of $7,168 ($200,000/27.9) by the end of the following year. The next year the factor is reduced by one and divided into the prior year-end balance. If there is a balance of $204,832 in the account at the end of that next year, then the RBD is $7,614 ($204,832/26.9) that is taken by the end of the next year. This continues until the retirement account is empty or the beneficiary dies. Federal and state income tax is paid only on the amount drawn each year. The funds left in the account grow tax deferred.

If the spouse is the beneficiary, she can use either of the above methods of withdrawal although the spouse can also use the recalculation method to calculate her payment each year if she opts for the life expectancy method. To recalculate each RBD, instead of subtracting one from the initial factor used in the calculation each year, the spouse would visit the single life expectancy table each year and use the factor for her corresponding age. In addition, the spouse may wait to draw payments from the retirement plan when the deceased would have turned age 70.5 if the owner dies before Required Minimum Distributions (RMD) begin, taking the distributions that the owner would have taken. Also and most likely, the surviving spouse can roll the funds into her own IRA. Once the assets are in her own IRA, she can name her own death beneficiaries.

After the death of the owner of the IRA the IRS regulations prohibit the distribution period from extending beyond the original non-spouse beneficiary's life expectancy. The RBDs continue to successor beneficiaries after the death of the beneficiary. All RBDs to successor beneficiaries are based on the original beneficiary's life expectancy, not on the life expectancy of the next beneficiary. This allows for the exhausting of an IRA proceeds since the original beneficiary's life expectancy factor decreases each year, eventually reaching 1.0 or less, which then requires a full distribution that year.

A non-spouse IRA beneficiary may want to name a successor beneficiary, if one has not been named, in order to pass distribution rights to a specific person. This allows an IRA to accumulate additional tax deferred income as explained above. Having no successor beneficiary will result in a single sum distribution when a beneficiary dies. But a beneficiary should first determine if the agreement between the deceased owner of the IRA and the custodian permits the naming of a successor beneficiary.

Beneficiaries are allowed to disclaim retirement accounts according to the code. This is very useful when there are multiple beneficiaries to a tax deferred account. According to the IRS account holders do not have to be designated until the year following the owner's death. So, beneficiaries can elect to disclaim their share of the account and let ill remaining beneficiaries receive the distributions. When trusts or estates are beneficiaries of a tax-deferred retirement plan distributions are based on the Single Life Expectancy factor for the deceased owner had he lived and is reduced by one each year thereafter.

TABLE 1
Single Life Expectancy Factor for 57 Year-Old Equals 27.9

Year	Factor	RMD	Taxes	RMD – Taxes	Portfolio Value
					$200,000
2006	27.9	$7,168	$1,792	$5,376	$204,832
2007	26.9	7,615	1,904	5,711	209,507
2008	25.9	8,089	2.022	6,067	213,988
2009	24.9	8,594	2,148	6,445	218,234
2010	23.9	9,131	2,283	6,848	222,197
2011	22.9	9,703	2,426	7,277	225,825
2012	21.9	10,312	2,578	7,734	229,063
2013	20.9	10,960	2,740	8,220	231,847
2014	19.9	11,651	2,913	8,738	234,107
2015	18.9	12,387	3,097	9,290	235,767
2016	17.9	13,171	3,293	9,879	236,742
2017	16.9	14,008	3,502	10,506	236,938
2018	15.9	14,902	3,725	11,176	236,252
2019	14.9	15,856	3,964	11,892	234,572
2020	13.9	16,867	4,219	12,657	231,770
2021	12.9	17,967	4,492	13,475	227,710
2022	11.9	19,135	4,784	14,351	222,237
2023	10.9	20,389	5,097	15,292	215,183
2024	9.9	21,736	5,434	16,302	206,358
2025	8.9	23,186	5,797	17,390	195,553
2026	7.9	24,754	6,188	18,565	182,533
2027	6.9	26,454	6,614	19,841	167,031
2028	5.9	28,310	7,078	21,233	148,742
2029	4.9	30,356	7,589	22,767	127,311
2030	3.9	32,644	8,161	24,483	102,306
2031	2.9	35,287	8,819	26,458	76,166
2032	1.9	38,509	9,627	28,881	39,048
2033	0.9	41,391	10,348	31,043	0

Total of RMDs $530,530   After Tax Total of RMDs $397897

DISTRIBUTION IMPLICATIONS

There may be wide difference in the amount of total distributions depending if either a non-spouse beneficiary decides to take the IRA proceeds five years after the death of the IRA owner or instead selects to stretch the IRA distributions over his life expectancy. In the following example, the distribution amounts and federal income tax payable using both payout techniques are calculated. For the example it is assumed that the owner of the IRA dies on December 31, 2005 with $200,000 as the balance in the IRA. The beneficiary is a son. He is filing a joint income tax return, is 57 years old in 2006 and has $61.300 in taxable income beside the distribution from his father's IRA. The 2006 federal income tax table is used for the income tax calculations (Table 3). In addition, it is assumed that the IRA portfolio grows at 6 percent per year and withdrawals are made on December 31 of the year. The son's duties to execute distributions from the IRA after the father's death involve notifying the custodian of the father's IRA, showing them the death certificate, and opening a beneficiary IRA with the custodian. The funds from the deceased IRA go into the inherited IRA but the deceased father's name stays on it. Then the beneficiary receives RBDs based on his life expectancy using the Single Life Expectancy Table. He also has the option to take all proceeds by the fifth anniversary of his father's death.

RESULTS

According to Table 1, the non-spouse beneficiary would draw Required Beneficiary Distributions (RBD) from 2006 through 2033 as long as he is alive. If the non-spouse beneficiary dies before 2033, his beneficiary would receive the RBDs as scheduled in Table 1. Notice that the total RBDs equal $530,530, and after tax the total is $397,897 when stretching the IRA. By taking the distribution of the IRA's proceeds by the fifth anniversary of the death of the IRA owner results in a payout of $267,645 and an after tax total of $187,552 in 2011 (Table 2) to the beneficiary. If the after tax payouts from Table 1 were to be invested, assuming the funds receive an after tax return of 4.5 percent when invested, the total of the payouts plus the dollar return from them equals $640,184 by the end of year 2033. Using the after tax payout in 2011 from Table 2 and growing it out to the end of the year 2033 at the same after tax return yields $493,868. This difference is nearly $150,000 more when stretching the IRA compared to taking a lump sum in the fifth year, assuming all after tax proceeds are reinvested.

TABLE 2
Take Funds at the Five Year Anniversary of the Owner's Death

Year	Distribution	Federal Tax	Distribution Less Tax	Portfolio Value at End of Year
2006	$0			$206,000
2011	$267,645	$80,093	$187,552	$0

TABLE 3
2006 Federal Income Tax Schedule Married Filing Jointly

10% on income between $0 and $15,100
15% on income between $15,000 and $61,300 plus $1,510.00
25% on income between $61,300 and $123,700 plus $8,440.00
28% on income between $123,700 and $188,450 plus $24,040.00
33% on income between $188,450 and $336,550 plus $42,170.00
35% on income over $336,550 plus $91,043

CONCLUSION

A non-spouse beneficiary upon the death of the owner of an IRA has the options of either taking distributions from the IRA by December 31 of the year of the fifth anniversary of the IRA owner's death or stretching the IRA by receiving payments over the beneficiary's life expectancy. It appears from the example that the beneficiary will receive substantially more in distributions after tax by stretching the IRA instead of opting for a total pay out. Using the assumptions of the analysis, if the non-spouse beneficiary desires to maximize his wealth, stretching the IRA is the viable option for him.

NOTES

1. Lloyd, M., R. Parker, and F. Bragdon, "Required Minimum Distributions: New Proposed Regulations," Journal of Pension Planning and Compliance, Fall 2001, p. 1–19; Monippallil, M., "New Rules for IRA Distributions," Journal of Accountancy, December 2001, p. 59–62.

An Examination of Delaying Social Security Retirement Benefits*

by Clarence C. Rose, PhD[†]

Abstract: When individuals still have employment opportunities and the desire to work, many factors should be considered before making the decision to begin Social Security retirement benefits. The decision of when to begin benefits can have a major impact on an individual's total percentage of income replacement in retirement and directly affect the worker's standard of living, spousal benefits, benefits of other dependents, and the benefits of the worker's eventual survivors. This article examines the economic value of delaying Social Security retirement benefits.

INTRODUCTION

For the vast majority of the baby boomers in the United States who are starting to reach retirement age, Social Security retirement benefits will be the greatest source of retirement income. However, the average monthly Social Security retirement benefit for retired individuals in January 2008 was only $1,079, and for married couples where both husband and wife receive benefits, the average combined monthly benefit was only $1,761. In spite of the relatively low level of average Social Security retirement benefits, for approximately one out of every five retired Americans in 2008 Social Security is the only source of retirement income. For approximately one out of every three retirees, Social Security retirement benefits provide 90% or more of the total income received in retirement. Furthermore, for approximately two out of every three retirees, Social Security benefits provide more than half of the total income received.[1] These statistics are not expected to change dramatically in the foreseeable future. By the year 2030, Social Security retirement benefits are still expected to be approximately the same portion of total retirement income received by individuals and the major source of aggregate retirement income in the United States.

Currently, of all the aggregate retirement income received by retired Americans, Social Security benefits provide approximately 42.5%, individual savings and personal investments provide approximately 36%, and employer and individual retirement accounts provide approximately 21.5%.[2] In addition to being the major source of retirement income for most Americans, Social Security may be the only stable source of retirement income for many retirees. The changing pension environment including the dramatic shift from defined-benefit plans to defined-contribution plans over the past several decades has increased the uncertainty of retirement income for many individuals. With defined-contribution retirement plans, individual workers and retirees are responsible for managing their own retirement accounts and determining the withdrawal rates from their accounts in retirement.

---

*Reprinted with permission. Copyright © 2008, Society of Financial Service Professionals. All rights reserved.
[†]Clarence C. Rose, PhD, is a professor of finance and director of the MBA and Academic Outreach Programs in the College of Business and Economics at Radford University in Radford, VA. Dr. Rose can be reached at crose@radford.edu.

Financial market volatility is also on the rise resulting in greater risks and increasing the chance of retirees outliving their retirement assets.[3] Also, health care inflation was reported to be 6.7% in 2006 and is expected to continue to outpace the consumer price index in the future.[4] Retirement is the time when health care costs usually rise dramatically for individuals. An estimated 80% of Americans aged 65 and older have at least one chronic disease.[5]

With all the financial demands and uncertainty faced by retirees, 60% of workers in the United States elect to begin Social Security retirement benefits at age 62, the youngest eligible age, and approximately 70% of workers retire before reaching full retirement age, resulting in a permanent reduction in Social Security retirement benefits. See Table 1 for the reduction in Social Security benefits for early retirement.

TABLE 1
Benefit Reductions for Early Retirement at Age 62 Based upon a Primary Insured Amount of $2,000 per Month at Full Retirement Age

Year of Birth	Early Retirement Years	Normal (or full) Retirement Age	Number of Reduction Months	Primary at Age 62		Spouse at Age 62	
				Amount	Percent Reduction	Amount	Percent Reduction
1943-1954	2005-2016	66	48	1,500	25.00%	700	30.00%
1955	2017	66 and 2 months	50	1,482	25.83%	690	30.83%
1956	2018	66 and 4 months	52	1,466	26.67%	681	31.67%
1957	2019	66 and 6 months	54	1,450	27.50%	674	32.50%
1958	2020	66 and 8 months	56	1,432	28.33%	666	33.33%
1959	2021	66 and 10 months	58	1,416	29.17%	658	34.17%
1960 and later	2022 and later	67	60	1,400	30.00%	650	35.00%

Source: U.S. Social Security Administration, "Benefit Reduction for Early Retirement," http://www.ssa.gov/OACT/quickcalc/earlyretire.html (last visited January 30, 2008).

When individuals still have employment opportunities and the desire to work, many factors should be considered before making the decision to begin Social Security retirement benefits. The decision of when to begin benefits can have a major impact on an individual's total percentage of income replacement in retirement and directly affect the retiree's standard of living, spousal benefits, benefits of other dependents, and the benefits of the primary worker's eventual survivors. This article examines the economic value of delaying Social Security retirement benefits.

MAINTAINING FINANCIAL SECURITY IN RETIREMENT

In order to build financial security and maintain economic independence in retirement, financial planners typically recommend that individuals build their retirement plans around three main sources of retirement income: 1) Social Security, 2) employer and individual retirement accounts, and 3) personal savings, which should include short-term liquid investments for emergencies and long-term investments for growth. Financial planners also recommend that individual retirement goals should be set to include 70% to 80% or more of income replacement during the retirement years with provisions to increase retirement income to keep pace with inflation. Unfortunately, the vast majority of Americans will not come close to meeting the recommended retirement income guidelines.

In 2008, approximately 20% of U.S. workers still have a traditional retirement pension plan, and half of all private-sector workers do not have access to an employer-sponsored retirement account or are not enrolled to participate. Only 7% of U.S. workers contribute to an individual retirement account (IRA), and the percentage of U.S. households with adequate savings for retirement continues to decline.[6] In 2007, only 66% of U.S. households were saving and investing for retirement, and the total retirement savings of many U.S. workers over age 55 is inadequate to maintain financial independence in retirement. Twenty-six percent of U.S. workers over age 55 have total retirement savings of less than $10,000, and 41% of U.S. workers over age 55 have less than $50,000 in total retirement savings. See Table 2 for the amount of retirement savings of U.S. workers over age 55.[7]

TABLE 2
Total Retirement Savings of U.S. Workers (55 years old and older)

Total Retirement Account Balance	Percentage of Workers in Range
$0 to $9,999	26
$10,000 to $24,999	6
$25,000 to $49,999	9
$50,000 to $99,999	11
$100,000 to $249,000	20
$250,000 or more	28

Source: Ruth Helman, Jack VanDerhei, and Craig Copeland, "The Retirement System in Transition: The 2007 Retirement Confidence Survey," http://www.ebri.org/pdf/briefspdf/EBRI_IB_04a-20075.pdf.

The lack of personal savings and the lack of participation in retirement account opportunities available today for U. S. workers have made Social Security by default the only reliable source of retirement income for millions of Americans and the major source of retirement income for most retirees. As a result, individual decisions affecting Social Security retirement benefits will have a major impact on the standard of living in retirement for the majority of future retirees in the United States.

DELAYING SOCIAL SECURITY RETIREMENT BENEFITS

The key variable concerning Social Security retirement benefits that many U.S. workers can control is deciding when to begin receiving benefits. This is a critical decision for most workers because electing to begin to receive Social Security retirement benefits before reaching full retirement age results in a permanent reduction in benefits for the primary insured and all others who may receive benefits based upon the primary insured's earnings.

Covered workers can elect to begin receiving Social Security retirement benefits as early as age 62 at a permanently reduced rate depending upon his or her year of birth (see Table 1), at full retirement age between ages 65 and 67, or any time up until age 70 with delayed retirement credits added on for each month retirement is delayed beyond an individual's full retirement age. Individual workers who defer collecting Social Security benefits beyond their full retirement age will receive more than 100% of the full monthly retirement benefit, depending on how long benefits are delayed. For individuals who reach full retirement age in 2008, the increase for each month of delay is two-thirds of 1% of the full retirement benefit, or an 8% increase for each year of delay. For example, if a person would have received $2,000 per month by retiring in 2008 at his or her full retirement age of 65 and 10 months, that person would receive $2,160 per month for waiting 12 months (to age 66 and 10 months) to collect Social Security in 2009. Delaying benefits past age 70, however, adds nothing to a person's monthly benefits.

In 2008, individuals who were born in 1946 can elect to begin receiving early Social Security retirement benefits one month after turning age 62. The differences in the monthly retirement benefits between starting early at age 62 and delaying benefits to full retirement age or delaying further to age 70 can be substantial as a source of income replacement in retirement for individuals at nearly every income level. Table 3 illustrates the estimated annual Social Security retirement benefits for individuals at different retirement ages for different levels of average annual earnings.

TABLE 3
Approximate Percentage of Income Replacement Provided by Social Security in Retirement for Individuals

Primary insured's average annual earnings	$20,000	$40,000	$60,000	$80,000	$100,000	$120,000
Annual Social Security Benefits						
Age 62 and 1 month	$6,888	$10,044	$13,212	$16,248	$17,736	$19,068
Income replacement	34.44%	25.11%	22.02%	20.31%	17.74%	15.89%
Age 66 in 2012	$9,528	$14,100	$18,684	$22,272	$24,420	$26,064
Income replacement	47.64%	35.25%	31.14%	27.84%	24.42%	21.72%
Age 70 in 2016	$13,044	$19,560	$26,076	$30,288	$33,348	$35,328
Income replacement	65.52%	48.90%	43.46%	37.86%	33.35%	29.44%

For comparison, benefits are estimated in today's dollars. An annual cost-of-living adjustment would be applied to future benefits. The maximum benefit for an individual at full retirement age in 2008 is $21,185. Future maximum benefits are adjusted for cost-of-living increases.

As can be seen in Table 3, the annual benefits increase considerably when the starting date is delayed. For an individual with average annual earnings of $60,000 who elects early retirement at age 62 in 2008, the annual Social Security retirement benefit is approximately $13,212 or 22% of income. Delaying retirement to age 66 in the year 2012 will increase the annual retirement benefit to approximately $18,684 per year or 31.14% of income. Delaying retirement to age 70 in 2016 will increase the annual retirement benefit to approximately $26,076 or 43.46% of income.

Figure 1 illustrates Social Security retirement benefits as a percentage of income replacement for a primary insured if benefits were to begin at age 62, age 66, or age 70. As can be seen in Table 3 and Figure 1, as a percentage of income replacement,

Social Security retirement benefits are considerably higher when delaying benefits at all levels of income, but especially at the lower income levels.

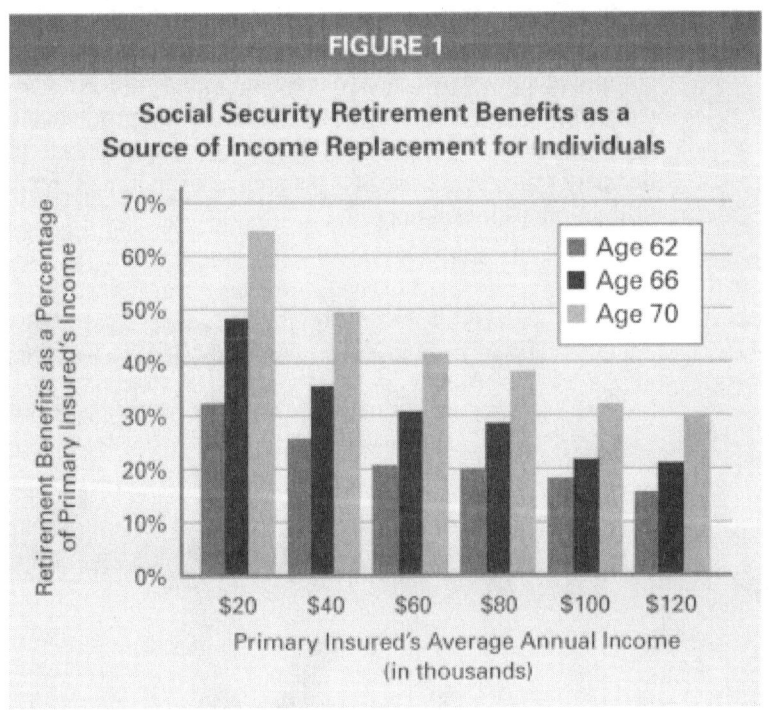

FIGURE 1
Social Security Retirement Benefits as a Source of Income Replacement for Individuals

The income replacement provided by Social Security retirement benefits for husbands and wives utilizing the spousal benefit is illustrated in Table 4. At full retirement age and beyond, an eligible spouse can receive his or her own Social Security retirement benefit or 50% of his or her spouse's Social Security retirement benefit, whichever is greater. Early retirement before reaching full retirement age reduces the spousal benefit as well as the primary worker's benefit. See Table 1 for the reduction in benefits for early retirement when utilizing the spousal benefit.

TABLE 4
Approximate Percentage of Income Replacement Provided by Social Security in Retirement for Husbands and Wives Utilizing the Spousal Benefit

Primary insured's average annual earnings	$20,000	$40,000	$60,000	$80,000	$100,000	$120,000
Combined Annual Social Security Benefits						
Age 62 and 1 month in 2008	$10,102	$14,732	$19,378	$23,830	$26,031	$27,966
Income replacement	50.51%	36.83%	32.30%	29.79%	26.01%	23.3%
Age 66 in 2012	$14,292	$21,150	$28,026	$33,408	$36,630	$39,096
Income replacement	71.46%	52.88%	46.71%	41.76%	36.63%	32.58%
Age 70 in 2016	$19,566	$29,340	$39,114	$45,432	$50,022	$52,992
Income replacement	97.83%	73.35%	65.19%	56.79%	50.02%	44.16%

Assumes that the husband and wife are the same age for calculating benefits. For comparison, benefits are estimated in today's dollars. An annual cost-of-living adjustment would be applied to all future benefits. The maximum Social Security benefit for a couple at full retirement age in which one spouse collects on the other's work record is $31,627.50 in 2008. Future maximum benefits are adjusted for cost-of-living increases.

As can be seen in Table 4, a primary insured with average annual earnings of $60,000 per year and a spouse who is eligible for the spousal benefit together would receive a combined annual retirement income from Social Security of $19,378 at age 62 or 32.3% of income replacement. Delaying the start of Social Security retirement benefits to age 66 (full retirement age) would produce approximately $28,026 combined annual income from Social Security or 46.7% income replacement. Further delaying the start of benefits to age 70 would produce a combined annual benefit of approximately $39,114 or 65.19% of income. Figure 2 illustrates the level of Social Security retirement benefits as a source of income replacement for married couples utilizing the spousal benefit.

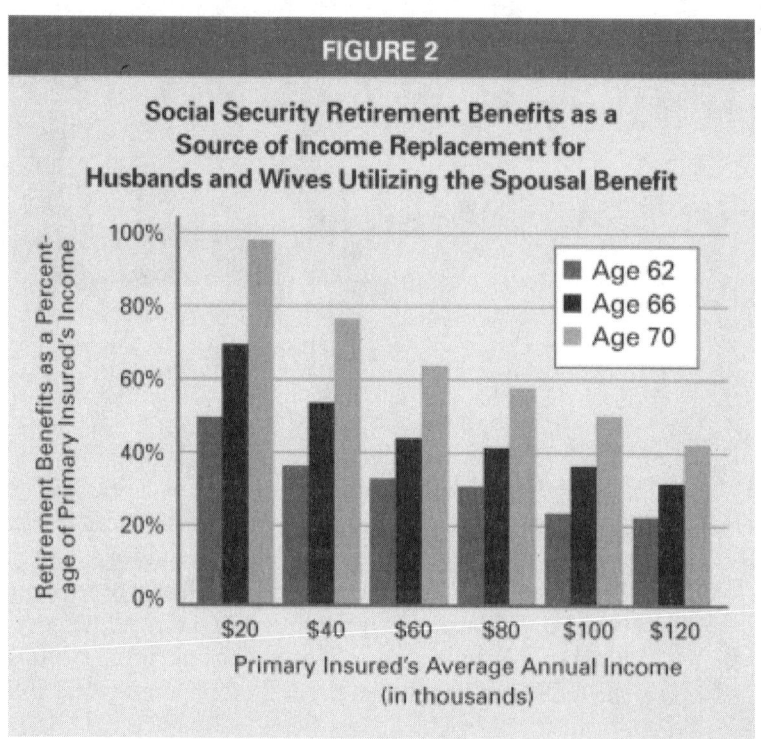

THE PRESENT VALUE OF DELAYING SOCIAL SECURITY RETIREMENT BENEFITS

If a covered worker elects to begin receiving Social Security retirement benefits at age 62, he or she will receive more monthly checks than if he or she had delayed benefits to full retirement age or beyond, but each check will be for a smaller amount. The exact amount of the reduction depends upon the individual's date of birth (see Table 1). In this analysis, the present values of the expected future benefits were calculated for three benefit starting dates: early retirement at age 62, full retirement at age 66, and delayed retirement at age 70. The analysis assumes no employment offset for benefits received prior to full retirement age and no taxes on benefits received. The life expectancy for men is assumed to be 79.5 years and for women is assumed to be 83.5 years. For this analysis, the expected Social Security benefits were used for individuals and for married couples with the primary insured's average annual income at various levels. The discount rate used in the present value analysis is 3.43%—the average U. S. inflation rate from 1913 to 2006.[8] For the calculations, the benefits are assumed to be received at the end of each year and all expected benefits are discounted back to age 62.

For benefits beginning at age 62, the present value of the future Social Security benefits is the calculation of a present value of an annuity for the specified time period using the annual benefits as the annuity payment. For benefits beginning at age 66 and at age 70, the present value of an annuity calculation is used to determine the value at the start of benefits; the values are then discounted back to age 62 using the present value of a lump sum. Table 5 is a summary of the results for individuals. Table 6 is a summary of the results for married couples.

TABLE 5
The Economic Value of Delaying Social Security Benefits for Individuals

Annual earnings	$20,000	$40,000	$60,000	$80,000	$100,000	$120,000
Annual Social Security Benefits for Retirement Age						
62 and 1 month in 2008	$6,888	$10,044	$13,212	$16,248	$17,736	$19,068
66 in 2012	$9,528	$14,100	$18,684	$22,272	$24,420	$26,064
70 in 2016	$13,044	$19,560	$26,076	$30,288	$33,348	$35,328
Present Value (2008) of Future Benefits for Men (Life Expectancy 79.5 Years)						
62 and 1 month in 2008	$89,518.97	$130,535.51	$171,708.00	$211,164.96	$230,503.56	$247,814.72
66 in 2012	$89,013.78	$131,726.94	$174,552.21	$208,072.51	$228,139.84	$243,498.65
70 in 2016	$88,181.23	$132,231.29	$176,552.21	$204,755.69	$225,442.18	$238,827.55
Present Value (2008) of Future Benefits for Women (Life Expectancy 83.5 Years)						
62 and 1 month in 2008	$103,564.28	$151,016.21	$198,648.56	$244,296.23	$266,669.01	$286,696.25
66 in 2012	$110,510.86	$163,539.37	$216,707.06	$258,322.61	$283,236.27	$302,304.26
70 in 2016	$121,861.43	$182,736.09	$243,610.75	$282,960.68	$311,548.23	$330,046.05

Present value of future benefits discounted to age 62 at a rate of 3.43% for number of years based upon current life expectancies.

As can be seen in Table 5, the economic value of the expected Social Security retirement benefits is very similar for men at the different levels of annual earnings based upon current life expectancies no matter when the individual elects to begin benefits. The reduction in benefits for early retirement and the increase in benefits for delaying benefits to full retirement age and beyond produce very similar present values when discounted to age 62 of the primary insured. The present values even are slightly higher when beginning at age 62 for men at the higher income levels.

However, for women, because of their longer life expectancy, the present values of future benefits increase considerably when benefits are delayed across the various income levels (Table 5).

Table 6 is a present value analysis of delaying Social Security retirement benefits for married couples using the spousal benefit. The analysis examines the present values of the combined expected future Social Security retirement benefits assuming that each spouse will live to his and her life expectancy. If the primary insured dies before the spouse receiving the spousal benefit, the surviving spouse would switch to the survivor benefit, which is the benefit amount of the primary insured for the remainder of his or her life. If the spouse receiving the spousal benefit dies first, the primary insured would continue to receive only his or her benefit.

TABLE 6
The Economic Value of Delaying Social Security Benefits for Married Couples Utilizing the Spousal Benefits

Annual earnings	$20,000	$40,000	$60,000	$80,000	$100,000	$120,000
Combined Annual Social Security Benefits for Retirement Age						
62 and 1 month in 2008	$10,102	$14,732	$19,378	$23,830	$26,013	$27,966
66 in 2012	$14,292	$21,150	$28,026	$33,408	$36,630	$39,096
70 in 2016	$19,566	$29,340	$39,114	$45,432	$50,022	$52,992
Present Value of Future Benefits						
62 and 1 month in 2008	$145,382	$212,012	$278,875	$342,947	$374,362	$402,469
66 in 2012	$155,755	$230,494	$305,429	$364,082	$399,196	$426,071
70 in 2016	$167,699	$250,584	$334,061	$388,021	$427,222	$452,587

Present value of future benefits discounted to age 62 at a rate of 3.43% for number of years based upon current life expectancies. Values assume changing to survivor's benefit or primary insured's benefit upon first to die.

As can be seen in Table 6, when using the average annual inflation rate of 3.43% in the present value analysis, married couples who utilize the spousal benefit increase the economic value of their combined future expected benefits by delaying benefits. The increase in value occurs across the various income levels. The differences in the economic values for married couples may be significant enough to influence the decision as to when to begin Social Security benefits.

Using a lower rate in the present value analysis of delaying Social Security retirement benefits would further increase the economic value of delaying benefits. Using a higher rate would reduce the economic value of delaying the start of benefits. For married couples, using a discount rate up to 6% still favors delaying benefits to at least age 66. Since most retirees use Social Security benefits for meeting living expenses, the average annual inflation rate appears to be the most appropriate rate to use in the decision as to when to begin benefits. As previously discussed, delaying Social Security retirement benefits also increases the income replacement percentage in retirement and, as a result, may influence the overall standard of living for retirees.

OTHER IMPORTANT FACTORS IN DECIDING WHEN TO BEGIN

In addition to increasing the present value of future benefits and the percentage of income replacement in retirement, there are many other factors that should be considered before electing to start receiving Social Security retirement benefits.

Employment

Social Security recipients who are younger than their full retirement age are allowed to earn up to $13,560 per year, the earnings limit, in 2008. Income above this limit for an individual would result in a $1 deduction from benefits for each $2 earned above the limit. For married couples utilizing the spousal benefit, the primary insured and spouse may each earn up to the limit before experiencing a reduction in benefits.

Any individual who expects to work after beginning benefits must be extremely careful when considering early retirement so as not to exceed the earnings limit.

In the year an individual reaches full retirement age, the earnings limit is $36,120. For every $3 over the limit, $1 is withheld from benefits until the month the individual reaches full retirement age. After the full retirement age is reached, there is no reduction in benefits for earnings.[9]

Social Security retirement benefits are included as taxable income for individuals and married couples. Individuals have to pay federal income taxes on benefits if total taxable income is more than $25,000. For married couples who file a joint return, Social Security retirement benefits are subject to federal income taxation if total income is more than $32,000.[10] Individuals and married couples who expect to be in the higher income tax brackets in retirement would generally benefit by delaying Social Security retirement past age 65.

Fringe Benefits

Health insurance and medical expenses are a major expense for most retirees. When an individual retires before eligibility for Medicare (age 65), consideration should be given to the increased costs of carrying health insurance and other fringe benefits, such as life insurance. Upon retirement, many companies transfer health insurance premiums and other fringe benefit costs to the retiree. Retirement before eligibility for Medicare insurance can result in large increases in health insurance costs.

Family and Personal Health History

Individuals eligible to begin Social Security early retirement benefits, who are still in good health and have a family history of longevity, would generally benefit more by delaying the start of benefits. While no one knows how long he or she will live, an individual in good health with a good family health history can expect to live beyond the normal life expectancy. As a result, the individual would increase his or her standard of living for a greater number of years by delaying benefits.

Spousal Benefits

A spouse cannot receive Social Security retirement benefits based upon the earnings record of a primary insured until the primary insured actually begins receiving benefits. Also, early retirement by the primary insured will permanently reduce the base amount upon which the spousal benefits are calculated. Married couples should carefully review the impact of early retirement on the total family benefits from Social Security.

Survivors Benefit

If the primary insured dies before the spouse, the spouse would change from the spousal benefit amount to the survivor's benefit, which would generally be the retirement benefit amount of the primary insured. Electing to receive early retirement will also reduce the eventual benefits paid to a survivor. Delaying Social Security retirement benefits past the early retirement age (62) will increase the base used to determine the spousal benefit and the survivor benefit for each month that retirement is delayed up to age 70. Delaying the start of benefits past age 70 results in no additional increases in the base amount of retirement benefits of the primary insured.

Other Funds Available

When an individual or married couple have other sources of retirement income or the funds available to provide the desired standard of living in retirement without major dependency upon Social Security, the decision maker's flexibility is greatly enhanced. The decision as to when to begin the start of benefits can be based upon personal preferences and retirement desires, not economic necessity.

CONCLUSION

While the majority of Americans continue to opt for early Social Security retirement benefits, serious consideration should be given to delaying benefits to full retirement age and beyond. The statistics indicate that many baby boomers will be facing difficult financial times in retirement as a result of many factors. The lack of adequate savings, the changing pension environment, continuing volatility in financial markets, increasing longevity, increasing health care costs, and the changes in the Social Security retirement benefits eventually delaying full retirement age to 67, all contribute to the importance of Social Security retirement decisions.

For covered workers, delaying the start of Social Security retirement benefits beyond age 62 increases the amount of income replacement in retirement and also increases the primary insured's base amount upon which the Social Security Administration determines the amount of benefits for eligible spouses, dependents, and the eventual survivors of the covered workers. Delaying benefits also increases the economic value of the expected future benefits for women and married couples as measured by the present value analysis of the expected future benefits.

NOTES

1. U.S. Social Security Administration, Benefit Calculators, *Retirement, Disability, and Survivor Estimates,* at http://www.socialsecurity.gov/cgi-bin/benefit6.cgi (last visited January 27, 2008).
2. U.S. Social Security Administration, "Retirement, Disability, and Survivor Estimates," at http://www.socialsecurity.gov/planners/calculators.html (last visited January 17, 2008).
3. Eleanor Laise, "Protecting your Nest Egg in Volatile Times," *Wall Street Journal* (January 16, 2008): D1, D9.
4. Steve Jacob, "U.S. retirees are in a fix," *The Roanoke Times* (January 20, 2008): Section H, page 1.
5. *Ibid.*
6. Bill Novelli, "Helping Americans Save," *AARP Bulletin* (June 2007): 22.
7. *Ibid.*
8. InflationData.com, "Average Annual Inflation by Decade," http://inflationdata.com/Inflation/images/charts/Articles/Decade_inflation_chart.htm (last visited February 5, 2007).
9. Kelly Greene, "Collecting on a Working Partner's Social Security," *Wall Street Journal* (January 26-27, 2008): B2.
10. U.S. Social Security Administration, Benefit Calculators, *Retirement, Disability, and Survivor Estimates,* at http://www.socialsecurity.gov/cgi-bin/benefit6.cgi (last visited January 27, 2008).

When Should Married Men Claim Social Security Benefits?[*]

by Steven A. Sass, Wei Sun, and Anthony Webb[†]

INTRODUCTION

Most married men claim Social Security benefits at age 62 or 63, well short of the age that maximizes the expected present value of the average household's benefits. That many married men "leave money on the table" is surprising. It is also problematic. It results in much lower benefits for surviving spouses and the low incomes of elderly widows are a major social problem. If married men delayed claiming Social Security benefits, retirement income security would significantly improve. This brief focuses on the potential gains from delayed claiming and the factors that may influence claiming behavior. It then considers possible policy responses.[1]

GAINS FROM CLAIMING LATER

Workers can claim Social Security benefits at any age between 62 and 70. For workers with average life expectancy, the expected present value (EPV) of benefits[2] is much the same from 62 to Social Security's Full Retirement Age (FRA). If a worker delays claiming, the shortened period of benefit receipt is offset by a higher monthly benefit.[3]

The EPV of benefits for married couples is much more complicated due to the special spousal and survivor benefits that Social Security provides. While both are alive, each is entitled to the greater of his or her own earned benefit or a benefit based on the spouse's earnings record, so long as the spouse has already claimed. Upon the death of a spouse, survivors are entitled to the greater of their own earned benefit or their spouse's earned benefit, subject to certain minimums and reductions if claimed before the FRA.[4]

Because most married women have lower lifetime earnings and outlive their husbands, spousal and survivor benefits are almost invariably received by women. The benefit wives receive while their husband is alive—whether their own earned benefit or a spousal benefit—is generally replaced by a survivor benefit upon their husband's death. The EPV of the wife's benefit received while her husband is alive is generally greatest if claimed at 62. The reason is that the increase in the monthly benefit from claiming later is generally too small to offset the reduction in her husband's remaining life expectancy.

The length of time wives can expect to receive the survivor benefit, by contrast, is independent of the age at which she or her husband claims. But her husband's

---

[*]Copyright © 2007. Center for Retirement Research at Boston College. Reproduction prohibited without publisher's written permission.
[†]All of the authors are with the Center for Retirement Research at Boston College. Steven A. Sass is Associate Director for Research. Wei Sun is a graduate research assistant. Anthony Webb is a research economist. This brief is based on a longer paper (Sass, Sun, and Webb, 2007)

monthly benefit, which generally becomes her survivor benefit, rises about 7 to 8 percent each year he postpones claiming up to the FRA, and up to that amount thereafter until age 70.[5] Since the resulting rise in the monthly survivor benefit is not offset by a reduction in the duration of benefit receipt, a husband's later claiming age has a large positive effect on the EPY of his wife's survivor benefit.

To study claiming behavior and the potential gains from delaying claiming, we selected a sample of households from the *Health and Retirement Study* (HRS), a nationally representative panel of individuals born between 1931 and 1941 and their spouses. Our sample is households in which both the husband and wife have retired before becoming eligible for Social Security. Households often conflate claiming with the much more complicated retirement decision; they essentially claim when they retire. By narrowing the focus to households that have left the labor force before age 62, 35 percent of the total, the determinants of the claiming decision can be better understood.[6]

FIGURE 1
Combination of Claiming Ages That Maximize the EPV of Household Social Security Benefits.

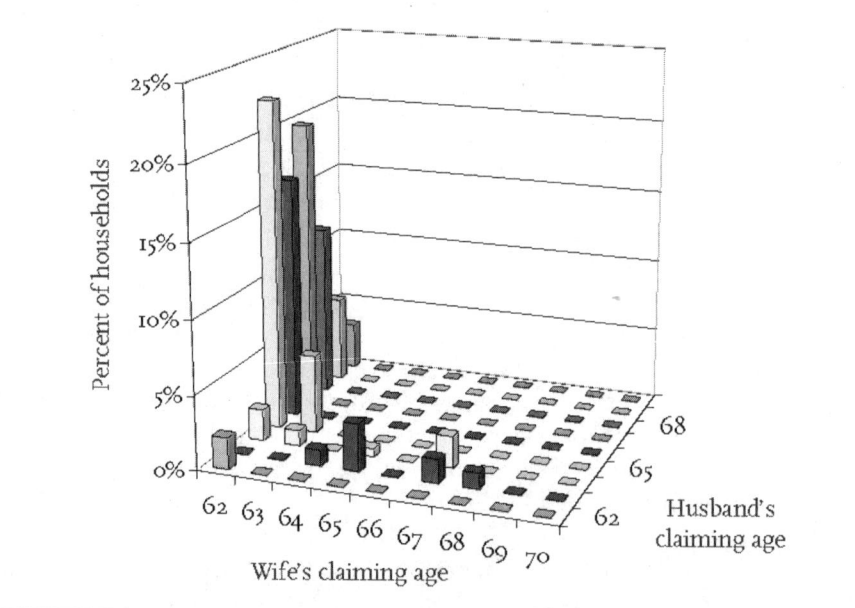

Note: These results are for 187 households in the HRS that retired prior to 62 for which sufficient information is available. Calculations assume a 3 percent rate of interest and population mortality based on each individual's birth year.

Source: Author's calculations from University of Michigan, *Health and Retirement Study*, 1992–2004.

Figure 1 presents the distribution of claiming ages that maximize the EPY of Social Security benefits for a sample of households retiring before age 62. Households, on average, maximize the EPY of benefits when the husband claims at 66 and the wife at 62. The maximizing ages show little variance for women but significant variance for men. While 84 percent of households maximize when the wife claims at 62, only 17 percent maximize when the husband claims at 66.

Over 90 percent of husbands in the sample actually claimed at 62, much earlier than the age that maximizes the EPY of household benefits.[7] It turns out that this choice has only a modest effect on the EPY of household benefits. For example, for a husband and wife who both claimed at 62, the median gain in household benefits from delaying until the maximizing age is only 4 percent.[8] However, as shown in Figure 2, this modest change masks a significant difference between the expected value of benefits received while the husband is alive—which is essentially unchanged—and the expected value of the survivor benefit—which rises by 25 percent. As the duration of receipt does not change, this reflects a 25 percent increase in the expected monthly benefit paid to a surviving spouse. Given this finding, the strong preference of men for claiming at 62 suggests that many do not take the survivor benefit into account when making their decision. The possible reasons are explored in the next section.

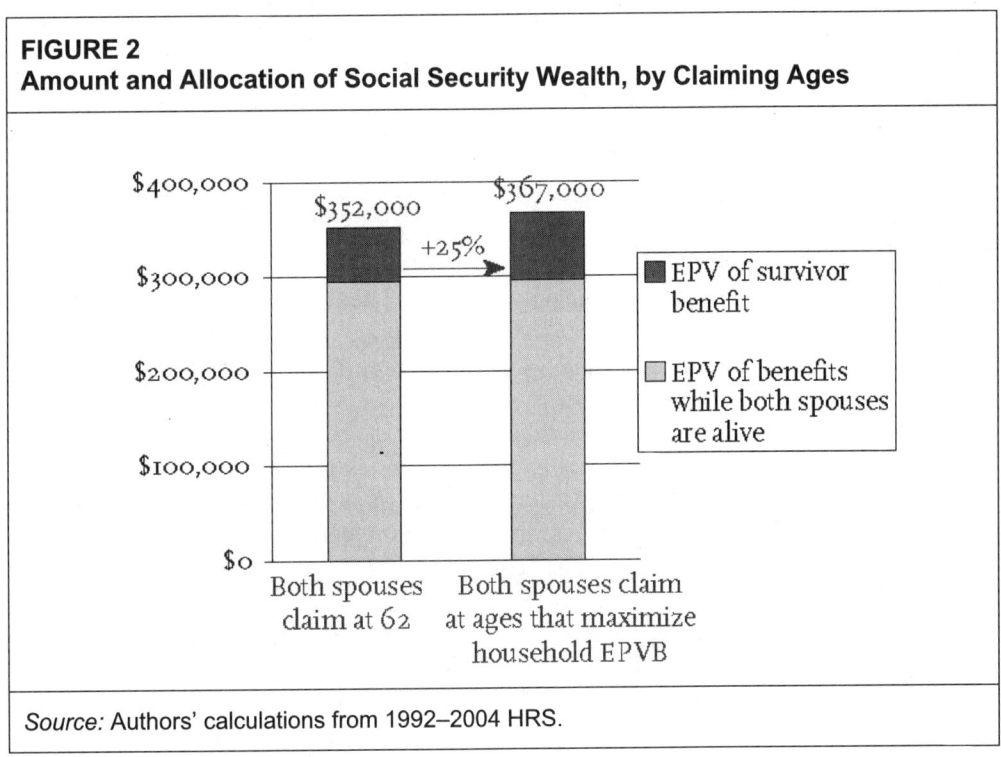

FIGURE 2
Amount and Allocation of Social Security Wealth, by Claiming Ages

Source: Authors' calculations from 1992–2004 HRS.

WHAT MIGHT EXPLAIN EARLY CLAIMING?

A regression analysis was used to examine factors that might influence the claiming behavior of married men. The sample size was just 340 households, so the results must be viewed as tentative.

Two factors that could plausibly explain early claiming by married men are ignorance and a caddish disregard for the well-being of their spouse. The regression controlled for factors identified in earlier studies as influencing claiming behavior; these included expected longevity, wealth, and time preference. The HRS does not provide good measures of time preference, ignorance, and caddishness.[9] The regression thus uses the household's financial planning horizon as an indicator of time preference. As a measure of ignorance (or its opposite, financial awareness), one regression uses three questions in the HRS that loosely measure finance/numerical literacy. A second regression uses educational attainment. The HRS does not attempt to measure caddishness. But it does ask husbands if they prefer to spend free time doing things with their wives, doing things independently, or some of each. A husband who prefers spending time with his wife may be more likely to care for her well-being, so this question serves as a proxy for caddishness. The analysis also uses information in the HRS on household decision-making power, testing whether husbands empowered to make important financial decisions are more likely to claim early.[10]

The regression results show no statistically significant relationship between early claiming and factors identified in earlier studies as influencing claiming behavior—household wealth,[11] expected longevity, and planning horizon. These earlier studies, however, identified only small and marginally significant effects. The lack of a statistically significant relationship in our analysis could also reflect our small sample.

The results also produced no evidence to attribute early claiming to caddishness, which is not surprising. Early claiming has essentially no effect on the EPV of benefits while the husband is alive. So caddish husbands have no real financial incentive to claim early. A husband aware of the financial implications would indeed need to be worse than caddish to claim early and expose his wife to a substantial reduction in survivor benefits.

The results do provide evidence that financial awareness has an effect. The regression with educational attainment found a statistically significant relationship between college education and later claiming. Husbands with a college education are 8.5 percent more likely to postpone claiming. A recent study, using questions asked in the 2004 wave of the HRS, reports similar results.[12]

While financial awareness is a plausible explanation for claiming later, ignorance is not a plausible explanation for claiming early. Something akin to social convention or mistaken information needs to motivate the general tendency to claim early. Households aware that social convention and the "conventional wisdom" lead to sub-optimal outcomes are the ones most likely to pursue a different path.

POLICY IMPLICATIONS

Early claiming has been a social convention for a quarter of a century. This convention is largely the result of the decline in the average age of retirement and the strong connection between retiring and claiming when employer defined benefit pensions were the primary source of private retirement income. Employer pensions are annuities designed to provide a supplementary stream of income, atop the retiree's Social Security benefits. Few retirees had the financial assets needed to top up their monthly pensions and postpone claiming for any length of time. So most had to claim when they retired.

With the shift from employer defined benefit pensions to 401(k)s, many more couples can control the drawdown of their private retirement resources. They can access their public and private retirement wealth sequentially rather than simultaneously, separate retiring and claiming, and thereby improve their retirement income security.[13] If greater recognition of these gains induces married men to postpone claiming, an educational campaign to raise awareness would be desirable. Although the evidence on the effectiveness of workplace financial education is mixed at best,[14] it would seem useful for Social Security's annual statements to participants to clearly indicate the impact of delay on the survivor benefit.

Given the public interest in retirement security and the threat posed by early claiming, policymakers could also consider changes in Social Security's rules, such as:

- Increasing Social Security's Earliest Eligibility Age from 62 to 64, in line with the rise in the FRA. This change would prevent the benefit some survivors will receive from falling due to the rise in the FRA.
- Requiring spousal consent for cases in which the higher-earning spouse claims before the FRA. Such a requirement would tend to establish the FRA as the default claiming age, as only then would higher-earning spouses not need to jump through a hoop to receive their benefits. Defaults have been shown to have a powerful effect on worker behavior in 401(k)s, a somewhat analogous setting. Requiring spousal consent would also provoke a much needed discussion between husband and wife about the consequences of claiming at various ages. And it would alter the balance of power within the household.
- Assure the lower-earning spouse a survivor benefit at least equal to the higher-earning spouse's benefit at the FRA. This policy could be made cost-neutral by reducing the benefits of the higher-earning spouse (or both spouses) who claim before the FRA. Figure 3 gives estimates of the adjusted monthly payable to higher-earning spouses at various claim ages when the FRA is 66.[15] The reductions would be less if the cost of the higher survivor benefit were financed by reducing both spouses' early retirement benefits, or by reducing early retirement benefits payable to all workers, whether married or single.

FIGURE 3
Benefit of Higher-Earnings Spouse as Percent of Full Retirement Benefits, under Current Law and Policy Alternative*

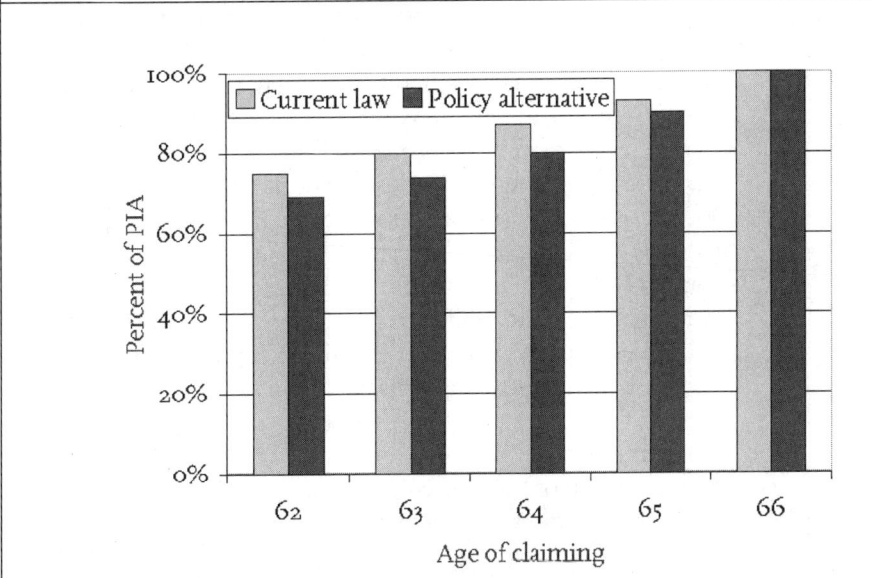

*The Full Retirement Age (FRA) used in this example is 66. Under the policy alternative, individuals who claim early have their benefits reduced in order to preserve the survivor benefit at 100 percent of the individuals Primary Insurance Amount. The estimates assume all survivor benefits are claimed after the survivor attains the FRA.

Source: Authors' calculations

If married men postponed claiming, Social Security's costs would rise. But the added cost would be small, given the modest increase in the EPV of household benefits. Moreover, later claiming can also be expected to result in later retirements, which would increase government tax receipts.[16] Later claiming thus could strengthen the finances of the federal government as well as the finances of the nation's households.

CONCLUSION

Raising the age at which married men claim Social Security benefits would significantly improve retirement income security. The improvement is most pronounced in the retirement income security of widows, currently a serious social problem. An analysis of married men who retired prior to becoming eligible for Social Security identified educational attainment, which is correlated with financial awareness, as a major factor in leading to later claiming. Although the prevalence of early claiming by married men produces a caddish outcome, the analysis did not identify caddishness as a causal factor. This suggests that an educational campaign that raises financial awareness could increase claiming ages. The significant public interest in assuring retirement income security suggests that policymakers may also wish to consider changes in the Social Security program that would raise claiming ages. These include raising the EEA, requiring spousal consent for early claiming, and reducing early retirement benefits of higher earning spouses to preserve the survivor benefit at its FRA level.

NOTES

1. For a more detailed description of Social Security's rules, the methodology used in this analysis, and other issues raised in this *brief* see Sass, Sun and Webb (2007).
2. The EPV of benefits is the present value of the sum of the payments discounted by annual survival probabilities and an interest rate. We follow the Social Security Administration in using a 3 percent real interest rate, which is somewhat above current levels.
3. The increase in monthly benefits has not been sufficient to offset the shortened period of benefit receipt at ages above the FRA, but the adjustment has been rising and will be sufficient for workers born after 1942.
4. The guaranteed minimum spousal benefit that each spouse can claim is based on their spouse's Primary Insurance Amount (PIA)—their earned monthly benefit payable at the FRA. If claimed at or after the FRA, the spousal benefit equals one-half of their spouse's PIA; if claimed before the FRA, the spousal benefit is reduced by a greater percentage than that applied to retired worker benefits. Survivor benefits are based on the deceased spouse's benefit. If claimed on or after the surviving spouse's FRA, the survivor benefit equals the deceased spouse's benefit, subject to a minimum of 82.5 percent of the deceased spouse's PIA; if claimed prior to the surviving spouse's FRA, the survivor benefit is subject to a milder reduction than that applied to retired worker benefits. Survivor benefits can be claimed as early as age 60; if claimed prior to the FRA, the survivor benefit is subject to a minimum of 71.5 percent of the deceased spouse's PIA.
5. For all workers born after 1942, the "delayed retirement credit" for postponing claiming after the FRA is 8 percent annually up to age 70. For workers born in 1942 or earlier, the delayed retirement credit is lower.
6. This approach follows Coile, et al. (2001). Additionally, the households in the sample are those in which: 1) both the husband and wife have matched administrative data that give their earnings histories; 2) neither husband nor wife claimed disability

7. benefit; and 3) the husband had at least the 40 quarters of covered earnings required for benefit eligibility and no quarters of uncovered earnings.
8. Coile et al. (2001) find a similar pattern in earlier cohorts.
9. These relatively small average gains are similar to those reported by Coile, et al. (2001) and Munnell and Soto (2005). There is, nevertheless, considerable heterogeneity in the gains among individual households.
10. The 2004 wave of the HRS asked participants who had not claimed questions that measure their awareness of the effect of claiming ages on monthly benefit amounts. A recent study that used these data to analyze expected claiming ages is discussed below.
11. Coile, et al. (2001) found a statistically significant relationship between early claiming and wealth. Both Coile, et al. (2001) and Hurd, Smith, and Zissimopoulos (2004) found a statistically significant relationship with expected longevity. Gustman and Steinmeier (2002) suggest that time preference is important in claiming decisions. A household's financial planning horizon has been shown to influence savings behavior in a manner similar to time preference (Lusardi and Mitchell, 2006). Educational attainment has been shown to be associated with financial literacy (Warner and Pleeter, 2001; and Lusardi and Mitchell, 2006). The HRS includes a module that measures a household's financial awareness, but few respondents participate.
12. This finding could be due to the fact that we measure household wealth differently. We use non-housing financial wealth while Coile, et al. (2001) also include housing wealth in their measure. Neither study included defined benefit pension claims in their household wealth estimates.
13. Delavande and Willis (2007) found that married men who were aware that later claiming increased monthly benefits, and who expected their wives to be relatively long-lived, reported older expected claiming ages.
14. In addition to the gains outlined in this brief, households that postpone claiming might also be able to reduce their tax burden (Mahaney and Carlson, 2006).
15. Lusardi (2005).
16. The estimates presented in Figure 3 assume all survivor benefits are claimed after the survivor attains the FRA. As noted above, survivor benefits claimed after the FRA cannot fall below 82.5 percent of the deceased spouse's PIA; survivor benefits claimed before the FRA cannot fall below 71.5 percent of the deceased spouse's PIA. To the extent that survivor benefits are claimed before the survivor attains the FRA, the required top-up needed to provide a survivor benefit equal to 100 percent of the deceased spouse's PIA, and the reduction in early retirement benefits needed to finance that top-up, would be greater.
17. Butrica, Smith, and Steuerle (2006).

REFERENCES

Butrica, Barbara A., Karen E. Smith, and C. Eugene Steuerle. 2006. "Working for a Good Retirement." Working Paper 2006–8. Chestnut Hill, MA: Center for Retirement Research at Boston College.

Coile, Courtney, Peter Diamond, Jonathan Gruber, and Alain Jousten. 2001. "Delays in Claiming Social Security Benefits." *Journal of Public Economics* 8: 357–385.

Delavande, Adeline and Robert J. Willis. 2007. "Managing the Risk of Life." Working Paper 2007-167. Ann Arbor, MI: Michigan Retirement Research Center.

Gustman, Alan L. and Thomas L. Steinmeier. 2002. "The Social Security Early Entitlement Age in a Structural Model of Retirement and Wealth." Working Paper 9183. Cambridge, MA: National Bureau of Economic Research.

Hurd, Michael, D., James P. Smith, and Julie M. Zissimopoulos. 2004. "The Effects of Subjective Survival on Retirement and Social Security Claiming." *Journal of Applied Econometrics* 19: 761–775.

Lusardi, Annamaria. 2005. "Saving and the Effectiveness of Financial Education." In *Pension Design and Structure: New Lessons from Behavioral Finance,* eds. Olivia Mitchell and Stephen Utkus, 157–184. Oxford: Oxford University Press.

Lusardi, Annamaria and Olivia S. Mitchell. 2006. "Financial Literacy and Planning: Implications for Retirement Wellbeing." Working Paper 2006-01. Philadelphia, P A: Pension Research Council.

Mahaney, James and Peter Carlson. 2006. *Innovative Strategies to Help Maximize Social Security Benefits.* Prudential Financial. Iselin, NJ.

Munnell, Alicia H. and Mauricio Soto. 2005. "Why Do Women Claim Social Security Benefits So Early?" *Issue Brief 35.* Chestnut Hill, MA: Center for Retirement Research at Boston College.

"Why Do Married Men Claim Social Security Benefits So Early? Ignorance, Caddishness, or Something Else." Working Paper 2007-17. Chestnut Hill, MA: Center for Retirement Research at Boston College.

University of Michigan. *Health and Retirement Study,* 1992-2004. Ann Arbor, MI. Available at: http://hrsonline.isr.umich.edu.

Warner, John T. and Saul Pleeter. 2001. "The Personal Discount Rate, Evidence from Military Downsizing Programs." *American Economic Review,* 91(1) 33–53.

Factors in Deciding to Relocate After Retirement

John J. McFadden

At retirement, you have to make many important decisions. One of the most significant is—where will you live? Most people—up to 90% in fact[1]—will, at least initially, stay where they are. If you have an established support network of family and friends, if your house is paid for (or mostly paid for), if you like your neighborhood, and have no mobility problems in your current location, the argument for staying put can be compelling. However, many other retirees will migrate elsewhere in retirement. The most common reason for moving is to be closer to children and grandchildren. The cost of traveling long distances to visit loved ones can be significant, and permanent relocation may be economically feasible or even advantageous, depending on costs in the old locality versus the new locality.[2] Finally, some retirees will take advantage of their new freedom to simply uproot themselves and seek out a new place to live, based on their vision of an ideal location. This article primarily addresses this issue—that is, how you determine what constitutes a better place for you to live, and how you get the information you need to make this decision.

Because the huge baby-boomer generation is heading rapidly toward retirement, there is an explosion of informational and service resources geared toward retirees. In particular, a vast amount of information is available on the Web regarding retiree relocation issues, some of it valuable, a lot of it superficial or advertising-oriented. This article will try to identify the issues involved in relocation in retirement, and discuss the ways in which retirees can find sources of information and assess the usefulness—to their own situations—of the information, they find.

The next step after the information-gathering process is not necessarily to call the movers. Most advisers suggest that, after you gather information about possible new home communities and settle on a few likely areas, you should visit these areas, rent an apartment or condo for an extended period, and try to get a feel for what it means to be a resident there and if it will work out for you. Then, but not before, you can put the actual relocation process into effect. Many retirees who plan to move have taken some of these steps already.

Finally, this article is not about whether you should move to a community that provides specifically for older residents in some manner, by providing special facilities, assisted living, or nursing home care. This is a separate and complex decision in itself; as a starting point, a useful website is <u>Assisted Living Facilities for Seniors</u>.[3]

FINANCIAL ISSUES

While the process of relocation often gets its energy from the emotional and spiritual quest for a dream retirement, there are bedrock financial issues that have to be resolved. For most retirees who have been settled in their current housing and lifestyle for a long time, relocation will often raise their monthly expenditure levels rather than lower them. Determining a realistic budget for the new living situation is critical. The most significant financial issues are housing prices, cost-of-living, taxes—and, for retirees who want or need to continue working in retirement, job opportunities.

Housing

The cost of housing in the new location is a major factor in the relocation decision. If you include property tax costs (discussed separately below), housing costs are almost always the most significant item in your annual budget in the new location. First, you need to determine what you can afford. Generally, the proceeds from the sale of your current residence will be the foundation for financing the new house. However, this raises an important question in the current housing market—is this a good time to sell? In a down market, you might not be able to realize the amount you planned, and will have to adjust accordingly. Since housing costs are down to some extent almost everywhere in the country, the prime problem is not necessarily the amount you can get for your old house. A more significant worry is that you might find it difficult to sell it in the amount of time you anticipate. This can just require a delay in your plans, or it could create a real crisis if you have already committed yourself to buying a house in the new location or taken on other expenditures of relocating. You may then find yourself in the position of using retirement fund assets—taxable if taken from your IRA or 401(k)—to cover transition costs with no prospect of replacing the funds in the near future.

There is much useful information available about housing prices in particular areas. One major website showing affordability data is provided by the National Association of Home Builders.[4] Websites from local real estate agencies will also provide much useful data. In looking at housing price data, it is also important to determine what the price trends[5] are so you are not stuck with a house that is difficult to sell and thus recover your costs in case things do not work out. One problem with the available data is that the most reliable figures are generally several years old, since the compilation process has not been completed for later years. For current years, the available data may consist of estimates or samples only.

In reviewing information from real estate agencies, a couple of caveats should be kept in mind. First of all, most real estate agencies are agents of their sellers and are trying to sell houses; their mission is not specifically to help you find your dream house. You may, however, be able to find a "home finder" like this one in Delaware[6] or a relocation specialist who offers to act as the buyer's exclusive agent. They are compensated by a fee or, more questionably, by fee splitting with the seller's agent. Most relocation specialists primarily serve corporate "gypsies" who move from corporate branch to branch as part of the career trajectory, and such relocation agencies may not be well oriented toward finding a dream home for a retiree. In any event, using a buyer's agent probably raises the cost of acquiring a new house in most cases.

Another issue is that information about houses that is presented by real estate agents is generally implicitly targeted to a specific group of buyers; otherwise, there would simply be too many offerings in most larger metro areas. If you are not in that targeted group, the information may not be helpful. As a simple example, if you are looking for an urban housing location, websites presenting exclusively suburban properties, as many do, are not going to be useful.

In reviewing price data, many websites provide median house prices for a large geographical area—for example housing costs by state.[7] This may be a misleading figure since you need information at the neighborhood level. Citywide or metro-area data are available on the Web for many areas but even that may not be too helpful. Often, in a low-median price city, housing in the most desirable neighborhoods costs far more than the median. For example, the median housing value in the city of Philadelphia is about $180,000, but in the center city neighborhood targeted by most new residents, the median exceeds $500,000. On the other hand, when you note that the median house price for the entire state of California is now more than $500,000, you can be pretty sure that any California house that you might like will also be pricy.

In finding housing, there's no substitute for an extended visit to communities you think you might like, connecting with local people—not just real estate agencies—as best you can and doing the legwork necessary to get the information you need. As a substitute for onsite legwork, you might try searching Google for a Web forum where you can chat online with local people about housing issues; e.g., City-Data Forum[8] for the Chicago area (the same site has forums for many other locations;) also look for local blogs sponsored by blogspot.com. and other providers (Google "blog" and the location). Craigslist also has local forums—for example, craigslist for Seattle[9]— that can be helpful. You may be surprised how many of your fellow retirees considering relocation are posing questions and contributing to these forums.

In addition to determining the initial cost of housing, it is important to make sure that the value of the new house will keep pace with the growth of housing costs in general. If the house is in a slow market, it will be more difficult to relocate in the future, if it becomes necessary, since the proceeds from selling the house may be less than required for a new house or less than needed for relocation to an extended-care facility or nursing home.

In general, housing that seems like a bargain probably will not appreciate in value at a rapid rate, unless the buyer is lucky enough to get in on the ground floor of an unpredictable real estate upswing, such as happened to some buyers of city property in deteriorated neighborhoods that became "gentrified" in later years. Taking a risk like this is probably not a suitable strategy for retirees. As with most types of property, the highest quality housing is generally most likely to increase in value at the market rate or above.

Cost of Living

Not surprisingly, the cost of living varies from place to place in this country and abroad. Housing costs and taxes are worth the separate discussions that they receive in this article, but there are many other elements in the cost of living. There is a great deal of information available, including "calculators" on the Web; The University of Michigan Library[10] site provides a recent collection of information resources based on government surveys and other reasonably reliable sources. Many websites that try to determine "best places" to live also include cost-of-living information—for example Best Places to Live 2007 - Money Magazine,[11] Sperling's BestPlaces,[12] ACCRA Cost of Living Index Calculator,[13] and others.

Apart from housing and taxes, what is the significance of cost-of-living data in deciding where to live? It could be important because retirees' budgets are sensitive even to small variations. In general, items like food costs[14] and gasoline prices[15] do not vary too much from one location to another. However, for some retirees it might be worth checking these hyperlinks for food and gas costs or similar websites. If, say, you expect that food or gasoline costs will be a major part of your budget—perhaps you'd like to run a part-time catering business, for example—you'll want to be careful about moving to a location where the prices for these items are "outliers"— that is, much higher than normal. For example, food and gasoline tend to be quite a bit more expensive in Hawaii than on the mainland.

Taxes

Taxes are often a major factor in retirees' deliberations about relocation. Federal taxes are not generally avoidable by relocating, since the United States, unlike most countries, imposes taxation on its citizens regardless of their location anywhere in the world. So avoiding excessive state and local taxes is the issue. A high tax rate, by imposing a steady burden on income from your retirement fund, can drain retirement asset accumulations in much the same way as high custodial costs or low investment returns, so attention is warranted. Sources of information will be discussed in some detail below, but a good summary of tax issues is found in Taxes by State[16] on the website of the Retirement Living Information Center.

One important caveat applies to all the currently available information on state taxes: much of it is out of date. All state tax laws are unfair, inefficient, inadequate to finance current and prospective state expenditures, and despised by the taxpayers. Consequently, state legislatures and tax administrators are constantly fiddling with the details of these provisions. As you read this, it is a near-certainty that some state or local lawmakers are in the process of revising or eliminating some tax provision or adding a new one. In reviewing state or local tax laws, keep this issue in mind and try to find out from local sources what recent changes in tax laws have occurred, and what changes you might be facing in the foreseeable future.

State and local taxes fall primarily into the following categories:

- Income taxes
- Sales taxes
- Property taxes

Income Taxes

In retirement, income is generally reduced at least to some extent, which reduces exposure to state income taxes. In addition, many states exclude retirement income, or provide credits or other benefits to retirees. The net result is that state and local income taxes may not be the most significant tax burden for retirees; in most areas, property taxes are more onerous. However, state and local income taxes cannot be ignored.

Currently, 41 states impose tax on personal income. State income taxes are highly diverse in structure, in the base for the tax, and in the rates of tax. Thirty-five states use the taxpayer's federal return as a starting point, by either using the adjusted gross income or taxable income from the federal return as a tax base, or computing the tax as a percentage of the federal amount. The others compute the base under their particular state tax law, sometimes as a result of state constitutional provisions that cannot easily be changed. For example, New Hampshire and Tennessee apply their tax only to income and dividends. Personal exemptions, deductions and credits are usually provided under state income tax laws. Generally, there are provisions that benefit over-65 taxpayers, but no uniform pattern exists. Some state taxes are graduated to some extent, while others provide flat or essentially flat rates. The top rate for 2007 for states with income taxes ranges from a low of 3% (Illinois—flat rate) to a high of 9.5% (Vermont—graduated tax, top bracket is $336, 551).[17]

A number of localities maintain a personal income tax, often on top of the state tax that applies. Most of these places are large cities like New York or Philadelphia, but other localities may have them as well, adding an additional layer of complication for retirees who plan to relocate. It is generally harder to get detailed information on these local taxes than for state income taxes. Local rates can sometimes be higher than state rates, as is the case for the Philadelphia tax (which, however, fortunately does not apply to income from retirement plans).

If you are looking for favorable places to relocate, you will want to compare tax burdens in some of the areas on your list. A number of websites provide comparative tax information; for example, a particularly useful one is maintained by the Federation of Tax Administrators.[18] However, these lists are only a summary of the tax rules that apply. Because of the wide variety of state income tax rules, and their complexity (some state tax laws are more complicated than the federal income tax) you may find it difficult to make an accurate estimate of what your actual state income tax burden might be if you locate to another state. One approach is to assume you have already relocated and figure your tax on that basis. Virtually every state has a website providing state income tax material, including forms and instructions, and if you are serious about moving to another state, it might be worthwhile for you (or your tax accountant) to take a look at these materials to identify problem areas, if any. Another way—not free—to get a handle on prospective state tax burdens is to buy tax preparation software—TaxCut, TurboTax, etc.—for the target state and work through a hypothetical return.

One final point—there are a few significant federal statutes that affect the state tax treatment of retirement income. These federal provisions will generally apply whether or not they are actually reflected in state law—that is, they are applicable even if state tax forms and instructions do not refer to them. Some examples:

- States may not tax US military retiree benefits if they exempt retirement income of state and local employees.
- States may not discriminate against pension income from federal government pensions—they must be eligible for the same tax rates and breaks applicable to other income.
- A state (for example, New York) may not tax retirement benefits paid to residents of another state (for example, Florida) on the ground that those retirees were residents of New York when the benefits were earned and the benefits were not taxed by New York at the time. This issue arises because many state laws allow a deduction or exclusion for 401(k)-type contributions or nonqualified deferred compensation plans at the time the benefits are earned during active employment. The state anticipates that the benefits will be taxable when they are ultimately paid. Federal law preserves the taxpayer's right to flee state taxes on these plans by moving out of the original jurisdiction after retirement.

How significant are low income taxes? An example might put the issue in perspective:

Example: Laura and Joe are both retiring at age 65. The couple's gross income in recent years has averaged $100,000 annually, and their major retirement asset is an IRA (rolled over from 401(k)s) valued at about $1 million. How much do they need (roughly) to replace their preretirement income? First of all, take Social Security taxes ($7,000) off the $100,000, because they will not pay FICA in retirement. Then reduce the amount further by the amount they don't have to save any longer—say another $15,000—and the amount needed to keep themselves whole is reduced to $78,000. If their Social Security benefit provides approximately $40,000 annually, they need to draw the IRA down by $38,000. This is about 3.8 percent—which probably will not deplete their savings too quickly. Suppose now, however, that we factor state income taxes into the picture. Let's say that they live in West Virginia, and have been paying state income taxes at a rate of about 5%. If they don't move, they'll continue to pay a tax of about 5% on their retirement income, since according to AARP,[19] West Virginia taxes both Social Security and pension income. If they move to Pennsylvania, however, the state tax rate of 3% does not apply to retirement income, so instead of $78,000 in income to maintain their standard of living, they need only $75,660. They'll need to draw their IRA down only by $35,660 or 3.6%. This doesn't sound like much of a difference—but at an 8% investment earnings rate, it represents an additional $30,000 in their retirement fund to provide earnings for other things—like going out to dinner occasionally.[20] Is this enough of an incentive to relocate in retirement? Probably not—other factors may dominate.

Note also that the example represents one of the more extreme cases—it's a move from a state with a relatively high tax on retirement income to a state with no tax on pension income. Many moves will produce a closer result or more of a state income tax "wash." In that case, consideration of other relocation costs as well as income taxes could move the financial advantages or disadvantages of the move in either direction. On the other hand, if a retiree has a lot of income that is not exempt from state taxes—for example, a lot of investment income not from retirement plans—the high-income-tax states like Vermont, California, or Hawaii could prove to be costly for relocation.

Sales Taxes

All but five states (Alaska, Delaware, Montana, New Hampshire and Oregon) impose taxes on sales. One reason for this is that politicians believe (unfortunately, with some accuracy) that taxpayers don't feel the pain of sales taxes as acutely as they feel other types of taxes. A sales tax can be sold to voters as a "voluntary" tax. This also means that the sales tax is one of the taxes most likely to be raised when a state or locality absolutely needs more tax revenue, a factor that makes it more difficult to get current information about sales taxes or plan ahead for sales tax costs.

Sales tax rates in 2007 varied from a high of 7.25% (California) to a low of 2.9% in Colorado, according the tables[21] published by the Federation of Tax Administrators.

One problem with predicting sales tax costs is that in many states, localities (municipalities or counties) are empowered to impose sales taxes in addition to the state tax, and thousands of localities do so. Local taxes may impose tax differently from the state's sales tax—for example, they may impose tax on items excluded from the state sales tax. The national tables referenced above don't cover these local sales taxes—to get information about them you need to do legwork similar to that necessary for housing costs or property taxes.

State sales tax laws differ in coverage and in the mechanics of collection. As the tables referenced here note, a majority exempt food and especially prescription drugs. In addition, states generally do not tax expenditures like rentals or payments for services. Some states provide refundable sales tax credits for low-income taxpayers. Comparative tables of state sales taxes that are available on the Web or in retiree publications sometimes omit important nuances. For example, the tables referenced above don't note that the Pennsylvania sales tax (like some others as well) exempts most clothing items, an issue that could be important to a retiree planning to open a retail fashion boutique as a retirement income supplement.

State sales taxes could very well be one of the more painful taxes for the retiree, since retirees tend to spend most of their income. However, the individual's spending pattern is important, because in some states—for example, a state where food, clothing, and prescription drugs are exempt—the individual pattern of expenditures might produce a relatively low sales tax burden.

Property Taxes

Local governments and local authorities like school boards are primarily supported through property taxes. Property taxes are often the most burdensome for retirees, since property taxes are not related to income, and are subject to unpredictable increases. There are thousands of taxing jurisdictions, and collecting nationwide information is a formidable task. Fortunately, the retiree needs only to determine this tax burden for those places that have been singled out as possible relocation areas. Finding this information is somewhat similar to determining housing prices, since real-estate agents and information services understand that the property tax burden is a large part of the cost of owning a house. There are some features of property taxes, however, that must be understood to develop a reasonable plan for dealing with this particular expense when relocating.

- Property taxes are determined by applying a tax rate to an assessed valuation. Thus, the tax rate for a given locality is relatively meaningless until you know how the value of your house is going to be assessed.
- Some localities actually attempt to determine fair market values for assessment purposes, while others use formulas that produce assessments of less than 100% of market value. In older jurisdictions, as a result of bureaucratic inertia and entrenched privileges, assessments may bear no consistent relation to actual fair market value, especially in neighborhoods where there is a lot of turnover or where housing values have risen sharply.
- Some areas with low property taxes also provide relatively few of the municipal services that some urban and suburban dwellers may be used to. For example, retirees may find themselves having to haul trash to a local landfill—or find a private hauler—if the municipality provides no trash pickup. Alternatively, there may be septic systems—for which homeowners bear the maintenance responsibilities—instead of municipal sewers.
- Baseline municipal expenses do not vary much from one locality to another. Therefore, in order to raise the money necessary for schools, sewers, or whatever, exclusive neighborhoods with expensive houses generally have

low rates of property taxes, while poor neighborhoods have high rates. This inequity is a source of constant friction in property taxation.
- Instead of trying to restore actual fairness and equity to property taxation by applying a uniform statewide rate and fair assessments, most states and localities have relief provisions for various groups. These include:
  - Property tax rebates, generally targeted to over-65 taxpayers or to taxpayers below a specified income ceiling, or both.
  - State or local provisions that cushion tax increases for long-term residents. Some areas have provisions that freeze assessed values at a specified age, or limit increases while a property owner stays in place. This may cause the taxes to jump noticeably when a new buyer steps in. Another type of relief provision allows property tax deferral to aged or low-income homeowners, which must be repaid when the house is sold. Relief arrangements are sometimes structured with a "circuit-breaker" that triggers the relief provision when the property tax reaches a maximum percentage of the owner's income. Relief provisions like these are common, and are found in the majority of states. In areas with these relief provisions, the existing property owner's property tax costs could be much less than the amount you would pay as a new owner, so determining the amount of current property tax bills is not enough.

Inheritance and Estate Taxes

State inheritance and estate taxes are not an immediate concern to retirees as part of the relocation process, but they should be investigated if passing a legacy to heirs is an important concern. The technical difference between inheritance and estate taxes is that inheritance taxes are based on the status of the recipient—they may differ depending on whether the recipient is a spouse, children or third parties. An estate tax, by comparison, is levied on the entire estate before it is distributed. In any event, however, the effect is to reduce the amount left for the heirs. In 2007, there were about ten states with taxes structured as inheritance taxes. These vary greatly in rates and exemptions from the base. Generally, inheritance taxes are imposed only on "probate" property, and some items that pass by operation of law, such as joint bank accounts, are not included. However, this is a matter of great technicality under local law.

If the state imposes an estate tax, it is generally based on the federal estate tax. However, because of changes in the federal estate tax—the increase in exemptions and the total phaseout scheduled for 2010—many states have "decoupled" their estate taxes. If the tax is decoupled, it is generally computed under the principles of federal estate tax law as it existed at the time of the decoupling, but it will not be affected by future changes in federal law.

A Web summary of current state inheritance and estate taxes is provided by McGuire Woods.[22] Like all published data on state taxes, it should be verified by an expert local advisor if the tax provisions are important for your own estate and financial planning.

Other Taxes

Finally, states generally impose a large variety of excise and other taxes and fees, sometimes lumped together as "nuisance" taxes. These include taxes on tobacco, licensing fees, etc. Generally, these taxes will not have a significant effect on the decision to move. However, if you're relocating, there's one of these miscellaneous taxes that could cost you some unexpected money—the real estate transfer tax. This tax varies widely, but could total up to 5% of the purchase price of a new house. Whether it is formally payable by the buyer or seller, it will increase the cost of the new house (and possibly slow the sale of the house if you decide to sell it in the future). Some states have both state and local transfer taxes. Because of poor documentation of some of the local taxes, you may have to go personally (or by email or telephone) to local authorities to find out about this potential expense.

Finally, if you're thinking about starting a new business in retirement, or relocating an existing business, be sure to consider state and local business taxes and business licensing fees very carefully. Some of these taxes are surprisingly burdensome, so much so that start-up businesses could be virtually unfeasible in certain localities.

Job Opportunities in Retirement

If you or your spouse wants to continue employment after retirement, for financial, social, or other reasons, then the job market in the target community becomes an important issue in relocation. There is a lot of information relating to specific communities available on websites like *retirementjobs.com*.[23] In general, the best job markets for retirees are the same as those for younger workers, and these tend to be higher-cost urban areas. However, some smaller communities popular with retirees, such as Ann Arbor, MI or Sarasota, FL had good job markets in 2007.

Retirement jobs include both part-time and full-time activities. In addition, starting a new small business is an option for some retirees. Retirement Jobs and Retirement Businesses at the Real Success Resource Center[24] includes a great deal of general information and advice for the retiree job seeker. This website notes a 2003 AARP survey finding that 80 percent of baby boomers expect to keep working in retirement jobs, and 15 percent would like to start their own business. The job most often mentioned as desirable, not surprisingly, is "consultant."

LIFESTYLE ISSUES

The issues summed up in the term "lifestyle" probably encompass the most important reasons why people relocate after retirement. Assuming that the financial issues already discussed here can be resolved, many retirees are looking for a place where they can find a way of living that is different, and hopefully better, than they had while they were working. Some of the desired aspects of the new dream location include:

- Culture and entertainment
- Recreational opportunities
- Easy transportation
- Good healthcare
- Congenial community
- Personal safety

Fulfilling these criteria is a personal decision. Many relocating retirees might find the best mix of all these advantages in a city downtown, while others, applying the same criteria, would choose a rural area for themselves.

Millions of non-retirees face relocation decisions, and there are many publications and websites that attempt to provide guidelines and information. For retirees, the websites of AARP The Magazine[25] and Retirement Living Information Center[26] have many studies of "best places" for retirees, based on lifestyle as well as financial criteria. Where to Retire Magazine[27] specializes in similar studies and recommendations. There are also many state-specific and locality-specific websites for prospective retirees; searching Google for "retirement relocation" produces sites covering practically the entire country and sites around the world.

For the general public, there are numerous "best places" websites, including Money Magazine,[28] Kiplinger's Best Cities[29], Relocate-America™,[30] and Sperling's BestPlaces.[31].= Many of these include questionnaires designed to develop priorities for making choices among localities. Some of the questionnaires seem simplistic. The Sperling site has one of the most comprehensive questionnaires, at Find Your Best Place,[32] and it can be a good guide to figuring out your real priorities. For example, how important is avoiding cold weather, etc. There are sites that specialize in certain issues, such as Morgan Quitno[33] and its crime studies.

Data from these websites is no substitute for on-site legwork. Just as average house prices don't necessarily indicate whether you can find an affordable house that meets your needs, overall statistics on other issues can be similarly misleading. For example, statistics about crime rates may not be helpful in relocation decisions, because even in the most dangerous cities, crime tends to be concentrated in neighborhoods that few retirees would consider for relocation, while the rest of the area has normal crime rates. Similarly, a locality's "health" rating might weigh the number of hospitals or physicians per capita along with items like the absence of local superfund sites (areas of historical ground pollution) or arbitrary measures of air quality, giving a result that might not coincide with what retirees are looking for when they indicate "health" as a major area of concern. However, the voluminous information in "best places" websites will reward close study, especially if you focus on the raw data rather than the place rankings for the "best city of the month."

ACQUIRING A SECOND RESIDENCE

Some retirees fulfill their retirement dream not by relocating permanently, but by acquiring a second residence (before or after retirement) to enjoy a better climate or specialized recreational or other opportunities (e.g., golf). Maintaining two residences is an expensive proposition, and the financial aspects must be carefully planned. In many cases, retirees may find that temporary rentals of condos or hotel accommodations in the target area is more realistic than actually acquiring a second (or third, etc.) home. This is particularly true for second homes outside the United States, since ownership of foreign property can entail endless complications that generally require the hiring of local advisors.

The issues in choosing a second residence are less critical than in relocating permanently because there is more flexibility. If the second residence doesn't work out, there is always the option of returning home or finding another second residence. Ultimately, if everything works out well, retirees may decide to stay in the second home permanently and abandon their primary residence.

Some of the issues discussed here do relate significantly to the second-home option, however. In particular, some attention needs to be given to tax issues. If the second home is in another state, the question of residency or "domicile" arises. Which state is the retirees' residence? Since "residence" or "domicile" is rarely defined clearly in state law, it is possible that the retiree may have to pay income taxes as a resident of both states. This extreme situation may be unlikely, but because state tax laws are promulgated completely independently from those of other states, the possibility of paying a greater total state or local income tax bill remains significant where there is a second home. State income tax laws are often not clear, and this issue should be investigated with a local tax advisor as part of the planning of the second home purchase.

State inheritance or estate taxes raise other issues. First of all, people who have moved to a tax-friendly state from one that is unfriendly (yes, we're talking about New York and Florida as the paradigm) want to make sure that their property is subject to inheritance taxes in the tax-friendly state. For example, a recent tax journal article noted that for 2005 a decedent with a New York domicile would pay $566,000 more in state and federal taxes on a $10 million estate than a Florida domiciliary.[34]

A worse case (though less common) problem is that both states may try to impose inheritance taxes on the same property of the decedent. The vague and inconsistent state definitions of "domicile" make this situation inevitable. This seems like a legal outrage, but the U.S. Supreme Court has generally upheld the rights of each sovereign state to define its inheritance tax scheme separately, even if double taxation results. For example, in a case involving the Campbell's soup heir, the Supreme Court refused to intervene[35] where both New Jersey and Pennsylvania claimed taxing jurisdiction over the property of the deceased Mr. Dorrance. More recently, the Supreme Court offered only some procedural help in resolving the claims of California and Texas in a legal wrangle over the worldly goods of the reclusive Howard Hughes.[36] In practice, states are likely to target only noticeably wealthy decedents for this kind of unwelcome attention, but the possibility should be addressed in retirees' estate planning. Careful attention to titling of property can help avoid problems; for example, the use of family corporations, partnerships, and trusts is often helpful. This kind of planning is a specialty among the Florida bar in particular—see the Florida[37] link.

CONCLUSIONS

Deciding to relocate in retirement takes careful planning and information gathering. While in most cases, cultural and lifestyle issues will probably be the emotional drivers for the move, the financial issues must be carefully studied. Housing costs (including current and future property tax burdens), taxes, and in some cases, the job opportunities in the new area need to be considered in the budget for retirement living in the new area. There is a great deal of information available on the internet, but there is no substitute for legwork on site in the new area and contacts with local people. Generally, it's wise to go on an extended "vacation" in the new locality before making a final decision about moving.

NOTES

1. "Hidden Tax Traps," Retirement Weekly Feb. 8, 2008; compare with survey of Virginia Polytechnic alumni that also shows 90% staying put initially, http://www.vchr.vt.edu/pdfreports/rtrptpub.pdf.
2. The mobility of children and grandchildren has to be taken into account, however; grandma and grandpa may find themselves once again far from loved ones if children must relocate far away for job reasons.
3. http://www.helpguide.org/elder/assisted_living_facilities.htm
4. http://www.nahb.org/page.aspx/category/sectionID=135

5. http://moneycentral.msn.com/content/Banking/Homebuyingguide/P85333.asp
6. http://www.exclusivebuyer.com/
7. http://www.midwestsides.com/stellent2/groups/public/documents/pub/mws_am_li_000927.hcsp
8. http://www.city-data.com/forum/chicago-suburbs/158181-anchorage-movin-chicago.html
9. http://seattle.craigslist.org/
10. http://www.lib.umich.edu/govdocs/steccpi.html
11. http://money.cnn.com/magazines/moneymag/bplive/2007/
12. http://www.bestplaces.net/
13. http://www.c2er.org/calculator.asp
14. http://www.ers.usda.gov/Publications/FANRR41/
15. http://www.gasbuddy.com/
16. http://www.retirementliving.com/RLtaxes.html
17. Federation of Tax Administrators, http://www.taxadmin.org/fta/rate/tax_stru.html
18. http://www.taxadmin.org/fta/rate/tax_stru.html
19. http://assets.aarp.org/rgcenter/econ/ib84_taxation.pdf
20. A more precise calculation of the annual and ultimate cost can be made with Steve Leimberg's Pension and Roth IRA Analyzer, 1-610-924-0515.
21. http://www.taxadmin.org/fta/rate/sales.html
22. http://www.mcguirewoods.com
23. http://www.retirementjobs.com/
24. http://www.real-success.ca/retirement_jobs.html
25. http://www.aarpmagazine.org/
26. http://www.retirementliving.com/
27. http://www.wheretoretire.com/freeinfo.cfm
28. http://money.cnn.com/magazines/moneymag/bplive/2007/
29. http://www.kiplinger.com/money/bestcities/
30. http://top100.relocate-america.com/
31. http://www.bestplaces.net/
32. http://www.bestplaces.net/fybp/quiz.aspx
33. http://www.morganquitno.com/cit00dang.htm
34. Surkin, Decoupling of State Estate Taxes, 101 J. *Taxation* 49 (2004).
35. *Dorrance v. Pennsylvania,* 288 US 617 (1933).
36. *California v. Texas,* 437 US 601 (1978).
37. http://goliath.ecnext.com/coms2/gi_0199-5155957/Domicile-planning-don-t-take.html

Age Banding: A Model for Planning Retirement Needs

Somnath Basu[†]

> The age-banding model, as proposed in this paper, provides a new approach to planning for retirement needs. The model reduces errors in estimating expenses, provides an algorithm to calculate the replacement ratio, allows easier incorporation of long term care benefits and significantly reduces funding needs. Two case studies are used to elaborate the model. Results, as compared to the traditional approach, show funding needs of an elderly couple are reduced by over 16% and contributions, for a 35 year old, are reduced by 42%. In neither case is the consequent increase in risk exposure greater than 2.5%. Finally, the model also incorporates case-specific risk management tools.

THE TRADITIONAL APPROACH TO RETIREMENT PLANNING

The traditional (this term denotes currently used methods) view of retirement planning begins with an estimation of the client's income immediately prior to retirement. The estimation depends on such variables as career path, industry condition, marital status (one or two incomes), etc. Planners then adjust this income downward (by about 10%–35%) not only to reflect the income necessary to maintain the client's standard of living but also to incorporate reductions in taxes and other work-related expenses, expenses that cease upon retirement. This reduction is termed the replacement ratio. The next step is to approximate the life expectancy during retirement, again adjusted for the client's current health, family medical history etc. Planners then extrapolate annual living expenses through the years in retirement, assuming that living costs increase at the Consumer Price Index (CPI) rate of inflation. Planners also assume that funds allocated exclusively for retirement expenses be generally invested in safer investment vehicles (lower risk securities like guaranteed contracts, agency securities, etc.) and by using the rates on such vehicles, estimate the amount of money the client should accumulate at retirement. Finally, planners estimate how much the client needs to save every year until retirement, such that these compounded savings eventually add up and grow into the required retirement fund. The annual savings are invested after taking into consideration the client's age, risk profile, other plans, (e.g. social security, employer pension plans) as well as any other wealth dedicated to retirement.

PINPOINTING WEAKNESSES IN THE TRADITIONAL APPROACH

There are four inherent weaknesses to the traditional approach to retirement planning: in short, they are:

1. The assumption that living expenses during retirement increase at the rate of inflation.

---

[*] Copyright © 2005, Association for Financial Counseling and Planning Education. Reprinted with permission from the Financial Counseling and Planning Journal.

[†] Program Director, Financial Planning, Associate Professor of Finance, California Lutheran University.

2. The investment of retirement funds mostly in less risky securities and assets.
3. The downward adjustment of pre-retirement expenses as an initial estimate of annual retirement costs.
4. The lack of ease in incorporating plans such as Long Term Care (LTC) plans.

These weaknesses are now described in greater detail. The assumption that costs increase at the inflation rate (CPI) during retirement reflects a notion that these costs follow a simple dynamic. Stern (2000) and Tiffany (2003) both use the (CPI) inflation rate to estimate retirement expenses. Smith (1997) considers issues in estimating retirement expenses and spending estimates using the same inflation rate. The widespread use of the CPI rate to estimate expenses is also well documented (Bell and Rauf (1998), Hager (1999), Levy and Young (2002) and Tiffany (2003). However, a closer observation of the spending patterns during retirement reveals that expenses do not follow this simple linearity. Retirees will tend to spend more on leisure immediately after retirement than at more advanced ages, simply because with age, many leisure activities are not possible for health reasons. Similarly people generally spend more on health related costs the older they get. The Health Insurance Association of America (2002), in a brief, reports that health-related costs increased by over 10% per year during the decades of the 1970s and 80s. In the 90s, while hospital services costs decreased to about 5%–6% per year (mainly due to managed care services), prescription drugs continued to increase by 16% annually. Further, the brief also projected healthcare costs to increase at higher rates in the near future. Similar projections can also be found in the reports from United States Department of Health and Human Services (2001) and The Centers for Medicare and Medicaid Services, Office of the Actuary (2002). The United States Census Bureau (2000) Statistical Abstracts shows that expenditures on Recreation increased at the rate of 7.14% between 1990 and 1998. Thus, the bundling of all retirement expenses creates a problem for the planner since the substantially higher inflation rates for leisure and healthcare (about 7.0%/year over the last 15 years) cannot be explicitly used to extrapolate these component costs.

A *second* weakness is the placement of funds in conservative and low-risk investments. It is true that retirees generally are more risk-averse as they are averse to considering a loss in the standard of living during retirement. However, to be invested in low-risk, low-yield securities for long time periods belies the basic relationship between investment horizons and risk tolerance, as equated by return expectations[1]. This has the potential to be problematic if investment returns are lower than the inflation rate of some underlying component costs. The need to diversify across asset classes for retirement planning has been widely studied. Both Smith (1997) and Stein (1999) observe the problems in excess allocation in bonds while Blair and Sellars (1995), Everett and Anthony (1996) and Betts (2003) all note the importance of including stocks in retirement portfolios. Benartzi and Thaler (1999) attribute the lack of higher-yielding assets (stocks) to client ignorance about the relationship between long-term portfolio horizons and asset returns.

Two additional points to note: first, explicit risk analysis should be conducted if any proposed method advocates greater risk-bearing for retirees. Second, when looking at low risk securities, planners need to consider that the long term historic average rate may cause problems of timing market entry when prevailing rates are lower than the historic average. An expansive study of the problem of retirement portfolio risk increases due to additional equity assets and issues regarding the management of risk can be found in Blair and Sellars (1995).

The *third* weakness in the traditional method is the lack of a definitive method to reduce pre-retirement income to an amount sufficient to maintain the existing lifestyle during retirement. In financial planning terminology, the percentage by which the income is reduced is referred as the *replacement ratio*. Traditionally, planners typically extrapolate current income to find both pre-retirement income and the living standard that such income may afford. Next, planners consider the expected lifestyle changes in a client and then *estimate* the reduction amount. The replacement ratio concept and problems regarding its calculation have received considerable attention (see, for example, Palmer (1994), Anonymous (1998), Stern (2000) and Levy and Young (2002)). However informed this estimate may be, the lack of an objective estimation technique still exposes the estimate to an error from any bias in the planner's own position (conservative or aggressive). Errors in estimating pre-retirement income and expenses (living standards) at this initial stage (> 0–35% range!) have the potential to explode, when extrapolated far in the future.

According to Haas (2001), "… determining what it will take to maintain your client's standard of living is important in the financial-advising process and is greatly desired. Replacement ratio and actual expense are two methods that can be used to determine a client's retirement income needs in order for him to maintain his pre-retirement standard of living." Tacchino and Saltzmann (1999) also note that planners may use either the replacement ratio or expense method to determine retirement expenses and that a conservative replacement ratio is generally 80 percent. In the age-banding model, the expense method of estimating retirement costs (consumption hypothesis) is used.

The *fourth* weakness of traditional planning concerns the lack of ease in incorporating vital contingency instruments such as long-term health care policies. Under the current technique of lumping all living expenses in retirement, planners can neither isolate nor integrate the differential cost-benefits of such policies. LTC policies have separate features (adult day care, home services, nursing home care,) and these vary by policies. The inability of the traditional method to incorporate the timing and the extent of the policy benefits and costs becomes another source of error. In the next section a model is developed that addresses all the above limitations.

DEFINING THE AGE-BANDING MODEL

In developing the age banding model, some (non-limiting) simplifying assumptions are made and two case studies are utilized to explain the model's structure. One simplifying assumption is that a typical retiree lives about 30 years in retirement (65 to 95). Another such assumption is that a retiree goes through a life style change (dynamic) every 10 years, at ages 65, 75 and 85. This latter assumption is critical as it allows the construction of a dynamic retirement planning model. The 10-year period is arbitrary and for ease of exposition only. As will be seen later, the 10-year time period can be customized for each client.

The *first phase* of retirement is assumed to commence when the individual retires. This phase is identified not only by a marked increase in leisure related expenses but also by a significant decrease in taxes (discussed later in greater detail) and a moderate decrease in basic living expenses. Note that a significant change in basic living expenses may occur when the residential mortgage is paid off; when this happens depends upon when the mortgage was initiated as well as its maturity term. While some clients may have paid off their mortgage fully before retirement there are others who may do so within the first 10–15 years of retirement. *Phase two* can be thought of as a transitional phase with reductions in leisure expenses and further increases in medical expenses. The third (and last) phase is marked by a sharp increase in healthcare expenses, negligible leisure expenses, and possibly small changes in basic living expenses.

APPLYING THE ALTERNATIVE AGE-BANDING MODEL TO A CASE STUDY

We begin with the computation of pre-retirement expenses, but instead of the traditional lumping of all expenses into a single number, the costs are segregated into four expense groups: basic living expenses, taxes, leisure expenses, and medical expenses. In developing the results of the age banding model, the computations are presented in two tabular panels. Panel A is constructed to always show the result of the computation when conducted along traditional times. Likewise, Panel B always shows the calculations termed the "Alternate view", which reflects the age-banding approach, as expounded in this paper. In the first case, it is assumed that the client is a couple (Mr. & Mrs. Smith), both around 60 years old and expecting to retire in 5 years. The current annual expenses of the Smiths are shown in Table 1.

Table 1	
Costs of Living at Age 60 (Today)	
Taxes	28000
Basic Living	36000
Healthcare	6000
Leisure	<u>5000</u>
Total	75000

Table 2A: Traditional View				
	Costs at Age	5 Yr. Growth (Inflation Rate)	Multiply by factor	Costs at Age
	60			65
Total	75000	3%	1.159	86925

It is also assumed that over the next 5 years, none of the items (or income) will change in any significant manner. Table 2A shows the projected expenses (using the inflation rate) of the Smiths just prior to retirement, i.e. at age 65.

Table 2B: Alternate View				
	Costs at Age	5 Yr. Growth & Inflation Rate	Multiply by factor	Costs at Age
	60			65
Taxes	28000	3%	1.159	32452
Basic Living	36000	3%	1.159	41724
Healthcare	6000	7.00%	1.403	8418
Leisure	5000	7.00%	1.403	7015
Total	75000			89674

Table 2B shows the age-banded projection of the same annual expenses just prior to retirement, but segregated by expense type and adjusted by differential inflation rates. Next, planners estimate the replacement ratio, i.e. adjust downward the income, the adjustment depending mainly on client-specific information. As mentioned earlier, no algorithm exists to aid planners in this adjustment. Planners adjust these expenses downward by about 10%–35%. Table 3 shows the revised expenses for the Smiths as they commence retirement. In this example, a conservative 20% reduction Tacchino and Saltzmann (1999) is assumed for the traditional model. The adjustment for the alternate view is discussed below.

Table 3A: Adjustments-Traditional View			
Total	86925	0.8	69540
Table 3B: Adjustments-Alternate View			
	Pre-retirement	Post- retirement	Post- retirement
	Costs at Age	Life-Cycle factor	Cost at Age
	65	at Age 65	66
Taxes	32452	0.5	16226
Basic Living	41724	0.7	29207
Healthcare	8418	1.15	9681
Leisure	7015	1.5	10523
Total	89674		65702

In the age-banding model, it is assumed that the commencement of retirement is a lifestyle change and this change manifests itself through annual expenses. In this model it is also assumed that each expense item changes by a factor whose value varies around 1. For example, leisure related expenses increase 50% upon retirement; hence the leisure factor, set to 1.5, is used to adjust pre-retirement leisure expenses. Similarly, the tax factor in this example[2] is 0.5 to reflect the elimination of FICA and reduction in taxes on salaries. The basic living expense factor is set at 0.7 expressing work related expense reductions and the possibility that the mortgage on the house may be paid off during the next decade. Finally, the health factor is set at 1.15 to reflect *minimal* expected increases in healthcare expenses during this first decade in retirement. Note that at this point only expenses during retirement are only being considered. Inflows such as social security income, healthcare benefits, etc will be discussed in a later section.

It is important to note two points in the above depiction. First, the age-banding model allows planners to objectively estimate the replacement ratio. Second, projections of future expenses can now be made *while* incorporating item specific inflation rates. Both applications should mitigate estimation error problems.

Table 4A shows the traditionally computed projection of expenses during retirement. These projections are simply the annually compounded values of the pre-retirement expenses, compounded at the rate of inflation.

Table 4A: Projected Costs for 3 Decades: Traditional View										
Unadjusted Costs										
65	66	67	68	69	70	71	72	73	74	75
69540	71626	73775	75988	78268	80616	83034	85525	88091	90734	93456
75	76	77	78	79	80	81	82	83	84	85
93456	96260	99147	102122	105185	108341	111591	114939	118387	121939	125597
85	86	87	88	89	90	91	92	93	94	95
125597	129365	133246	137243	141361	145601	149969	154468	159102	163876	168792

As discussed earlier, leisure and health related costs have increased at a rate of about 7% per year over the last 15 years. For the age banding model, it is assumed that projected health/ leisure expenses are compounded at this rate of 7% (rate assumption discussed later) while basic living costs and taxes are projected to increase at the standard and reasonable 3% inflation rate

This method of segmenting expenses item-wise and then projecting their future values has some very interesting implications. First, alternate lifestyles during retirement can be evaluated by alternate expense structures. Observing various cost configurations will lead to greater control over the finances since the benefit of altering life styles can be weighed against the costs in retirement expense (affordability) changes[3]. Further, segmentation allows the observation of the proportional affects of component costs over time. To elaborate this point, consider healthcare expenses. While planners may advise that larger outlays for healthcare be made for the latter years of retirement, they cannot explicitly capture the true dynamics of that advice in their expense projections. By the age banding technique, planners can visually depict the relationship amongst aging, healthcare and healthcare cost inflation.

Table 4B shows the three phased expense projections by the age banding technique. Appendix 1 contains illustrations of the computational details of age-banding calculations and explanations of how life cycle factors are used to adjust the costs. It is important for planner to note that the life cycle factors are controllable objective reflections of their clients and the proper assessment of these factors are crucial for realistic projections.

Life-Cycle Adjusted Costs	Table 4B: Projected Costs for 3 Decades after Life-Cycle Adjustments									
65	66	67	68	69	70	71	72	73	74	75
65702	68413	71330	74395	77617	81005	84569	88319	92266	96422	100801
75	76	77	78	79	80	81	82	83	84	85
86409	90329	94461	98815	103406	108249	113360	118753	124449	130464	136819
85	86	87	88	89	90	91	92	93	94	95
128568	134877	141546	148599	156059	163954	172311	181159	190530	200458	210978

A comparison between the two panels in Table 4 shows the impact of the differential inflation levels. Since the growth rates of expenses projected by the alternate technique are greater, the age banded expenses are considerably higher than their traditional counterparts. The following cost comparison illustration shows the differences in expense projections between the two methods.

Table 4C: Cost Comparisons Between Methods					
66	75	76	85	86	95
71626	93456	96260	125597	129365	168792
68413	100801	90329	136819	134877	210978
4.70%	-7.29%	6.57%	-8.20%	-4.09%	-20.00%

As mentioned earlier, an additional benefit of the age banding model is the ability to observe the component cost dynamics during retirement. Figure 1 illustrates this benefit. Planners should note that such a realistic visualization should be an immensely powerful counseling tool. Figure 1 shows only the breakdown of costs within the categories. From Table 4C we observe that the age banded estimates of retirement costs are higher; thus a significant portion of expenses are being allocated to the latter stages of life, which reflects the greater estimation accuracy of the proposed model.

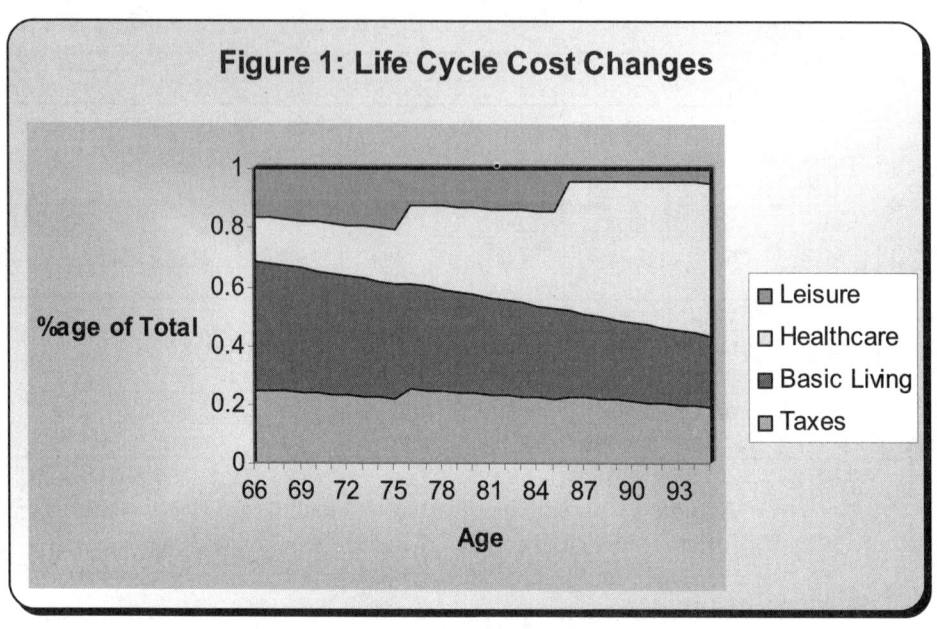

At this point the effects of the traditional bundling of expenses can be better appreciated. It induces estimation error problems at every planning and implementation stage. Another problem arising from bundling expenses is that it prevents the smooth incorporation of contingent policies like long term care. In the age banding model, the segmentation of retirement provides exactly that benefit. For example, care features such as adult day care and home health care are more likely to be a choice in the transitional decade while nursing home care is a *more likely scenario* in the latter decades. In this example, if the Smiths own a LTC policy, then the planner can not only change the medical factors to reflect the clients' health but also net health expenses to LTC benefits. This process can be further fine tuned by decomposing medical expenses into sub-components such as prescription drugs, hospitalization, etc and integrate them with the policy features. Alternately, an approximate estimate can also be obtained by adjusting downward the life cycle factors for healthcare costs. It is worthwhile to note that owning a LTC policy should have a significant impact on the amount of funding required for retirement, given both the significant increases in costs of healthcare products and services and that greater amounts of healthcare products and services are consumed at the latter stages of life. The age banding technique can thus incorporate LTC policy benefits more accurately within the retirement planning framework.

In the traditional scheme, planners now generally assume a greater risk aversion for retirees and advocate more secure but low-yielding investments. This assumption allows planners to use a proxy rate (such as agency or treasury bond rates, 6% in this example) to discount the projected expenses and compute the total amount of money needed to fund the retirement. For the Smiths, this would amount to $1,030,474 as shown in Table 5A. Note that the expenses are increased at the CPI rate (3%) while the cash flows are discounted at 6%. This amounts to a net discount rate of 2.9126% (i.e. (1.03) * (1.029126) = (1.06)). The discount factor 19.83 represents the present value factor at 2.9126% for 30 years. The factor 0.747 shown in the second last column of the table represents the present value factor at 6% for 5 years.

Table 5A: Traditional View of Funding Requirements							
		Factor	Amount Needed At Age		Amount Needed At Age		Amount Today (Age 60)
Post retirement need	69540	19.83	65	1379006	60	0.747	1030474
Increases annually at	3%						
Safe rate of Investment	6%						

Now consider the retirement fund for the Smiths as computed by the alternate method. By computing the expenses using the *age-banding technique*, three portfolios are constructed, each dedicated to funding expenses in the three phases. For the planner, this segregation has another major benefit. For the Smiths case, the planner has 15-25 years to manage the performance of the latter two portfolios. Finally, note that once assets are allocated within the three portfolios, they can be integrated as one portfolio; the difference, being that the single portfolio will contain assets dedicated for different time phases

In the age-banding model, each of the three dedicated portfolios has its own term. Thus, for the Smiths, the portfolio for the first decade needs to be fully accumulated in 5 years whilst the subsequent two portfolios have 15- and 25-year terms, respectively. The primary benefit of this division is that it allows the retiree to seek somewhat higher rates *and higher risk* for the longer-term portfolios. In turn it is assumed that the higher rates will mostly mitigate the effects of future medical costs. The analysis of the change in exposure to risk is considered in detail in a latter section of this paper.

Since seeking higher rates means assuming higher risk, explicit inclusion of an analysis of risk is a necessity. However, from a behavioral point, it is one thing to develop a model where a retiree holds some equity for better planning and quite another to persuade a retiree, especially during a dismal period of equity performance, to consider purchasing equities to hold in a retirement portfolio. To alleviate this condition a bit further, it is assumed that the dedicated portfolios be fully funded 5 years before they are actually needed. For example, the funds needed for expenses for the 76–85 and 86–95 decades be in safe investments at age 70 and 80, respectively. This can be considered analogically as an additional cushion to allay the risk perceptions of individuals. Table 5B, shows the amounts needed to be accumulated at ages 60, 70 and 80 to fund retirement expenses for the 3 decades beginning at age 66, 76 and 86. A 6% rate of growth is assumed for the funds during the cushion years, e.g. 60 to 65 or 70 to 75. The growth rates for the accumulation period are described in the following paragraph.

Table 5B: Funding Needs-Alternate View			
Amount Needed At	PV of CFs	Amount Needed At	PV 5 Yrs. Earlier
65	602102	60	449926
75	805644	70	602024
85	1222067	80	913199

At age 60, the Smiths need to have the funds earmarked for the first decade in a safe investment. For the next two portfolios and excluding the cushioned years, the Smiths have 10 years and 20 years, respectively, to accumulate the necessary funds. Assume that the Smiths seek a return of 8% for the second portfolio and 10% for the final portfolio. These return expectations are more consistent with the investment term and are also amenable to client specific adjustments. For the sake of simplicity assume also that the Smiths will use only two classes of assets as investment vehicles, lower risk bonds and large cap stocks. It is assumed that the bond rate is 6% and the large cap stock rate is 11.5%.[4] Table 6A shows the amounts of funds that the Smiths should need at age 60 to fund all 3 portfolios. In this example, the amount ($449,926) is placed in a "safe" (cushioned) investment while the rest can be invested to earn somewhat higher rates. The added risk from these investments is discussed in greater detail in a later section. Note that the asset allocation decision when cash flows are specified does not need optimization techniques since it falls out of the cash flow requirements. This can be considered as an added benefit, albeit as a byproduct.

		Table 6A: Alternate View				
	Amount Needed At		Earnings Rate	Factor	Amount Needed At	Amount Today
Today	60	449926		1.000	60	449926
10 Yrs Later	70	602102	0.08	0.463	60	278890
20 Yrs Later	80	901439	0.10	0.386	60	133993
Total						862809

Recall that the two methods start with retirement expenses that are similar to each other and that the expenses along the alternate lines become considerably higher at the latter stages of retirement. What is quite amazing from the above table is that the alternate method now actually leads to a much smaller funding requirement *(about $167,665 less,* i.e. $1,030,474 – $862,809) than the traditional method. This is of course the effect of age-banding for investment. *Age banding not only provides a more accurate portrayal of expenses, etc. but also leads to a significant reduction in funding needs!*

In the example above, what if the client was an individual aged 35? What would be the effect for such an individual? Such a scenario becomes the second case illustration. For the sake of simplicity, assume that the expenses the Smiths face are also what the 35-year old (Ms. Jones) will be facing. Obviously, this assumption is not correct, but it does not require the derivation of Ms. Jones's expenses at retirement- an exercise whose depiction would be redundant for planners who conduct such calculations routinely.

For Ms. Jones, the funds required for the 3 portfolios are 30, 40 and 50 years away. Since this is a long time away, assume that Ms. Jones does not need the same five year safety cushion like the Smiths as she has ample time to manage portfolio risk. Also assume that, given her age, Ms. Jones is willing to take more risk than the Smiths and to include small cap stocks in her portfolio. Given the latter assumption, investments in the three portfolios (30, 40 and 50 year portfolios) can be expected to earn average returns of 12% (same as the traditional), 13.5% and 15%, respectively. Table 7 shows both views of the contributions that Ms. Jones will need to make annually to fund her retirement portfolio. Note that the time-varying return requirements are client-sensitive. The required return will eventually depend both on the client's risk tolerance and the amount they can contribute towards retirement.

Table 7A: Contributions-Traditional View				
Amount Needed	At Age		Exp Rate	Annual Contribution
30 Yrs Later	65	1379006	0.12	$5,714.13

Table 7B: Contributions-Alternate View				
30 Yrs Later	65	596175	0.12	$2,470
40 Yrs Later	75	796720	0.135	$683
50 Yrs Later	85	1206746	0.15	$167
Total				$3,321

The alternate method results in a *42%* (1 – ($3321/$5714)) reduction in contribution for Ms. Jones. This is a significant reduction from the traditional view. Note that for a less risk tolerant investor, lower required rates of return may be expected; however, as long as the portfolio funding needs are considered to be 30 – 50 years away (as opposed to the 30 year traditional schedule), the implications regarding reduced contributions will remain unchanged. Further, given the long-term perspective of her investments, she has ample time to manage her portfolio risk and return characteristics.

RISK ANALYSIS

Retirees are especially averse to increasing their portfolio risk. There are two main reasons for this aversion. First, consistent with their age and life-cycle, retirees generally exhibit a greater aversion. Second, retirees implicitly understand that a failure in their portfolio would imply a loss in their living standards; this loss is viewed as more painful in retirement than at any other stage in their lives. The study of risk starts by analyzing the change in Ms. Jones's portfolio risk. Subsequently, a discussion of risk issues for the Smiths is provided, since it requires a more detailed explanation.

To begin with, the portfolio standard deviation is used as the measure for risk. Table 8 shows the changes in risk between the two methods for both Ms. Jones and the Smiths.

Table 8: Risk Analysis				
Ms. Jones	Bonds	Large Caps	Small Caps	P'fol Risk
Traditional View	0	100	0	20.40%
Alternate View	0	85	15	22.95%
The Smiths				
Traditional View	100	0	0	7.96%
Alternate View	78.79%	21.21%	0	10.07%

The 2.5% increase in risk[5] for Ms. Jones is contained entirely in the two portfolios dedicated to the last two decades of retirement since the returns for the initial portfolio is the same for both methods. This provides Ms. Jones with a 40–55 year window to manage this increase in risk. On the other hand, the effect of the 42% reduction in contributions is *immediate* in terms of added utility.

For the Smiths, too, the portfolio risk increases by about 2%, as shown in Table 8. Given the advanced age of the Smiths, a more detailed discussion of the increase in risk is desirable. *First* observe that about 52% of the Smiths' portfolio is dedicated to funding the first phase (66–75) of retirement. Since this segment has the same characteristics as the traditional portfolio, there is no difference in risk; the Smiths' immediate retirement needs (next 15 years) are as assured as in the traditional portfolio. Decomposing the risk further, it is observed that the risk increase is derived equally from the composition changes in the 2nd and 3rd dedicated portfolios. The benefit of a reduced retirement funding need *is* the result of taking on additional risk. However, this assumption of additional risk and its consequential effect must be managed over the 10-35 year (age 70 to age 95) window. Like Ms. Jones, however, the benefit of a fund which requires about 16% less funds than that computed by the traditional method, is immediate.

Second, the Smiths' portfolios include a 5 year cushion for risk management. The investment advisor has time to monitor the performances of the dedicated portfolios and make appropriate readjustment decisions as business cycles and portfolio values dictate.

Third, the reduction in expense estimation error considerably increases the chance of plan success, which also aids in reducing risk. *Finally*, note that the alternate method provides the Smiths with a savings of about $167,000. If the Smiths set away $50,000 each in two 6% bonds maturing in 15 (age 75) and 25 (age 85) years, the investments would be worth $120,000 and $215,000 respectively. Such an investment would dramatically reduce the increase in risk. Further, the Smiths would still retain a savings of $67,000 in funding their retirement plans.

Note that if a client has sufficient funds, then living through retirement is unlikely to lead to financial worries. The age banding model provides advisors with a way to fund retirement that help clients with wealth constraints to also plan effectively while retaining the ability for greater risk control.

ISSUES IN ADAPTING THE MODEL TO INDIVIDUAL CLIENTS

The model as developed above requires and is amenable to some fine tuning at the individual level, as discussed in the following:

a) Income Netting: If individuals expect to receive income in the form of fixed annuities (e.g. Social Security income or other benefits), then such income can be netted out of expenses before computing funding needs[6]. Note, however, that if the annuity was in the form of a guaranteed annuity contract (GAC) but was issued by a firm with some default risk, then that stream of cash flow would need to be adjusted for the default risk before income netting.

b) Atypical cases: The case study involving the Smiths is of course an unique example, even though the changes during their retirement (from greater leisure to greater healthcare needs) years may be experienced by many retirees in general. However, many atypical cases also exist. For example the spouses may vary greatly in age or one of the partners may experience the onset of serious illness at an earlier stage in retirement. The model allows easy incorporation of such unique circumstances. For example, the retirement period can be extended to a much longer time period to accommodate varying ages of spouses or greater longevity of life. Alternately, if contingencies (such as premature health problems) can be expected then the factors can be changed to reflect such events. If unexpected, the breakdown of the retirement years into phases with changing factors provides the planner with a robust tool to accommodate this change, unlike the traditional method. The breakdown into phases, the life cycle factors and the differential inflation rates can be used in different combinations to address most unique circumstances that arise for various retirees. As in any model, exceptional situations will exist that cannot be solved by a given model. The reader is urged to consider such possibilities as further research topics and help expand and fine tune the model's capabilities.

c) Point Estimates: In considering differential inflation rates for healthcare etc., the planner may wish to use an estimation range (e.g. 6%–9%) instead of the 7% point estimate. Since predicted rates may contain error, using point estimates may expose the client to four different sources of estimation errors, rather than one. Moreover, range estimates will allow financial planners to work within bands (ranges) of projected expenses and thereby cushion the effects of estimation errors. More astute planners may also use statistical analysis (expected values, dispersion, z-statistics, etc.) to further mitigate the effects of estimation errors.

d) Micro-Management: The "decade" approach to age banding is flexible and can be changed to any other time span (e.g. 1 year, 5 years, etc.), just as medical costs can be broken down to component costs. Such micro-analysis should considerably increase the efficacy of the model. Micromanagement, however, while increasing accuracy, would also require additional effort.

e) Mathematical Modeling: Note that the model is very amenable to mathematical modeling in a continuous time framework as the four expense categories can be depicted as continuously differentiable functions or functions that may be smoothed for differentiation. However, the desirability and usefulness of such rigor is debatable when applications are so subjective.

CONCLUSION

The age-banding method of retirement planning expounded in this paper shows planners an alternate way of thinking about retirement planning. The method provides marked benefits over the traditional plan in terms of more accurate expense projections, much smaller resource requirements and greater flexibility in managing risk. When applying this model, there are two additional noteworthy points to consider. First, a planner adopting this method needs to continuously monitor and manage the portfolio over time since the portfolio is dynamic. This is no different from *servicing* any other client by any other method. Second, planners need to understand that portfolio returns are uncertain and that their clients may very well live a much longer life than assumed. Both these issues are very critical in a dynamic retirement plan and are left for future research.

APPENDIX 1: COMPUTATIONS BY THE AGE-BANDING TECHNIQUE—AN ILLUSTRATION

In the following illustrations, the computational technique to project future expenses at varying rates for the first decade of retirement is shown in Table A1. Costs are broken down into different categories and extrapolated over the retirement years at the differential inflation rates. At the beginning of each decade (starting at age 65), the costs are adjusted by life cycle factors to reflect changes in life styles during retirement, albeit at finite points in time. The life-cycle factors that were used in generating the retirement expenses for the Smiths are shown in Table A2.

	Post-retirement Costs at Age 65	Inflation Factor	Age & Costs/Yr									
			66	67	68	69	70	71	72	73	74	75
Taxes	16226	3%	16713	17214	17731	18263	18810	19375	19956	20555	21171	21806
Basic Living	29207	3%	30083	30985	31915	32873	33859	34874	35921	36998	38108	39251
Healthcare	9681	7%	10358	11083	11859	12689	13578	14528	15545	16633	17798	19043
Leisure	10523	7%	11259	12047	12891	13793	14758	15791	16897	18080	19345	20699
Total	65702		68413	71330	74395	77617	81005	84569	88319	92266	96422	100801

Table A1: Cost Computations-Alternate View

Table A2: Life-Cycle Factors			
Age	65	75	85
Taxes	0.5	1	1
Basic Living	0.7	0.8	0.9
Healthcare	1.15	1.2	1.25
Leisure	1.5	0.5	0.25

REFERENCES

Anonymous (1998). Retirement Planning. *Tax Management Financial Planning Journal,* 14, 46-48.

Bell, J.H., & Rauf R.C. (1998). A graphical approach to retirement and estate planning. *Journal of Finance Service Professionals,* 52, 72-81.

Benartzi, S., & Thaler, R.H. (1999). Risk aversion or myopia? Choices in repeated gambles and retirement investments. *Management Science,* 45, 364-381.

Betts, A. (2003). The value of asset allocation. *Texas Banking,* 92, 22.

Blair, D.T., & Sellars, A.T. (1995). More than investment education. *Journal of the American Society of CLU & ChFC,* 49, 64-71.

Centers for Medicare and Medical Services Office of the Actuary (2001). *National Health Expenditures Projections: 2001-2011.*

Everett, M.D., & Anthony M.S. (1996). Abstract retirement planning using Modern Portfolio Theory. *Journal of Asset Protection,* 1, 65-71.

Haas, Donald Ray. (2001) Assessing Retirement Income. *Advisor Today* Aug 1999 Vol. 96, Issue 8, 78-79

Hager, G. (1999). Want a shock? Do the numbers online. *The Washington Post,* H 07.

Health Insurance Association of America (2002). *Issue Brief: Why do health insurance premiums rise.*

Levy, J., & Young, M. (2002). Replacement ratio redux. *Benefits Quarterly*, 18, 22-31.

Palmer, B.A. (1994). Retirement income replacement ratios: An update. *Benefits Quarterly*, 2Q, 63-66.

Smith, K.V. (1997). Stocks versus bonds in retirement planning. *Journal of Financial Planning*, 10, 87-90.

Stein, M.K. (1999). Getting to 'yes' in retirement planning. *Journal of Financial Planning*, 12, 30-31.

Stern, L. (2000). Do you really need millions to retire. *Better Homes and Gardens*, 78, 21-25.

Tacchino, K. & Saltzmann, C. (1999). Do accumulation models overstate what's needed to retire? *Journal of Financial Planning. Feb 1999, Vol 12, Issue 2, 62-74*

Tax Management Financial Planning Journal (1998). *Retirement Planning*, 14, 46-49.

Tiffany, G. (2003). Public employee retirement planning. *Employee Benefits Journal*, 28, 3.

The United States Census Bureau (2000) Statistical Abstracts of the United States, Parks, Recreation and Travel.

United States Department of Health and Human Services (2001). *Health Care Financing Administration*.

NOTES

1. Retirees investing all their retirement funds in a less risky and lower yielding portfolio is a general assumption. Certainly, there are many planners who also advocate the holding of stocks in retirement portfolios. The example in this paper represents a base case, for simplifying purposes only. However, from the point of view of the model being presented, the generality of the results are not changed for any other asset allocation schedules.
2. Note that taxes in this case represent the average tax rate and not the marginal tax rate. The average tax rate is computed as (total tax/total income) whereas the marginal tax rate is computed on the adjusted gross income. This factor must also be customized for each client. Most of the taxes paid are on income from pensions, 1099 income, etc.
3. Note that the age-banding model can incorporate many more categories of expenses than the four shown in this paper. A larger number of categories would be required to assess the implications of changing expenses to their impact on life styles changes.
4. The assumed returns are based on the long-term average returns (1926-2002) for AAA rated bonds and the S&P 500 stocks, respectively.
5. The historic standard deviations used in the computation for the long bond, large caps and small caps are 7.96%, 20.4% and 40.44% respectively. The correlation between bonds and stocks are assumed at 0.80 and large caps vs. small caps are assumed to be 0.90. Readers will note that the correlation figures are quite a bit higher than what is generally known—the error is intentional. The point being made is that even with this overestimation error, the increase in the "alternative" portfolio risk is still marginal.
6. In table 4B, subtract the social security income from the projected expenses for each year and then proceed to calculate funding requirements.

Medicare's Financial Condition: Beyond Actuarial Balance*

American Academy of Actuaries

Each year, the Boards of Trustees of the Federal Hospital Insurance (HI) and Supplementary Medical Insurance (SMI) Trust Funds report to Congress on the Medicare program's financial condition. The Medicare program provides health coverage for the aged and for certain individuals with disabilities. The trustees' report is the primary source of information on the financial status of the Medicare program, and the American Academy of Actuaries proudly recognizes the contribution that members of the actuarial profession have made in preparing the report and educating the public about this important issue.

The projections of Medicare's financial status in the 2008 Medicare trustees' report are consistent with the projections in the 2007 report. The HI trust fund, which pays for hospital services, will be depleted slightly earlier in 2019 than was previously projected. HI expenditures will again exceed HI non-interest income this year. In addition, Medicare expenditures will continue to consume an increasing share of federal outlays and GDP. The trustees conclude, "The projections shown in [the] report continue to demonstrate the need for timely and effective action to address Medicare's financial challenges—both the long-range financial imbalance facing the HI trust fund and the heightened problem of rapid growth in expenditures."

This issue brief examines more closely the findings of the trustees' report. The American Academy of Actuaries' Medicare Steering Committee concludes that the Medicare program faces serious short-term and long-term financing problems. As highlighted in the 2008 Medicare trustees' report:

- *The HI trust fund fails to meet the test of short-range financial adequacy because HI trust fund assets will fall below annual expenditures within the next 10 years.*

- *The HI trust fund also fails to meet the test of long-range actuarial balance. HI expenditures will exceed HI non-interest income this year. By 2019, when trust fund assets are projected to be depleted, tax revenues would cover only 78 percent of program costs, and this share will decrease rapidly thereafter. The trust fund depletion date is projected to arrive slightly earlier in 2019 than was projected last year, due in part to slightly lower projected payroll tax income and slightly higher expenditures than previously estimated.*

- *The value in today's dollars of the HI deficit over the next 75 years is $13 trillion. Eliminating this deficit would require an immediate 122 percent increase in payroll taxes or an immediate 51 percent reduction in benefits, or some combination of the two. Delaying action would require more drastic tax increases or benefit reductions.*

---

*Copyright © 2008. Reprinted with permission from the American Academy of Actuaries, Washington, D.C. Reproduction prohibited without publishers' written permission.

- *The SMI trust fund includes accounts for the Part B program, which covers physician and outpatient hospital costs, and for the Part D program, which covers the prescription drug benefit. The SMI trust fund is expected to remain solvent only because its financing is reset each year to meet projected future costs. Projected increases in SMI expenditures will require significant increases in beneficiary premiums and general revenue contributions over time.*

- *Medicare's demand on the federal budget, measured as the HI income shortfall and the general revenue contribution to SMI, is projected to increase rapidly.*

- *For the third year in a row, the difference between Medicare outlays and dedicated revenues exceeds 45 percent within the next seven years, thereby again triggering the Medicare funding warning. As a result, the next president must propose legislation to reduce this share within 15 days of the next budget submission. Congressional action is not guaranteed, however, and depending on what action, if any, is taken, other financing problems could remain.*

- *Medicare expenditures are also projected to increase rapidly as a share of GDP and of total federal revenues, thereby threatening Medicare's long-term sustainability.*

- *The increasing costs of the Medicare program reflect the increasing costs of the health care system as a whole. Efforts to control spending in the Medicare program should be considered within the broader context of the entire health care system.*

The committee recommends that policymakers implement changes to improve Medicare's financial outlook. The sooner such corrective measures are enacted, the more flexible the approach and the more gradual the implementation can be. Failure to act now may necessitate far more onerous actions later.

SHORT-TERM FINANCING OF MEDICARE

To assure short-range financial adequacy of the HI trust fund, the Medicare trustees recommend that trust fund assets equal or exceed annual expenditures for each of the next 10 years. This level would serve as an adequate contingency reserve in the event of adverse economic or other conditions. For the next several years, the trust fund assets are expected to significantly exceed annual expenditures. However, trust fund assets are projected to fall below annual expenditures during 2012. As a result, the HI trust fund fails the test of short-range financial adequacy.

LONG-TERM FINANCING OF MEDICARE

The Medicare program has three fundamental long-range financing problems:

1. Income to the HI trust fund will soon become inadequate to fund the HI portion of Medicare benefits;

2. Medicare's demands on the federal budget are increasing; and

3. Paying currently promised Medicare benefits will place an increasing strain on the U.S. economy.

Each of these problems is discussed in more detail below.

Medicare HI Trust Fund Income Will Soon Become Inadequate to Fund HI Benefits

In terms of trust fund accounting, Medicare consists of two parts, each of which is financed separately. Hospital Insurance (HI) pays primarily for inpatient hospital care (Part A); Supplementary Medical Insurance (SMI) pays primarily for physician and outpatient care (Part B) and prescription drugs (Part D). Like the Social Security program, Medicare makes use of trust funds to account for all income and expenditures, and the HI and SMI programs operate separate trust funds. Taxes, premiums, and other income are credited to the trust funds, which are used to pay benefits and administrative costs. Any unused income is added to the trust fund assets, which are invested, as required by law, in U.S. government securities, for use in future years. Note, however, that the trust fund assets represent loans to the U.S. Treasury's general fund. As a result, the buildup of Medicare trust funds is essentially used to fund other government spending.

The 2008 Medicare trustees' report highlights the long-term financing problems facing the program:

- The HI program is funded primarily through earmarked payroll taxes. From 1998 through 2004, HI payroll taxes and other non-interest income exceeded HI expenditures, and the trust fund accumulated assets. In 2005, however, HI non-interest income fell below HI expenditures and has continued to fall short since then. Beginning in 2010, HI expenditures are projected to exceed all HI income, including interest. At that point, the HI trust fund will need to begin redeeming its assets—U.S. government securities—in order to pay for benefits. If the federal government is experiencing unified budget deficits at the time these securities need to be redeemed, either additional taxes will need to be levied to fund the redemptions, or additional money will need to be borrowed from the public, thereby increasing the public debt.

- By 2019, HI trust fund assets are projected to be depleted. At that time, tax revenues are projected to cover only 78 percent of program costs, with the share decreasing further thereafter. The HI trust fund depletion date is projected to arrive a little earlier in 2019 than projected in the 2007 Medicare trustees' report, due in part to slightly lower projected payroll tax income and slightly higher expenditures than previously estimated.

- The value in today's dollars of the HI deficit over the next 75 years is $13 trillion, or 3.5 percent of taxable payroll over the same time period. Eliminating this deficit would require an immediate 122 percent increase in payroll taxes or an immediate 51 percent reduction in benefits, or some combination of the two. Delaying action would require more drastic tax increases or benefit reductions. Projections over an infinite time horizon would increase the shortfall to $34 trillion, or 6.1 percent of taxable payroll. Given the uncertainty of projections 75 years into the future, however, extending these projections into the infinite future can only increase the uncertainty, so that these results can have only limited value for policymakers.

- The SMI program is financed through beneficiary premiums that cover about a quarter of the cost. Federal general tax revenues cover the remaining three quarters.[1] The SMI trust fund is expected to remain solvent, but only because its financing is reset each year to meet projected future costs. Projected increases in SMI expenditures, therefore, will require increases in beneficiary premiums and general revenue contributions over time.

Medicare's Demand on the Federal Budget Is Increasing

Another way to gauge Medicare's financial condition is to view it from a federal budget perspective. In particular, this assessment determines whether Medicare receipts from the public (e.g., payroll taxes, beneficiary premiums) exceed or fall short of outlays to the public. Under this approach, interest income on the HI trust fund assets and contributions from general revenues to the SMI program are ignored, because they are essentially intragovernmental transfers between the general fund and the Medicare trust funds. As a result, the difference between public receipts and public expenditures for Medicare reflects any HI income shortfall and the general revenue share of SMI.

Table 1 reports the HI income shortfall and the general revenue contribution to the SMI program in 2007 and projections over the next 10 years. Recall that the SMI program is designed for about three-quarters of its expenditures to be funded through general revenues. In 2007, Medicare expenditures already exceeded public receipts by $174 billion. This amount is expected to grow over the next 10 years; the cumulative difference between Medicare expenditures and public receipts is projected to total $2.9 trillion over this period

TABLE 1
HI Income Shortfall and SMI General Revenue Contribution (Billions of Dollars)

| Calendar Year | HI Trust Fund | | | SMI Trust Fund | HI Income Shortfall Plus SMI General Revenue Contribution |
	Income[1]	Expenditures	Shortfall	General Revenue Contribution[2]	
2007	$207.1	$203.1	–$4.0	$178.4	$174.4
2008	204.8	229.5	24.8	186.2	211.0
2009	230.9	245.5	14.6	208.4	223.1
2010	243.0	260.5	17.5	192.3	209.7
2011	255.4	276.0	20.6	217.5	238.2
2012	268.1	294.7	26.6	234.9	261.4
2013	282.0	315.6	33.6	258.2	291.8
2014	296.2	337.8	41.6	273.3	314.9
2015	310.5	361.4	50.9	313.9	364.8
2016	325.7	386.8	61.1	302.2	363.3
2017	341.7	414.9	73.1	353.3	426.4
TOTAL					
2008–2017	$2,758.3	$3,122.8	$364.5	$2,540.0	$2,904.5

1. HI receipts exclude interest income.
2. SMI general revenue contribution includes Part B and Part D general revenue contributions.
   Source: American Academy of Actuaries' tabulations based on 2008 Medicare Trustees' Report tables III.B4 and III.C1

Beginning in 2010, when HI expenditures are projected to exceed HI public receipts plus interest income on trust fund assets, the HI trust fund will need to begin drawing down its assets, further increasing Medicare's demand on the federal budget. Unless payroll taxes are increased or benefits reduced, HI trust fund assets are projected to be depleted in 2019. There is no current provision allowing for general fund transfers to cover HI expenditures in excess of payroll tax revenues.

For a longer-term view of Medicare's demand on the federal budget, Table 2 reports the HI income shortfall and the SMI general revenue contribution over the next several decades, as a share of GDP. The HI income shortfall and SMI general revenue contribution are projected to grow dramatically—from 1.4 percent of GDP in 2008 to 7.8 percent of GDP in 2080. This will increase considerably the pressures on the federal budget, unless HI income shortfalls or SMI general revenue contributions are reduced.

TABLE 2
HI Income Shortfall and SMI General Revenue Contribution (Percentage of GDP)

Calendar Year	HI Shortfall	SMI General Revenue Contribution[1]	HI Income Shortfall and SMI General Revenue Contribution
2007	0.07%	1.29%	1.36%
2010	0.10	1.21	1.31
2020	0.47	1.86	2.33
2030	1.14	2.72	3.86
2040	1.80	3.23	5.04
2050	2.22	3.55	5.77
2060	2.58	3.91	6.48
2070	2.97	4.23	7.21
2080	3.31	4.49	7.79

1. SMI general revenue contribution includes Part B and Part D general revenue contributions.
Source: Social Security and Medicare Boards of Trustees Summary of the 2008 Annual Reports, Chart E.

A provision of the *Medicare Prescription Drug, Improvement, and Modernization Act of 2003* (MMA) intends to address these financial challenges. Basically, if in two consecutive trustees' reports general funding sources are projected to account for more than 45 percent of Medicare spending within the next seven years, the administration is required to recommend ways to reduce this percentage.[2] Options would include reducing spending (e.g., benefit cuts, delayed eligibility, reduced provider payments), increasing revenues (e.g., raising payroll taxes, raising beneficiary premiums), or some combination thereof. The president's proposal must come within 15 days of the next budget submission. The provision was first triggered in 2007, and in response President Bush submitted legislation in February 2008. Congress is now required to consider the legislation on an expedited basis. There is no requirement, however, that any legislation be enacted.

The 2008 Medicare Trustees' Report projects that the 45 percent threshold will first be reached in 2014. Because last year's report also projected that the threshold would be reached within seven years, the requirement is triggered again this year. The triggering of this provision draws attention to the need to manage the demand Medicare places on the federal budget, and provides policymakers the opportunity to address the financial situation of the program and to limit the burden the program places on the federal budget. Congressional action is not guaranteed, however, and depending on what action, if any, is taken, other financing problems could remain. For instance, legislative changes reducing general revenue funding might have no impact on HI solvency.

Medicare Is Projected to Place Increasing Strains on the Economy

A broader issue related to Medicare's financial condition is whether the economy can sustain Medicare spending in the long run. To gauge the future sustainability of the Medicare program, we examine the share of GDP that will be consumed by Medicare. As shown in Table 3, total Medicare spending is projected to consume a greater share of GDP over time. In 2007, total Medicare spending was 3.2 percent of GDP. Spending is expected to rise to 6.3 percent of GDP in 2030 and 10.7 percent of GDP in 2080. (Notably, this measure understates the share of the economy devoted to health spending among the elderly and disabled, because Medicare imposes cost sharing and does not cover all health products and services utilized.)

TABLE 3
Medicare and Social Security Expenditures as a Share of GDP (Percentage)

Calendar Year	Medicare	Social Security	Medicare Plus Social Security
2007	3.2%	4.3%	7.5%
2008	3.2	4.3	7.5
2009	3.3	4.4	7.7
2010	3.3	4.4	7.7
2020	4.4	5.3	9.7
2030	6.3	6.0	12.3
2040	7.6	6.0	13.6
2050	8.4	5.8	14.2
2060	9.2	5.8	15.0
2070	10.0	5.8	15.8
2080	10.7	5.8	16.5

Source: American Academy of Actuaries' tabulations based on 2008 Medicare Trustees' Report (plot points for Figure II.D.1) and 2008 Social Security Trustees' Report (plot points for Figure II.D.5.)

Considering Medicare spending in conjunction with Social Security spending further highlights the strain these programs place on the economy. Social Security spending as a share of GDP increases more modestly than Medicare over the next several decades, and as a result, Medicare spending is expected to exceed that of Social Security in 2028. Combined, Medicare and Social Security expenditures equaled 7.5 percent of GDP in 2007. This share of GDP is projected to increase to 12.3 percent of 2030 and 16.5 percent in 2080.

Medicare and Social Security expenditures are even more striking when considered relative to total federal revenues. The trustees report that total federal revenues have historically averaged about 18 percent of GDP. Using this average, about 40 percent of all federal revenues in 2008 will be used to pay Medicare and Social Security benefits. If no changes are made to either program and federal revenues remain at 18 percent of GDP, this share is expected to increase to nearly 80 percent in 2050, and by 2080, Medicare and Social Security spending would equal over 90 percent of total federal revenues.

These projections highlight the increasing strains that Medicare, especially in conjunction with Social Security, will place on the U.S. economy. Moreover, increased spending for Medicare may crowd out the share of funds available for other federal programs.

If we are to avoid this trend, reforms must be made to address the rapid growth in Medicare expenditures. It is important to recognize that the problem of rising health care spending in the Medicare program reflects spending growth in the U.S. health system as a whole. Therefore, unless spending in the health system as a whole is addressed, implementing options to control Medicare spending may have limited long-term effectiveness.

CONCLUSION

The American Academy of Actuaries' Medicare Steering Committee continues to be very concerned about Medicare's long-range financing problems. HI non-interest income is already falling short of outlays this year and the HI trust fund is projected to be depleted as soon as 2019. Medicare will likely place increasing demands on the federal budget, even with the provision that alerts Congress when the program's reliance on general revenue sources is becoming large. The program's sustainability is also called into question as currently promised benefits will require increasing shares of both GDP and total federal revenues.

The committee recommends that policymakers implement changes to improve Medicare's financial outlook. We agree with the 2008 trustees, who state in their report:

> "The sooner the solutions are enacted, the more flexible and gradual they can be. Moreover, the early introduction of reforms increases the time available for affected individuals and organizations—including health care providers, beneficiaries, and taxpayers—to adjust their expectations.

NOTES

1. Part B beneficiaries pay monthly premiums covering about 25 percent of program costs (beginning in 2007, Part B premiums became income-related, with higher income enrollees paying more than 25 percent of costs); general revenues cover the remaining 75 percent of costs. Part D premiums will be set at about 25 percent of Part D costs. However, because of low-income premium subsidies, beneficiary premiums will cover only about 9 percent of total Part D costs in 2008. State payments on behalf of certain beneficiaries will cover about 14 percent of costs and general revenues will cover the remaining 77 percent of costs.
2. More specifically, a determination of "excess general funding" is triggered if for two consecutive trustees' reports the difference between Medicare outlays and dedicated financing sources (HI payroll taxes, HI share of income taxes on Social Security benefits, Part D state transfers, and beneficiary premiums) exceeds 45 percent of Medicare outlays within seven years of the projection.

Spending in Retirement: Easing the Reins or Pulling Them in[*]

Richard F. Stolz[†]

Helping clients achieve a successful retirement is typically the primary goal of a financial plan, and the focal point of the ongoing financial planning relationship. But when clients ultimately retire, the work is hardly over. Indeed, in some respects, the planner's role at that turning point becomes even more critical—and the work more challenging.

This is particularly true when clients' personal instincts, financial delusions, or ingrained patterns of economic behavior threaten their well-being in retirement—either by outliving their assets through overspending, or denying themselves the pleasures of a comfortable material standard of living they can easily afford.

Indeed, more often than not, retired clients don't live within their economic means—typically by being overly frugal. Less common but perhaps more disturbing are the cases of profligate spending by retirees, which lead to dire financial consequences.

What can planners do to guide both kinds of retired clients down the path of fiscal responsibility? Insights can be gleaned from CFP® certificants who work extensively with retirees, through a combination of innate skill, trial and error, and training, have developed creative and effective tactics to keep clients from defeating themselves—at least most of the time.

Some situations defy remedy.

CONFRONTING OVERSPENDERS

The crucial task of at least attempting to get retired clients on track is at the core of a planner's duty to clients, according to Judy Hagar, CFP®, of Wolters, Hagar & Pratt Financial Planning in San Diego, California. "If we see our clients spending too much, or they have extra money and they're not being efficient with it, we have an obligation to point that out. It's our job to tell our clients the bad news," she says.

And how does Hagar define excessive spending? For starters, she emphasizes the importance of weighing the unique personal circumstances of each client. "There is no formula that works for everyone," she says. "It cracks me up when people do these inordinately detailed studies of which percentage is the right percentage so a portfolio can be sustainably distributed over time. That's nonsense."

---

[*] Reprinted with permission by the Financial Planning Association, *Journal of Financial Planning,* March 2008.
[†] Richard F. Stolz is founder of Publishing Services & Strategies, a communications consulting and marketing services provider based in Rockville, Maryland. He has been writing about personal and corporate finance topics for 28 years.

Indeed, planners say, not all clients intend for their portfolio to outlast them—but the overwhelming majority of portfolios do.

While Hagar accepts the commonly accepted 4–5 percent range as a starting point, she offers an example of a situation in which she endorsed a higher, albeit temporary, distribution rate. "We had a client who had breast cancer and beat it, but told us, 'Frankly, I want to spend money now because I may not be around in ten years.' She wanted to travel while she was still healthy."

Hagar has similarly endorsed above-benchmark spending for certain retirees with substantial home equity who, "if need be, could do a reverse mortgage," or for clients whose portfolios have performed significantly above long-term expectations.

But after factoring all of the relevant variables, if it's clear to Hagar that a client is overspending in retirement, she will confront them. "I try to do it gently," she says. "But I lay out all the numbers right in front of their faces."

Hagar and her partners prepare a cash-flow report for clients, with negative numbers highlighted in red. "I ask, 'Is this what you're spending?'" and allow them to draw their own conclusions. "If they don't look at that number and express some sort of dismay or shock, they're in denial."

Indeed, "in denial" seems to describe the typical overspending client (whether before or in retirement). William Burns, Jr., CFP®, CLU, ChFC, REBC, of Burns Matteson Capital Management in Corning, New York, has a few retired clients who fit that description. "One client is a perpetual optimist; he believes an inheritance will bail him out"—even though the anticipated size of that uncertain inheritance is relatively modest.

Another client, who habitually spends more than she can afford in supporting her adult children, believes they will soon be "on their feet," and that her dwindling retirement portfolio will then magically swell. Still another client believes that selling her modest home will turn the financial tide—without accepting the fact that she'll still have to pay rent somewhere.

"They just don't seem interested in doing the things they need to do," Burns laments.

When Burns told a client how much she had withdrawn from her retirement portfolio in recent months and she refused to believe him, he documented the client's stated purpose for each withdrawal. Not only can Burns meticulously document each disbursement, but "now we have the ability to tell her what she wanted to do with the money" when reviewing prior transactions.

CODE RED

Burns also has employed a color-coding system on financial reports to capture the attention of clients whose spending is putting their financial health at risk. For example, for a particular 72-year-old client, Burns determined that drawing down the portfolio at a $10,000 monthly pace would deplete his funds within a decade. "We code this red for the 'danger zone,'" Burns explains. If the portfolio is tapped at a more moderate $7,000 monthly pace, Burns projects it will have a 14-year life, and the color indicated would be yellow, for "caution."

That client would need to maintain a $5,000 monthly withdrawal rate to reach the safety of Burns's green zone. "We were comfortable defining the green zone as a set of assumptions that should allow the portfolio to last until his age 92," Burns says.

Beyond simply trying to bring spendthrift clients back to the reality by focusing on specific numbers, planners strive to keep them mindful of the big picture, and the possible ultimate consequence of their behavior. Says Thomas C. Scott, CFP®, CEO of Scott Wealth Management Group in Irvine, California: "I'll tell clients to imagine themselves 82 years old, in fairly good health, but in no position to go out and look for a job, and all of a sudden, their portfolio plummets and they can't just pull that money out anymore. Sometimes they just look at you, and the light bulb goes on."

But it's rarely sufficient merely to confront such clients with a vivid and alarming description of the doomsday financial scenario. So Scott seeks to engage overspending retirees in a dialogue. "If a client's expectation of portfolio performance is way too high, I'll say, 'You're probably going to run out of money at 76,' and I'll just look at the client and ask, 'What do you think about that?'"

Scott continues, "His response will be, 'I don't like that.' And I'll say, 'What do you want to do?'" and proceed to lay out realistic alternatives, and pursue the conversation.

CONCERN WITHOUT SHAME

Chris Brown, CFP®, of Snow Creek Wealth Management LLC in Nashville, Tennessee, also seeks to engage clients in identifying an appropriate solution, but his tone may be somewhat gentler. "We don't want the client to feel ashamed. We want to show our concern, and just try to be as genuine as possible and say, 'Here's the situation. We need to see if there is something we can constructively come up with together either to reduce spending, or find another way to structure the portfolio.'"

That "something," Brown says, may be an immediate annuity, to insure the client a base level of monthly income for life and to shift financial market risk to the issuing insurance company.

In recent years, insurance companies have increased the flexibility of annuity products. Thomas Scott says he's "excited" about guaranteed withdrawal benefits on variable annuities that can give his clients "the opportunity to have equity exposure, and at the same time, a baseline stream of income with the possibility of increases that, once they happen, are guaranteed from that point on.")

Engaging overspending retirees (or any other clients, for that matter) in a serious dialogue about the perils of their behavior doesn't guarantee a positive response, of course. In fact, it may kill the relationship. That has happened on more than one occasion to Diana Simpson, CFP®, of Fee-Only Planning Professionals LLC in Birmingham, Alabama. "Sometimes you tell clients what they don't want to hear, and they don't come back," she says.

PARTING COMPANY

What if retired clients are headed for financial disaster, but ignore warnings and advice, and still wish to maintain the professional relationship? While some planners will take pains to put clients on record acknowledging, in writing, that they have disregarded the guidance they have received, Simpson believes she's better off parting company with them. "I really feel I have an obligation to keep the client from doing something harmful. If they aren't going to listen to me, I just can't keep them," she says.

Simpson is also skeptical that getting a client to sign an acknowledgment of disregarding her advice would take her off the hook legally should some kind of malpractice claim ultimately arise. "The client can always say, 'I didn't know what I was doing. I didn't know what it meant,'" she says.

But William Burns says he and his partners are prepared to stick with a handful of retired clients who appear to be poverty-bound. "We don't think they'd be better served by ending the relationship," he says. "I'm prepared for the day their money is all gone. I think they're going to need us more than ever at that time, even if it's on a pro bono basis. Maybe we can delay the inevitable by a year if our management is better than the clients would achieve on their own."

NEEDLESSLY FRUGAL CLIENTS

Thankfully, the more typical problem for planners whose retired clients stubbornly resist their advice is the opposite: clients have more money than they need but simply fail to believe it.

Yet even an imaginary state of poverty can be a tragedy for retired clients, as Thomas Scott explains. He describes the "inability of clients to comfortably spend down their assets" as a "massive roadblock to executing a successful retirement strategy."

One of Scott's clients, a widow, recently died in her nineties. At the funeral, her children lamented the fact that she had never taken the European trip "she had fantasized about for so many years." Yet her portfolio would have generated a $400,000 annual income until she was 120 years old, Scott says.

While perhaps an extreme example, it vividly illustrates the challenge of helping clients ease their tight grasp on the purse strings—when appropriate. Faced with a similarly needlessly frugal retired client sitting on a $2 million portfolio, Burns was able to achieve a happier outcome. The 70-plus-year-old former engineer and his wife were sitting in Burns's office several months ago reviewing their investments, and their 50th wedding anniversary was fast approaching. The couple's traditional winter escape from the frigid upstate New York winter had been renting a mobile home in Florida for two months.

Burns suggested a more ambitious alternative: celebrating their 50th with a cruise to Hawaii.

Anticipating that his client's reaction would be that such a trip would be too expensive, Burns framed the affordability issue this way. "Their portfolio had already risen $150,000 year-to-date," he recalls. "I asked them, if it had only gone up $140,000 instead, would you really have noticed the difference?"

The thrifty client took the point—but needed another nudge. "So I asked my client, 'If you don't think your fiftieth is a big enough occasion to take the trip, do you think you'd have an interest in doing it for your hundredth?'"

After three weeks of deliberation, the couple decided to take the cruise. The good news is they were able to relax enough about the money to enjoy the trip, Burns says. "They met some people on the boat whom they're probably going to travel with again."

Burns is now working on another comfortably retired client who is making big home improvements, but has balked at putting $15,000 into new floors, on the basis that those dollars wouldn't be recouped when the home is sold. "My response is to tell him that if he thinks he'll live there another ten years, and he enjoys the new floors, it's okay."

But Burns says he doesn't try to impose his personal priorities on his clients. Meeting with them on a quarterly basis and talking to them on the phone between meetings, Burns is confident of his ability to assess the kind of spending decisions they would ultimately want to make—once they're reassured they're not bound for destitution.

Also, planners don't necessarily want to have to weigh in on every significant spending decision a retired client has to make. Ideally, retirees can enter retirement with an overall comfort level that makes individual decisions easier. One approach Scott will take is to ask clients, "How much money do you want to arrive in your mailbox every month, without a doubt?" Having identified that need, he says, "we take a certain amount of retirement assets and make sure that core need is taken care of." (For particularly skittish clients, that could be accomplished with an annuity, for example.)

"Once that's done," Scott adds, "we can play a little with what's above and beyond that." In theory, retirees can consider the excess as retirement mad money.

RETIREE 'PAYCHECKS'

In some cases, recently retired clients—particularly those without a defined-benefit pension—simply feel financially disoriented by the lack of a regular paycheck. For them, there's a simple solution, notes Chris Brown. "We have the client's monthly withdrawals from their retirement portfolio directly deposited into their checking account so they have a sense of that paycheck continuing on. It alleviates a fear of running out of money" for some clients, he says.

Often an underlying element to frugal clients' worries about exhausting their assets is a fear that inflation will flare up and erode their purchasing power. "We can model those inflation scenarios for them, but it takes clients a while to get used to hearing that they've saved enough," says Robert Schmansky, CFP®, of Focus Financial Planning LLC in Bingham Farms, Michigan.

"There have been times of high inflation, but it's our job to help clients understand the history of it, over longer periods of time than the 1970s or early 1980s when we had those brief periods of high inflation," he says.

ROLE OF CHILDREN

Sometimes retired clients' children can help reassure them that they don't need to cling tightly to all of their investments. Having a client's child or children attend a routine portfolio-review meeting can be helpful, says Diana Simpson. Her clients are primarily "independent women, either by choice or circumstance," with assets in the $250,000–$300,000 range.

She will encourage clients to bring in children, in part because "I want them to see that Mom's getting good advice." But the approach can backfire, she warns, in situations where selfish children "are much more concerned about conserving the assets for their own inheritance" than encouraging their parents to enjoy their retirement, Simpson adds.

But clients' natural desire to pass on residual assets to their children can be used to motivate them, for example, to spruce up their homes, as Judy Hagar explains. "With our clients who are not used to spending, we may ask them if there are things they'd like to do to the home that would make their lives more pleasant or easier."

If they balk, Hagar might "talk to them about the fact that if they don't keep their home up, it won't sell for full value, and that will reduce their kids' inheritance. They don't like to hear that, so sometimes they will go ahead with a project that has been long overdue."

Ultimately, there's a limit to how far planners can go—or should attempt to go—to encourage retirees to spend if they simply aren't inclined to do so—particularly the older ones. "Once you reach a certain age, you're set in your ways," says Simpson. "These folks who have been frugal all their lives aren't suddenly going to start going crazy and buying diamonds and furs."

FINDING EMOTIONAL REWARDS

Thomas Scott states, "It's not my job to be my client's psychoanalyst. It's my job to say, 'I can assure you that this income is going to last as long as you live. Without a doubt, you're never going to run out of money, and that includes taking a cruise every year.' If she doesn't want to take a cruise, that's none of my business, but at least I'm letting her know she's secure, and that she can take the trip."

And some clients may have very sound nonfinancial reasons for maintaining a job and, in the process, accumulating assets after giving up full-time work, according to Schmansky. "Many keep part-time work for the satisfaction of remaining active."

Well-funded but frugal clients looking more for emotional rewards than material comfort are also often very open to conversations about charitable giving opportunities, planners say. "I'll point out to them that even if they're not planning to spend their money on themselves, somebody is going to spend it," Schmansky says. "That's a good way to get the conversation going on whether they have any charitable thoughts. We can help them decide how much to give."

Often, the "charity" they're most interested in is their own children and grandchildren. While delivering funds to offspring ties into basic gift and estate planning strategies, clients can be urged to consider other possible approaches. For example, in the high-priced southern California real estate market, retired clients of Judy Hagar have explored with her the tax-efficient ways they could help grandchildren buy homes in their community.

And as for gifts to traditional charities, it is not always apparent to frugal retirees that they're in a position to contribute. "Most people will say, 'I can't afford to gift anything,'" says Judy Hagar. "And they're thinking in terms of writing a check. You have to educate them."

That education may involve identifying assets or life insurance policies that are no longer needed that can be contributed. When Hagar senses possible interest, she asks clients for the names of any charity they may be interested in, then contacts the charity's director of planned giving to give a presentation. "That opens people's eyes," she says, when they learn they can continue to receive income, and also a tax deduction, from planned giving transactions.

Once William Burns has opened his retired clients' eyes to these possibilities, he sometimes works with them to establish donor-advised charitable funds. "We manage the charitable assets, along with their regular assets," he says. Among other advantages to the approach, it allows clients to get their children involved. Burns continues, "We've helped clients set up a matching gift program for their children."

A child wishing to make a charitable contribution to a particular organization can see their gift matched by their parents. The idea is to instill in children the same charitable-minded traits of the parents.

Another approach Burns has used with comfortably retired clients to achieve the same result is to have them give children a "gift certificate" that allows them to direct the parents to contribute the stated dollar amount to the charity of the child's choice.

Having helped clients achieve the kind of financial security in retirement that creates the "problem" of needing to prod penny-pinching retirees to contribute surplus assets to charity—or simply indulge themselves—is perhaps the best kind of problem for a planner to have.

"One of the greatest moments in our profession," says Chris Brown, "is when we are able to sit down with a client and show them that it's okay to take additional money out of their portfolio in order for them to enjoy their retirement even more."

Richard F. Stolz is founder of Publishing Services & Strategies, a communications consulting and marketing services provider based in Rockville, Maryland. He has been writing about personal and corporate finance topics for 28 years.

DEFINING—AND ACHIEVING—A 'SUCCESSFUL' RETIREMENT

Working with retired clients whose spending habits are out of whack with their financial resources can prompt financial planners to reflect on the basic question of the ultimate purpose of retirement planning.

"Our goal," says Thomas C. Scott, CFP®, CEO of Scott Wealth Management Group in Irvine, California, "is to achieve a successful retirement." But what does "success" really mean to his clients? Or perhaps what should it mean, after purely dollar-denominated answers are addressed?

Scott believes most of his clients, if they could look back on their retirement "post-mortem," would like to be able to say, "I had peace of mind. I had comfort. I enjoyed myself."

Yet the ability to achieve that kind of success requires more than the mere fact of having a healthy investment portfolio. "If you want your clients to be 'successful' in retirement, it's really important not only that you give them security, but that they understand the security they have," he says.

Adds Robert Schmansky, CFP®, of Focus Financial Planning LLC in Bingham Farms, Michigan: "It's always our job to relieve our clients' fears. Their state of mind is probably the most important asset they have, along with their health."

Of course, planners' ability to give clients peace of mind in retirement begins with having developed a basic level of understanding, rapport, and trust essential to leading them toward making appropriate financial decisions. That's less challenging with some clients than others, of course.

For example, Scott knows that his "cautious and conservative" clients are easier to work with because they "know how important it is that the retirement plan work," and therefore follow his recommendations during the run-up to retirement.

In contrast, says Scott, those people who "have no fear at all and say, 'let's be aggressive' haven't comprehended what the transition to retirement is all about," and make it harder for Scott both to help them to afford to be able to retire when they want to, and to live within their means once they do.

Continue Your Journey of Learning

Please visit TheAmericanCollege.edu
to learn more about our continuum of education

Success Skills

LUTCF Insurance Skills (6 courses)
Taught by experienced financial services leaders, LUTCF classes put you on the fast track for success. By combining essential product knowledge with basic planning concepts, the LUTCF has helped thousands of insurance professionals boost their production by as much as 40 percent.

FSS Financial Services Skills (6 courses)
FSS classes are taught by moderators with years of sales experience, helping you quickly establish a thriving financial services practice. As an FSS student, you'll gain fundamental product knowledge while learning practical sales skills that have been shown to increase production by as much as 40 percent.

Retirement and Wealth Transfer

CASL® Retirement Planning (5 courses)
CASL is the most robust designation available in the specialized retirement coaching field. It provides comprehensive knowledge on psychological and sociological issues confronting older clients. Completing this rigorous program prepares you to lead clients from middle age through retirement and assist them with wealth management and wealth transfer.

CLU® Insurance Specialty (8 courses)
This prestigious course of study helps advance your career by providing in-depth knowledge on the insurance needs of individuals, business owners, and professional clients. CLU designees average up to 51 percent higher production income than their peers.

CAP® Philanthropy (3 graduate-level courses)
The CAP provides you with the knowledge and tools you need to help clients and prospective donors reach both financial and philanthropic goals. It enables you to work effectively with and for all types of nonprofit organizations and donors.

Financial Planning

CFP® Certification Education (6 courses)
These courses expand your financial planning knowledge by covering all of the 89 topics outlined by the CFP Board that you must understand to pass the CFP Certification Examination. The American College is the industry's #1 provider of education for individuals who plan to sit for this exam.

ChFC® Financial Planning Specialty (8 courses)
The ChFC provides comprehensive coverage of the key financial planning disciplines, including insurance, income taxation, retirement planning, investments, and estate planning, that will help you succeed in this competitive field. ChFC designees average up to 51 percent higher income than their peers.

RHU® Health Insurance (3 courses)
The RHU is the premier credential for professionals serving a wide range of health insurance needs. It broadens your knowledge of managed care and medical, disability income, and long-term care insurance to help you succeed in the health insurance field.

REBC® Employee Benefits (5 courses)
The REBC designation enhances your competitive edge in the dynamic field of employee benefits. You'll gain a thorough understanding of pensions and retirement planning, group medical plans, long-term care, executive compensation, and personnel management.

Leadership and Management

CLF® Field Leadership (7 courses)
The CLF program provides managers with the knowledge they need to achieve key organizational goals, such as recruiting and retaining top performers, developing business plans, and motivating others. CLF courses feature practical field applications and seminar-based programs.

Master's Degrees

MSM Executive Leadership (10 courses)
The MSM is designed for executives who want to refine and deepen their essential leadership skills in such areas as managing group behavior, strategic leadership and influence, and organizational and crisis communication. The MSM is an accelerated one-year program that combines residency and on-line distance learning.

MSFS Advanced Financial Planning (13 courses)
The MSFS provides comprehensive tools to help you analyze, plan, and implement integrated strategies to protect, conserve, and/or distribute financial assets and/or human life values. The program combines convenient distance learning with faculty and peer interaction, helping you gain entry to advanced markets, corporate clients, and larger cases.

To order additional copies of this publication please remit U.S. $20.00 per copy plus $9.95 postage and handling to:

The American College Press
270 S. Bryn Mawr Avenue
Bryn Mawr, PA 19010

To place an order by phone or to obtain information about bulk ordering policies, contact The American College Press at 610-526-1350 or email Textbooks@TheAmericanCollege.edu.

The New York Life Center for Retirement Income

The goal of the New York Life Center for Retirement Income at The American College is to produce state-of-the-art education concerning retirement concepts and strategies for financial service professionals. Funded in 2007 by a generous gift from The New York Life Insurance Company, the Center pursues several objectives on behalf of professionals seeking to elevate their financial services practice. These include:

- We will generate this collection of cutting edge research in the fall of each year in order to help you provide state-of-the-art service as a planner. The ideas in each article are expected to represent new and promising concepts for retirement security.

- We will produce a website replete with videos featuring thought leaders discussing the articles from this book as well as other retirement issues. For more information on our website please go to www.theamericancollege.edu and click on the link for the New York Life Center for Retirement Income.

- We will package this book, some website readings, and our expert videos so that it is possible for financial service professionals to receive continuing education credit.

- We will bring leading experts together for seminars on important matters to the retirement planning industry.

- We anticipate creating a Certificate of Advanced Retirement Studies from The American College. Development of this project and the details concerning it should be available on our website starting in January 2009.

Our objective is to elevate the technical knowledge of financial advisors and agents in matters related to the complex and numerous options related to retirement income.

We welcome your feedback. Please email Kenn.Tacchino@theamericancollege.edu or write to:

Kenn Beam Tacchino, Director
New York Life Center for Retirement Income
The American College
270 South Bryn Mawr Avenue
Bryn Mawr, PA 19010-2196

Your Bridge to a Lifetime of Professional Achievement

We encourage you to take advantage of knowing more about The Alumni Association. Together we can create a stronger community and explore new opportunities for professional success.

Call us at (610) 526-1200
e-mail: russell.figueira@theamericancollege.edu